You're Not a Fucking Bachelor Anymore

By

Michele A. Fabiano

KCM PUBLISHING
A DIVISION OF KCM DIGITAL MEDIA, LLC

CREDITS

KCM Publishing
a division of KCM Digital Media, LLC

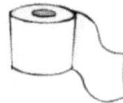

To my husband Joe

for the love, laughter, inspiration,
and having a sense of humor

Contents

*"Somewhere on your path to glory
you will write the story of your life"*

Harry Chapin, *Story of A Life*, Sequel, 1980

Introduction

I never intended to write this book.

I never intended to put what was happening in my life down on paper.

I've written about other people, their hobbies, interests, and art. I even had the opportunity to interview country singer Aaron Tippin about how he makes time for staying in shape with his busy schedule. What other people are doing or creating always seemed more interesting. There was nothing interesting about my life that I would even consider putting down on paper *or* think people would want to read about. But then again, everybody has a story.

The manuscript I was working on at the time (*The Agony Continues: Michelangelo's Search for Art in 20th NYC*) took place at the World Trade Center. After the Sept 11th attacks on the World Trade Center I packed it up in boxes. There was no way I could publish that story. I was frustrated; all my work had gone down the drain. What was I going to do next? My husband was getting aggravated with the boxes and the clutter in the house and wanted to know what I was doing with it all. He suggested I get rid of everything if I wasn't going to write! "Throw it out," he'd yell.

I started cleaning and re-organizing and came across two of my favorite articles, one about country singer Hank Williams Jr., and the other about trumpet player Erskine Hawkins written by my friend, writer, and mentor Bill Jarnigan. Bill was the director of university relations at the University of North Alabama, where I taught art history. He wrote about music in his weekly newspaper column and is also the former executive director of the Muscle Shoals Music Association. Not only does he know a lot about music, he could also write. I learned two important things from Bill. The first was about the art of writing. Writing is like painting or any other art form. In painting it's the placement of the colors, lines, shapes to help tell stories, convey messages, or evoke feelings. Writing is all about words. Bill is a wizard at tightening up thoughts and forced me to look at the art of creating paragraphs and sentences; like how to say something in two sentences instead of three paragraphs while still capturing the attention of the audience. I have not yet mastered the technique and may never come close, but I will never forget the day he edited three paragraphs into one, and totally changed my story for the better. The second thing he taught me was about the process of writing. While it may be frustrating, difficult, challenging, you have to keep writing to get better. Every day Bill would say, "What are you doing? Did you write anything today? You need to write every day. Every day you need to keep at it." As I stared at two of my favorite articles he wrote, his deep voice and southern drawl in every word echoed through my head as I recalled how he always encouraged me to keep writing.

I smiled as I stared at his stories. It was my epiphany.

I cleaned up the boxes, re-organized, and took out two files of notes for two different manuscripts – nothing. I simply added more notes, more characters, and more in-depth story lines. What a mess. For me, when that happens, I know it's just not the right time and I packed those stories away. More boxes, more clutter. Ugh!

So now what? What to write about?

Ironically, it was my husband who decided for me.

It started when I ran out of the bathroom, naked, enraged like a lunatic, and screaming nonsensically at my husband as to why he couldn't put the roll of toilet paper on the holder. My Master's degree meant nothing as I attempted to debate logically about the function of a plastic roller and toilet paper! Like a lawyer I'd provide endless, rational arguments for this simple task to no avail. The arguing eventually escalated to other mundane tasks of everyday living: the television remote control, laundry, putting the toilet seat down, shopping, cooking, money, and other routine responsibilities. When had we become so unreasonable? When had I become so irrational?

I couldn't believe we were starting our married life together arguing about toilet paper.

In between the bickering, I began to see the humor in every situation. "I should write this down," I said to my husband one afternoon as I laughed more. He was *appalled* that I even considered it. We argued about that too.

The more I thought about it, the funnier it all became. I grabbed a pad from my desk. In less than fifteen minutes I had outlined the chapters. Within the hour I had written two chapters. And from that day forward, every time something happened, I'd smile, reach for my pad and start writing.

My husband knew the look on my face – it was like I'd won the lottery. He'd say sarcastically, "Oh, what? Are you going to put that in the story?" He became accustomed to the red leather-bound journal I carried in my pocketbook. When I pulled it out his eyes would widen with alarm, challenging me not to but secretly knowing that it was good material and I was going to write it down no matter what he said.

As the chapters materialized, I began thinking about the complexities of relationships, the real meaning of the word *compromise* and if couples really grasp the concept of *working as a team*? Do we understand what sharing space for the rest of your life *really* requires? And regardless of the type of relationship we are in, do we really comprehend the true meaning of a partner, spouse, or significant other?

While I am writing from my perspective, I am acutely aware that both *men* and *women* are equally at fault when it comes to some of the topics I address. With all our growth, development, technology, and evolution, it's perplexing and disconcerting that the root cause of failed relationships could be over toilet paper and the TV remote control that is worshiped like a piece of fine art.

Later, as the manuscript developed, I realized something was missing. I set the manuscript aside and to my husband's dismay, returned to the *Michelangelo* manuscript. Boxes and research filled the house once again. When finally published, I returned the *You're Not a Fucking Bachelor Anymore*, and it wasn't long before I figured out what was missing.

"While arguing about toilet paper, lint, and space, I blurted out, "You're just like my father!" Once the words were out, I couldn't help but think how this was eerily like my life growing up – a life I had so desperately tried to escape.

While the chapters comically highlight issues many couples encounter, they are connected by a thread or pattern of behavior that is discovered and referenced as I look back at my upbringing in the attempts to understand the full magnitude of the dysfunctional environment I grew up in and how it found its way into my married life.

It all began in New Jersey at Exit 145 off the Garden State Parkway and decades later would continue at Exit 74. Growing up the oldest girl in an Italian family was not easy. I was not only the *first* born, but, the first-born and only female. Since I was *not* the first-born male, I was given the female version of my great-grandfather's name Michael to Michele.

My father had a construction business and some of my early childhood memories are going to work with him on jobs or when they were building homes. I was only a substitute for the non-existent first-born male but limited to the work I was allowed to do because I was female.

Over the years my father would painfully remind me that because I was not the *first-born male*, my brothers would be entitled to certain heirlooms that had been passed down from generations past. Nothing would be easy for me, the first child. Later, something as simple as going to the movies would be difficult – my parents made sure I was not going to leave the house. My place in my adolescent development would often conflict with the demands and expectations of the first-born female in an Italian household. Should I be cleaning up at construction sites or cleaning the house? Was I being taught that my role was to serve men either at home or at work? And if I wasn't allowed out of the house, how was I ever going to get married? Which was my father's goal for me.

In addition to this confusion, my father continuously reminded me how angry he was at the world and what a hard day at work he had. The family suffered the effects of his hard days and life disappointments. No matter where we were, the Garden State Parkway, the New Jersey Turnpike, down the Jersey shore, the convenience store, or at home, there was always fighting, yelling, and obscenities – lots and lots of them. I thought this insanity was simply how all families functioned.

Fast forward - decades later. Here I am married and fighting with my husband about lint, toilet paper, and other random stuff!

What the hell had happened?

After taking a personal inventory, I realized it was inevitable that this behavior was already in my DNA and unbeknownst to me would manifest at some point in my life. Had I turned into the one thing I had vowed would never happen to me – *my parents*? Had I become just like *my parents*, who argued about everything?

And somewhere in between the quarreling and disputes, my husband and I began laughing at the absurdity of our behavior and how each of us had become so unreasonable.

Rules for laundry, shopping, bathroom etiquette, man caves, pets, money, vehicle maintenance, closet space, cooking, cleaning, spending habits, and other random stuff, are humorously explored through light-hearted banter and bickering as we both try to make sense of it all before solutions are agreed upon.

Advice from my mother and comments from my friends and co-workers are referenced as I search for answers in each chapter. The arguing and obscenities learned from my father surface.

As the manuscript developed further, I also began to think *more and more* about family life and its impact. Everyone has something: dysfunctional family members, parents had different ways to deal with children and how they were raised, how children are affected by childhood memories, or the fear of becoming like our parents. Are we really products of the environment we were raised in? How we try our best not to repeat bad behavior witnessed by family members or others we were raised with? Abuse, addiction, its impact growing up and later as an adult. What is the role of women in the family? Women fighting for a place in the work force and its effect on the family unit? Life after getting married.

Topics as old as time and some people spend a lifetime trying to figure out. Topics that are imbedded in the chapters which others have written about extensively but not my purpose to dig deeper into. I do however spend the first few chapters painting a quick picture of what comes to mind when I think of my childhood.

Idiosyncrasies of life growing up in New Jersey, and major attractions like the Turnpike and Parkway are imbedded in the story and like a painter painting a canvas, brush stroke after brush stroke, color after color, the memories, somehow surfaced into my married life as chapter after chapter connects and unfolds.

I love my husband. We are sort of like *Ralph Kramden* and *Alice* of the television show, the *Honeymooners*. The Honeymooners was a popular sitcom that ran from 1955-1956, which stared comedian Jackie Gleason as Ralph Kramden. Ralph and his wife Alice lived in a poor section of Brooklyn and Ralph is always yelling at Alice, as she refuses to listen to another get-rich-quick-scheme. Ralph frequently says, "One of these days you're Going to the Moon Alice, right to the moon." He is a teddy bear at heart and always makes up with Alice at the end, stating, "Baby You're the Greatest."

My husband is funny, and I'm not. He is always ready with a humorous and clever retort that I can't match. He also has a sarcastic sense of humor and knows how to provoke me. When he does something unusual or outlandish, I can feel my eyes narrow as I stare at him in utter disbelief and say, "Seriously. Why would you do that? What the hell is wrong with you?" The obscenities and gesturing my father taught me pepper the conversations.

I'm also a realist and like to get right to the point, which is how I grew up. In the Italian household you just came right out and said what was on your mind. There were no sit down quiet conversations about behavior modification or how a family matter was going to be dealt with. Situations were handled or discussed immediately.

And after he was done with verbal beating the phone calls would start and within an hour the entire family knew what was going on. After he was done telling the family, anyone he ran into heard about it next. This continued until something else happened and then he would start all over again anytime one of us did something wrong.

And that is exactly how I am with my husband. What happens in our life is discussed with my mother and friends. Like my father, stories are repeated until we have something else to talk about.

And like *Alice* of the *Honeymooner*s, I also get right to the point when we are discussing something or figuring out how to complete a task or deal with any given situation. While my husband usually has some sort of wild scheme or unique way of accomplishing tasks or will take ten steps to complete projects. His reasoning for the things he does is incomprehensible and at times exhausting. For instance, why cover the countertop with wood and put a step stool on top of the wood to paint the kitchen ceiling? Why not just bring the eight-foot ladder inside? Like *Ralph* he was always going to find a better way and *Alice* was there to keep him grounded by telling him how it was going to be.

I am deeply indebted my friends, family, coworkers, and early readers, who all shared funny stories - solidifying that I was not suffering alone and at times admitting that they too are part of the insanity that occurs in their own homes. I pay homage to them by simply making reference to everyone as, my best friend, or my best girlfriend throughout the story.

Each had their own unique voice as they discussed and offered suggestions – I am humbled and grateful for their contributions and the laughter as we talked about the foolishness in our lives. I can't thank you enough for your feedback, sharing stories, and finding humor in the reality *and* oddities of life.

I am especially grateful and indebted to my dear friend Laura Coffey, for taking time out of her extremely hectic schedule for the preliminary read once completed. Your feedback was invaluable. I can't thank you enough for your support, encouragement, and more importantly your continued friendship.

And like Rex Harrison (Pope Julius II), who yelled up to Charlton Heston (Michelangelo), "when will you finish," while painting the Sistine Ceiling, in the movie, *The Agony and the Ecstasy*, there was my friend Joann Eletto, asking the same question, "Are you done yet?" Always encouraging me to finish the book, sharing stories, laughing at life and always adding a bit of levity to the day.

The Agony and the Ecstasy was a movie released in 1965 and based on the book by Irving Stone. The movie featured Charlton Heston as Michelangelo and Rex Harrison as Pope Julius II and examines the commission of the Sistine Ceiling by Pope Julius II, a commission that Michelangelo did not want and vehemently refuses. Pope Julius II constantly badgers Michelangelo as he is painting the ceiling always asking, "When are you going to finish."

To my 'soul sister' Brandi Braden, thank you so much for the friendship and being part of the journey. I will never forget that one hot summer day we stood outside and I was explaining that I had to go home and finish a manuscript I was working on. Instead of telling her what it was about, I simply stated the title. Without hesitation she understood and immediately and began listing the habits of her boyfriend. I laughed and asked, "Is he related to my husband?" As she shared stories, she gave me added confirmation that I was not suffering alone. You are most definitely my 'soul sister' and truly a friend for life.

There are not enough words or space to thank my friend Bill Jarnigan, who inspired and helped me to imagine more. THANK YOU!!!!

To the team at KCM Publishing for their guidance and support and making the story better. The journey is always challenging and rewarding!

Deepest gratitude to my brother Michael for the patience, laughter and understanding it all! There is really nothing else to say!!!

Special thanks go to my mother – She really is the greatest. What would I do without her? She is an amazing person and I don't know how she survived, but she did. Like so many have told her, she is a saint for putting up with it all. I thank her for reliving the stories, arguing about dates and events that occurred, and still finding humor in it all. Laughter is really the best medicine and we are still laughing.

Finally, and most importantly, I need to thank the love of my life, my husband Joe for learning to laugh with me, at one another, and at himself as we navigate life together. I couldn't have a better partner. I appreciate you more than I can say. Whether I'm making art or writing you always support me. I especially thank you for helping out around the house while I took time to write, edit, again and again and again. I dedicate this book to Joe and our incredible journey. To the stories we learned to laugh about, to the stories not told and the stories yet to come.

Thank you, Joe, for the love, laughter, and putting up with it all!

You're Not a Fucking Bachelor Anymore

Do we understand what sharing space for the rest of your life *really* requires?

CHAPTER 1

How it All Began

Although I don't remember the day or the month, I do recall, rather vividly, the incident.

My husband was relaxing on the couch in the living room watching television. He jolted upright when the door slammed loudly into the wall as I came running out of the bathroom, half-naked and screaming, "Do you see this?" I shouted angrily.

The blank look on his surprised face indicated he had no idea what I was talking about.

My adrenaline peeked. I could feel the blood rushing to my face. I was furious. "Do you see this?" I yelled again as I held the roll of flower-patterned toilet paper in one hand and the sleek bronze roller it attached to in the other.

His eyes twinkled with guilt. He brought his hand to his face to cover his mouth – an attempt to avoid laughing.

I shook my head in disbelief; infuriated that he found the situation entertaining. Hand gesture's cut through the air before I shouted, "What the hell is wrong with you? Do you see this?" I screamed for the third time and began demonstrating the object lesson, "TOILET PAPER GETS PUT ON ROLLER AND THEN SLIPS INTO THE TOILET PAPER HOLDER! Do you get it? YOU'RE NOT A FUCKING BACHELOR ANYMORE!"

And so it began –

CHAPTER 2

It's All Part of Our DNA

I am an educated, rational, intelligent person who quarrels with my husband over inconsequential matters such as **NOT PUTTING THE TOILET PAPER ON THE ROLLER!** Our home is a battleground over routine, mundane tasks of everyday living!

Next to arguments over money, the inability to insert a roll of toilet paper on the roller (with the paper forwards not backwards), I believe is undoubtedly the underlying reason people get divorced! While my best girlfriend and I agree that toilet paper is at the top of the list, it's even more disturbing that we spend time talking about it daily. The conversation always starts out like this, "Do you know what *he* did last night...?"

The *he* refers to our husbands, boyfriends, significant others – you get the picture.

The, what *he* did stories, begin when I arrive at work and continue in the corridors, in the lunchroom, throughout the entire day and later on the phone or at gatherings. My co-workers are predominantly female and the few men that perchance witness these conversations depart immediately – an indisputable sign of their guilt.

If it isn't the toilet paper causing problems it's possibly a combination of someone's laundry, cooking, cleaning, or eating habits. If you and your significant other are able to reach a compromise in any of the aforementioned areas, it may make disputes over shopping, money, the television remote control, or the clutter in your home seem much easier to deal with.

Finally, if you can survive all that, you probably have reached the point where you are ready and eager to welcome the idea of the "man cave" either into your home by converting a room or by building an additional structure somewhere on the corner of your property, preferably at the furthest end of it!

What the hell is wrong with *me* I started to contemplate after yet another disagreement over his bathroom habits or lack of them!

Or, was it *him*?

Who was to blame?

During my tirades my husband would chuckle and simply say, "Babe, why are you getting so upset? It's only a lint trap," or "It's only a roll of toilet paper."

"My point exactly," I shouted. "So why can't *you* just remove the lint from the dryer and attach the toilet paper to the roller?"

Like a lawyer, trying to plead a case in front of a jury, I would offer countless debates and logical reasoning, only to find wads of lint jammed in the lint trap or the roll of toilet paper sitting on the sink and floor, symbols of defeat.

Conversations with friends and colleagues revealed the same circular discussions were occurring in their households as well! The, *"WHY CAN'T YOU PUT THE TOILET PAPER ON THE ROLLER,"* was always at the top of the list!

No wonder the country is in such a mess! If men and women can't achieve a reasonable compromise over toilet paper, how the hell can they possibly develop successful policies, formalize budgets, cut taxes, or solve any other serious economic matters? How can countries stop fighting with one another if we can't stop disputing over trivial issues in our own homes?

Think about it! People in conflict over lint, toilet paper, or the television remote control! How did we lose perspective? What is wrong with *us*?

How the hell did *I* reach this point, I thought after yet another battle over putting the toilet paper on the roller.

The entire disagreement was perplexing and yet ridiculous!

What is so difficult about this? Were all men like this? And if so, why didn't my mother tell me? Hell, she warned me about everything else that was possibly wrong with men!

How come I didn't know this *before* I was married? I'd been in the dating field long enough to discover this flaw. I spent time with many colorful and interesting characters so how could *this* have eluded my attention? Perhaps something was wrong with *me* I continued to wonder as the fighting intensified.

While thinking of ways to correct my husband's lack of regard for the function of the toilet paper holder, I desperately wanted to know how *I* turned into this irrational and unreasonable person! Why was *I* wasting my breath having outlandish conversations about the lint trap, laundry, and shopping, wasting money and, of all things, a plastic attachment for toilet paper!

Well the answer as to how it all began revealed itself to me late one evening when the obscenities started between my husband and I over, once again, the toilet paper issue and then escalated to laundry.

"You should really calm down," my husband suggested, annoyed that I was interrupting an episode of fishing for Alaskan crabs. "Who cares about why the toilet paper is not on the roller? I'm tired of fuckin' talking about it. It's just paper and really no big deal," he shrugged.

"No big deal?" I shrieked. "Get serious. The bathroom isn't a fucking outhouse! And I don't recall hiring a cleaning service for our seventeen hundred square foot mansion!"

The fits of uncontrollable laughter that he burst into were the driving force for what occurred next.

Somewhere buried deep in the recesses of my brain, lying dormant and waiting for the right moment to spring forth, it happened. The words were out of my mouth before I even thought about them. And it all made sense when I yelled back, "You're just like my fuckin' idiot father! He did the same stupid stuff. My mother and he argued over the same damn things!"

I am being too kind when I use the word argue. It was war – a war that carried on for decades. I had a seat on the front-line of their continuous battles. I don't remember a time when they were not engaged in some type of conflict, which was usually perpetuated by my father.

My husband smirked, looked at me with raised eyebrows over his coffee cup, and stated a bit smugly, "So I guess that would make *you* just like *your* mother or perhaps *you're* more like that *crazy* fuckin' father of yours!"

Ugh! The thought makes me ill. I retreated to the bathroom and reached for the jar of aspirin and swallowed two before our dispute continued.

I returned to the living room and without hesitation responded, "And if *you* don't think *you're* not like *your* father and *your* mother, *you* have another thing coming," I snapped.

My husband laughed easily at my ill-attempted comparison.

"The man is dead…you didn't even know him."

He shook his head in disbelief before playfully throwing a pillow across the room at me as I rambled on.

I snapped my fingers for emphasis. "I heard all about *your* father from that crazy uncle…and remember when *your* mother made those comments at the church and indicated all the crap that happened in *your* house…and remember that time we went to visit your aunt and *she* told me…"

My husband stared at me with his mouth hanging open. "How the *fuck* do you remember all that?" he interrupted.

"It's one of the gifts God bestowed upon women - we never forget a thing," I grinned innocently as I continued to recall his family issues.

And on and on it went.

There would be *years* of obscenities, disagreements, and analysis of the impact each of our strange and bizarre childhoods had on our lives.

Understanding the magnitude of the dysfunctional environment *I* was raised in and its effect began to make sense as to why *I* turned into something resembling an unrecognizable alien straight from a science fiction movie as we bickered over ordinary household tasks of daily living.

Our behavior was ridiculous!

The obscenities, slamming of doors, and vicious disputes over such trivial things like toilet paper, laundry, shopping, clutter, cleaning, cooking, leaving the toilet seat up, and the television remote – this *was* how *we* began our married life together.

But this fighting didn't *really* happen overnight. How *we* became so foolish and unreasonable began way before *we* knew one another…not only was it learned behavior but I believe was somehow already part of our DNA.

Before I start to highlight the absurd things we were fighting about and our ludicrous behavior, I first have to take a quick look back at *where* and *who* I learned it all from.

The next four chapters take a look at my years before marriage where it all really began.

CHAPTER 3

The Early Years

As a child my father made me painfully aware that I was going to accomplish three things. First, marry someone who was Italian. Second, marry someone who was a registered, active, participating, voting democrat in the state of New Jersey. And third, live locally; hence, my father would not have to experience the terrible calamity of traveling farther than twenty miles to visit - as he hated driving long distances. This included travel on two of New Jersey's major highways of transportation: The Garden State Parkway and the New Jersey Turnpike. Needless to say, we rarely went anywhere and when we did it wasn't far from home.

Traveling with my family was always a process and required weeks of preparation. Getting ready to go somewhere was like running a marathon. I always felt like an outsider looking in as the scene before me unfolded. Apparently, he suffered from agoraphobia or some fear of traveling. I don't quite know what it is but he was deathly afraid of all types of travel.

The year was 1974. We were heading down the shore to Seaside Heights for a vacation. My father preferred the Garden State Parkway as opposed to the Turnpike and weeks before the trip would purchase enough tokens for the next millennium. This was well before the days of any sort of EZ Pass technology.

Tokens overflowed from a huge cup that rested in the cup holder on the consol. His philosophy was that if he had huge amounts of tokens in the vehicle he didn't have to worry about running out. Second, if the state raised the price, he believed those who had tokens would be allowed to use them up since they were already paid for. He was always trying to stay one step ahead of the government.

While my father was worrying about the government, my mother began packing. This process took the entire week. My father also made sure the car was serviced. There could be absolutely nothing wrong with the vehicle and it still went somewhere to be checked and re-checked. This ritual took days to complete too.

Tension and anxiety escalated daily. Throughout the week there was arguing. I heard fragments of conversations, which included: why we needed to go on vacation, money or rather the lack of money, where we were going, or why we just couldn't remain home. Cigarettes and bottles of Rolaids were replenished and put in the front seat next to the overflowing plastic cup of tokens. There was always too much *stuff* and the arguing continued. Once packed, the *stuff* was quickly crammed in the car by my father and then removed by my mother who told him he didn't pack it properly and proceeded to reposition it all.

Beverages were spilled in the back seat before we left the driveway, my father was always screaming for my mother, who was *always* the last to enter the vehicle. We were *always* late. Obscenities from my father drifted through the cigarette smoke swirling about his head and the entire vehicle.

The atmosphere was tense and everyone was anxious and nervous; especially my father who had issues driving far distances. I never really understood it. Many understand being afraid of Friday the thirteenth, or walking under a ladder, but to be afraid of a highway and the traffic and being away from your normal surroundings – well, it was a severe phobia my father wrestled with and one he thankfully would not pass on to his children.

With the brown station wagon loaded, we pulled out of the driveway and headed toward the highway.

Like participants in a video game we crept off route 280 and slowly merged toward the East Orange toll plaza. The family all held our breaths as we silently waited for the sound of tokens to hit the metal basket, signaling victory, before falling to some unknown depth below the concrete.

The congestion would continue as five lanes merged into one and we slowly rounded the curve and the station wagon finally surged forward, cutting in front of other vehicles – success at last as we were now officially on the Garden State Parkway.

CHAPTER 4

What Exit Are You From?

Anyone who has lived in or near New Jersey knows the quickest way to travel is via the Garden State Parkway or New Jersey Turnpike. People in Jersey don't ask what town are you from, rather we say, "What's your exit? Or, what exit are you from?"

My exit was 145 off the Parkway and 15W on the Turnpike.

In New Jersey you are defined by your exit whether you live in either north, south, or central Jersey. The north, south, or central is a serious debate and further intensified when more area codes were added. I grew up in North Jersey. We went down the shore (i.e. the beach, the seashore) and anything past Seaside was south. Others will disagree.

Folks in New Jersey are said to have an edge. It may very well be caused by anyone of the major roadways, like the Garden State Parkway, where you automatically become a different person. Your hands immediately grip the steering wheel forcefully and your back straightens as you move closer to the dashboard. Your entire body is tense and your head constantly moves in all directions, looking in mirrors, and out windows as you attempt to join the race on the highway. Signs and speed limits are only suggestions as driver's speed, disregard signs, and pass in the wrong lanes as they attempt to get to their destination.

The atmosphere in the vehicle was nerve-racking as my father struggled to concentrate on driving and his fear of traveling away from the home intensified. Conversations in the station wagon between my parents were always the same. My father yelled and my mother didn't say too much except for, "you have to calm down."

The script went something like this: "Where's the fucking exit...I need a token...fuck you (to someone beeping their horn), I missed the exit and need to turn around...why didn't you tell me to turn...give me the token...dammit...which way should I go... the directions are wrong...why can't you read them correctly... where is the fucking change...why can't you have it ready...what the hell is wrong with you...don't tell me to take it easy...and look at this fuckin' traffic...and all fuckin' potholes...now I have to fix the tire...this is why we don't go anywhere...we should have stayed home...we should never have left at this time... fuckin' traffic...damn state...fuckin' construction..."

And on and on it went.

While the shouting from my father seemed like normal behavior, I would secretly laugh at his ridiculous antics. Didn't all kids think their parents were crazy and weird? Years later we would understand more about the effects of bullying, travel fears and other addictions. To my brothers and me it was a comedy show, which we much later vowed was *never* going to happen to us. The screaming at my mother was so loud the toll collectors could probably hear him down the length of the Garden State Parkway to the very last exit! Seriously, did he actually think my mother had control over the traffic, potholes or the cost of the tolls?

Traffic in New Jersey - it was inescapable. Whether you went north, south, east, or west - traffic, congestion, and tolls were unavoidable. "Tell me about New Jersey," a friend living in Alabama asks. I sum it up in one sentence: "If you're not an offensive driver, can't drive like a NASCAR driver, or don't like driving at all, don't even bother."

My friend laughs, "It really can't be that bad."

"Fuh-ged-da-boud-it." I laugh.

"What the hell do you mean by that," my southern friend asks.

"You have to live here just to understand what I mean. The actor Jonny Depp in the movie *Donnie Brasco*, gives a thought-provoking explanation of the term. "It's like, you know, it's all good or never mind or you know, just for-get about it.""

Johnny Depp plays an FBI agent who infiltrated the Bonanno crime family in New York under the name Donnie Brasco. Life gets more and more complicated for the undercover FBI agent as he gets deeper and deeper into the inner circle of underworld characters and mod bosses. Fuh-ged-da-boud-it is said over and over by different characters in the movie. One of the FBI agents who listens to the tapes and hears the term daily asks Johnny Depp to explain what fuh-ged-da-boud-it really means. "It could be a good thing, or you agree with something or you think it is just plain crazy. Or sometimes it just means forget about it," as Depps's character clarified.

I continue, "Traffic, tolls, exits and congestion, are much, much more than a fragment of the landscape of the state. If you are willing to battle traffic, jug handles, potholes that can ruin your suspension and take tires off your vehicle, you will experience some of the greatest restaurants and fantastic food. We have the best bread, pizza, and *Taylor Ham or pork roll*, I grew up in the north, so we said Taylor Ham! Oh, and if you visit be prepared NOT to pump your own gas and be the recipient of the "Jersey Bird," I laugh.

My friend laughs. "This is why I don't travel."

So back to the station wagon; as we headed south, the script between my parents repeated itself down the parkway and we learned more about my father's eclectic vocabulary as the on-slaught of vulgarities continued. Before, after, or in between every word, sentence, or phrase, obscenity after obscenity pounded at us like a torrential hailstorm in the heat of the summer.

Smoke curled and floated throughout the car from the ciga-rette dangling from his lips…his face was beet red as he gripped the steering wheel…swearing at my mother for no particular rea-son and other cars that had the audacity to cut *him* off because he was driving too slow!

We held our breaths, as we knew what was coming next – *The Union Toll Plaza*!

As a kid it looked like an incalculable number of booths span-ning across the entire parkway both going north and south bound. The color-coded signs hung from the square workspaces reading Token, Exact Change, or Cash. The signs could be seen from any vantage point in the car. The goal was to get to the correct booth without getting into an accident. Horns blared and multiple deliv-eries of the *Jersey Bird* were demonstrated as drivers sped up, crossed over three or four lanes, and cut one another off just to reach the appropriate booth and pay the twenty-five-cent fee. Crossing four and five lanes and cutting people off to get to the opposite side just to pay the toll was normal. My father was a re-lentless participant in this chaotic ritual. It was amazing we never had an accident.

When he finally arrived at the tollbooth he would come to a complete stop. Throwing or I should say hurling the token into the basket and speeding back into traffic with what seemed to be the entire population of New Jersey *didn't* happen. Instead the scene went something like this: the window slowly opened or if the win-dow was broken, the door would open and he'd place his hand deep into the white, plastic basket and slowly drop the token in.

We sat in silence as he waited for the digital sign to read "THANK YOU" before he even thought about merging into traffic. The government was *watching* and he wasn't going to take any chances on getting a ticket! Of course this was long before the elaborate camera systems that are in place today. A picture of your license plate now comes in the mail with your ticket, administrative fees included, if you fail to pay the toll.

Anyway, I don't know what was worse, the failure of the sign not lighting up to acknowledge his token was received or the merging of the droves of vehicles back into three lanes.

The technological failure of the sign evoked a concert of screeching horns, hoping to alert some unseen employee, that money was deposited. My father followed with the standard oaths, more screaming, and then blaming my mother for taking the trip. The inevitable flip of the *Jersey Bird* or an assortment of lewd hand gestures to other motorists ensued as the journey continued and the behavior was repeated all the way down the highway.

One day I made the mistake of asking, "Did you think you were going to miss the basket? Is that why we stop all the time? Why can't you just throw it in like everybody else?"

I can still see the back of his hand as it came whipping around the seat toward me.

"You wanna get smart with me," he sneered.

My brothers took most of the hand as I eventually learned to sit behind my mother, out of his reach.

Calling the Division of Youth and Family Services, or DYFUS, was unheard of. The back of a hand, belt or wooden spoon, we just took it. And we never complained. It was like this for other kids we knew. If we did something wrong we knew what was coming. It was just part of growing up. We didn't care, it was routine, and nobody whined or complained for fear of initiating round two.

Lessons were learned immediately and only repeated if, according to my father, "you were just plain fucking stupid."

My mother, her voice loud and sharp, would politely but firmly intervene and yell for him to *STOP*. She would shout his name loudly as the expletives continued. Reminders of his foul language in front of the children were ignored.

If what researches say is true about the ability for children to learn while they are developing in the womb, then the moment I entered the world and took my first breath, I was fluent in profanity from A to Z in English *and* Italian!

Now that we are adults, my mother is constantly scolding us for using foul language. She says, "What is wrong with you. I didn't teach you to speak like that."

I reply, "You're right, you didn't but *he* did, how the hell could you forget?" Like popcorn popping from a machine the expletives flow quickly from my mouth. "Really, Mom, how could you forget about how we grew up?"

As a young child my father's behavior was inexplicable and, at times, just plain *fuckin'* bizarre! The absurdity of wanting to have a token in your hand, ready to throw it into the bucket when not only did you have at least thirty minutes until you reached the next toll, but there was a built in coin holder right on the dash board, inches from your fingers - it was madness! And the yelling… Well, we didn't know any different – whether in the car or the house, this was the way life was for us.

Laughing or keeping your mouth shut for fear of having a bar of Lava Soap shoved into it when you returned home was sometimes difficult to do. I didn't realize it until later that I was actually afraid of a cake of soap! To this day, I still can't buy a bar of Lava Soap! Again, DYFUS or child protective services were unheard of. My mother claims I didn't get my mouth washed out enough.

Even more preposterous was when I recently discovered an old token for the Parkway in my desk. I dropped it like it was a burning ember as it immediately transported me back in time to those moments driving with my father on the Garden State Parkway. The token was one of the bimetallic ones, with the brass center, which had replaced the original token. It was created to combat counterfeiting on the Parkway.

Why I have one in my possession, I don't recall. I call my mother and we re-live the stories driving with my father and argue about the cost to ride the parkway twenty years ago! My husband smirks. He is getting aggravated that we're even having the discussion. He irritably states that we both need help. I tell him to throw out the token. He tells me to put it on e-bay that it may be worth something!

Ugh! More madness.

I try to explain the insanity and the reason why Lava Soap and tokens, evoke such awful memories to my husband. How ridiculous! Not really, it was just another consequence of the dysfunctional environment I was raised in that would haunt me for decades to come and unbeknownst to me creep into my married life.

As a child, I didn't know any better. As an adolescent, I thought life was just was crazy. As a young adult, I just wanted to escape the idiotic behavior. Life would become complicated much later, and as an adult I would put the pieces together.

CHAPTER 5

What the Hell is Art History?

Change was never an option with my father and under his sovereign rule he was determined that I would live close by after I married an Italian who was a registered, active, voting democrat. When I was born, the compass was already placed on the map, the radius was drawn, and the exits off the Garden State Parkway would remain the same.

His master plan for my life included attending college, which seemed reasonable. But then, shortly after graduation, like a primate in the jungles of Africa, or a fish in the deep blue sea, I would have to choose a mate and get married!

This was *all* he ever talked about: me getting married. At the dinner table, on the phone or when he saw me the conversation was always the same – when I got married… where I was going to live…who I was going to marry…when was I going to get married… simply more madness.

Why, I wondered, did all parents have this rule? What was he going to gain, three goats and some land? Was there a swim upstream ritual included as well? Does ovulation miraculously start at the turning of the tassel? Was the appendage on the graduation cap a symbol for the hand on the biological clock that was ticking?

If all of this did take place, that would put me at approximately twenty-two years old.

To his disappointment, his master plan wasn't to be.

I did attend college and received a B.A. in art history.

"What the hell kind of fucking, stupid major is that? What the *fuck* are you going to do with a goddamn degree in art history?" he'd constantly argue every time he saw me, along with a lengthy, provoking list of what he considered my failures and under achievements. "Is this what I *fuckin'* paid for? What the *fuck* is wrong with you?

On the days I felt strong enough to aggressively attack his comments, I responded, "What the *hell* did you send me to college for, to major in household domestication? I have already mastered the art of cooking, cleaning, doing laundry and, let's see, I guess the only thing that's left on the list is childbearing – and I don't have to get married to do that," I'd snap.

His litany of obscenities echoed off the walls of the staircases as I sprinted to my room, on the third floor with tears streaming down my face, slamming and locking the door.

Punching the *on* button of the stereo was the only thing that could drown out the booming voice that continued to scream and rant nonsensically about a variety of miscellaneous and obscure events in his life, which as an adult, I finally understood to be more excuse driven behavior for his own failures fueled by alcohol. Hits from Jackson Brown, Eric Clapton, the Grateful Dead, or the Eagles played before he ended his diatribe with what a *fuckin'* hard day he had and the last thing he needed was to hear crap from his ungrateful, fucking kid! These were just a few of the kinder insults.

Other times I'd stare at him defiantly. "Does it really matter? *You* expect me to get married next - why do *you* care what I majored in anyway? *Your* plan comes first, right?" I finished sarcastically, like I was arguing as a teenager all over again.

As the years passed the conversation was always the same: "What the hell is art history...when are you going to find a husband and get married...when are you going to get the *hell* out of my house and have your own?"

First he wants me in the house then he wants me to leave. It was infuriating and confusing.

I'd respond with what I thought was an intelligent, college-educated answer, "Art history, it's the study of paintings... I'd like to teach...and travel...and learn about...you know Michelangelo... DaVinci..."

He was barely listening. He cut me off before I could finish a word about the *Last Supper*. Inflamed, with some alcoholic beverage, his face red as a jersey tomato, the ear-piercing banter continued, "Don't you fuckin' get smart with me,"... or, "you think just because you're in college now you are smarter than me...how dare you."

DaVinci's one-point perspective technique was similar to how my father jested, like a street, one way - untimely criticism and harmful banter.

CHAPTER 6

Why Can't You Find A Husband?

It was rarely quiet inside our home. I'm not referring to loud music, blasted by the stereos of pubescent teenagers. It was constant unrelenting yelling, fighting, and screaming, the product of severe dysfunctional family arguments, which resulted in confusion and a total breakdown in the family communication dynamic.

There was no such thing as quiet conversation. Perhaps some of it was cultural; the result of an immigrant grandfather passing on a mixture of Italian and some screaming broken English. Still, arguing seemed regular to all of us. It was the way we conversed, or rather how my father communicated; the rest of us, well, we thought everyone behaved this way. Then there was the shouting - at and above one another just to be heard – conversation was never simple.

On rare occasions tranquility filled the house already present with lustful fumes of pasta gravy masking the lingering obscenities. It was a cease fire to fuel up on a snack from the refrigerator, taste the simmering gravy on the stove, or sip a soft drink only to retreat to a shadowed dark recess of the three stories of what could have been a haunted house before the *monster* returned. The local clergy, I'm certain, were reluctant to enter for an exorcism of this kind could only be cast with great prayer and fasting. Nevertheless, when the yelling commenced, the script went something like the following.

My mother would intervene always shouting his name loudly and telling him to STOP IT, when he was out of control.

Obscenities flowed.

"What is wrong with you?" She would yell just loud enough so the neighbors wouldn't hear. She was always worried about what the neighbors would think.

Like a bomb ready to explode he ranted on and on…

He was past the point of reasoning…too much liquor…too many life disappointments…too much guilt…coping skills were non-existent…regrets and reminders of failures were present and confronted him daily….

The arguing rose to another level.

More obscenities…bullying…throwing items in his path….

I *never* understood *why* my mother kept a box of tissues on the corner of the counter in the kitchen. Like a projectile missile, it always went flying across the room, smashing and breaking objects in its path. Regardless of what was broken, the tissue box was always returned to the same spot on the counter.

More vulgarities…name calling…punching walls…throwing chairs…

"…*Fuck* those neighbors; I'll say what I want…"

The slamming of the back door and cloud of cigarette smoke lingering in the house signaled an end to the dispute…someone was always crying…someone was always hiding…

It would start all over again when he came home.

People in his inner circle don't believe me because outside, in public, he portrayed himself as a funny, likable, charismatic character and a lovable guy – that fun-loving, life of the party guy…

But behind closed doors…he was a different person…it was a different ballgame.

If one works at something long enough, one can master a trade or skill. My father could weave rivers of obscenities that intertwined so perfectly that it became a form of art, which, he mastered with the same accuracy and perfection as Michelangelo carved his sculptures. His language was unremittingly colorful, overflowing with scores of expletives – volumes – like the heaping piles of marble shavings surrounding the base as Michelangelo carved his beloved *David*.

I was really too young to understand the significance of the drinking, what the endless foul language really meant, and the reason for the constant fighting. What I really *despised* the most was the smoking. He would smoke two to three packs of Camel non-filtered cigarettes daily. Later switching to some obscure brands, thinking they would somehow lessen the effects of the nicotine he inhaled.

There was always smoke in our house. It was so bad that my nose hurt from inhaling it. We *all* hated it!

The smoke drifted and followed him from room to room.

It floated up the stairs from his basement office like a genie being released from a bottle.

I spent my entire childhood, adolescence, and part of my adult hood walking around with a shirt pulled over my face to avoid inhaling the smoke.

The smoke and acrid smell from the cigarettes was horrendous.

There was always a cloud of smoke swirling around his head.

There was always a cigarette in his hand.

My mother was always yelling, "PUT OUT THE CIGARETTE!" This always evoked more hostility, violence, obscenities, punching holes in the walls, damaging furniture, knocking over plants, or slamming doors…

***

So, can you guess where I wound up after graduation? Paris? London? Italy?

Unfortunately, it was only a short commute right back to exit 145 to the suburbs of New Jersey. A second term, living under *his* roof! Escape seemed hopeless from the smoke-filled floors of violence and contention. Just as two magnets being drawn together, I was back! Back to everything I was hoping to flee. Back to the perpetual arguing, abuse, obscenities, cigarettes, beer, violence, ever present fear, and a sense of impending doom. Anyone who lived under his roof, suffered silently.

I wondered how long I could continue being pulled into the darkness. When was enough - enough? Would I? Could I? Every doubt about succeeding, moving, clouded my judgment. I reasoned with God and recited prayers in desperation. This brown-eyed girl had a future, a career! Life was waiting! The world was calling and it wasn't going to be at exit 145!

Unbeknownst to my father, the master plan he had for my life was about to change. I had other ideas, which included furthering my education, teaching, and traveling.

It was my turn at bat so to say – the big league. I was nervous. The hour was upon me. My shoes felt like cleats on a runner stealing second base. It all happened so fast.

Vacating the premises without being at least engaged was unorthodox, too unconventional, but I was determined, the world was calling and I was moving forward with or without his blessing.

I will never forget his reaction when the moving van pulled into the driveway. My friends came and were all too happy to assist loading the cargo on the truck. They were glad I was escaping the insanity. The chore was complete in an hour. The back hatch came rolling down and the lock arm snapped tightly in place. The metal clink was like a cue for center stage.

Respectfully, I went to say good-bye, racing swiftly up the three deteriorating, green concrete steps, pulling the screen door open into the unfinished porch, knowing for sure the meeting would be dreadfully uncomfortable.

He was leaning against the worn, yellow Formica countertop, in the kitchen, waving his unfiltered cigarette in the air, screaming at me so loudly the neighbors who lived behind us and across the street, could hear him. Hell, St. Peter could hear him it was that bad!

This incident – well, I recall it like it happened yesterday.

He began and ended, "*If* you leave this fuckin' house, *you* will never amount to anything."

There was his goal for my life. To be subservient - just as he viewed our mother! If I wasn't confined to his home, following his rules – serving, cleaning his house - I didn't deserve anything else, and I was a disrespectful daughter.

His fist slammed hard into the countertop and then he threw a chair…the rest of the ear-piercing banter is simply not worth wasting space over.

In my determination to be free, I committed a dreadful sin. Not only did I move out, I moved in with my boyfriend! I must admit now, this was not the best choice. Parts of me adopted a rebellious nature to do the very things he tried to prevent. Damaged by his wicked nurturing, deciding to intentionally irritate him more by doing the very thing he tried to avoid - by not letting his Catholic, Italian daughter out of the house – seemed like a great choice!

Nothing mattered. Energized by freedom, yet at the same time clutched by guilt and a host of other issues, I was led to conclude: some wounds just never heal.

Ignoring the battle scars, I worked, went back to school and received a master's degree in Art History. I was lucky enough to travel and teach. At the age of thirty I still was not married. Over time a relationship from a distance became tolerable with my father to a degree; however, the *"WHY CAN'T YOU FIND A HUSBAND"* conversation was still a hot topic and continued until I finally married at the age of forty!

There, almost twenty years later, did I find my life-long partner - born in Rome, Florence or Venice?

No. Not even close.

So, guess whom I fell in love with and married?

A man of German descent. A man with absolutely *not* a drop of Italian blood running through his veins. A man who was a registered republican from Pennsylvania, who, of all things, had never even voted!

To my father, a life-long democrat, chairman of the democratic county committee and deputy mayor, I had committed yet another sin!

There would also be no grandchildren, as our children had four legs and fur. I even changed my voting status and became a registered republican.

To make matters worse we made our home, in south Jersey, off exit 74 on the Garden State Parkway, which happens to be approximately eighty miles and currently about five dollars in tolls one way on the parkway! By the time I finish this book and get it published it probably will increase significantly!

The mileage, and my father, no longer matters.

CHAPTER 7

Missing the Signs and Toilet Paper

As a survivor of a dysfunctional childhood, well vested in education, traveling, worldly affairs, work experience, the merit and disappointment of relationships, I considered myself well-rounded and ready for marriage and thought the time adjusting to life with my new husband would be effortless, uncomplicated, and trouble-free! My spouse, only a year older than me would also be ready for marriage, as he would have gone through dating mishaps and mid-life crisis events. He too would be well past all those stages of relationship debacles, and chapter after chapter of lessons learned, some of them harder than others, would all be behind him.

Furthermore, since he owned a home and had lived on his own, the know- how's of daily living, cooking, cleaning, laundry, spending money and yes, having a regard for one's feelings about putting the toilet paper on the damn roller, would not be a concern. Adapting and compromising would also not be difficult.

Here is how it turned out...

The wake up call for us materialized shortly after the wedding and honeymoon. My girlfriend summed it up simply. "Just face it, you were sucked in like a late night television infomercial!"

I don't know what happened or how I missed the signs. We had lived together a short time before we were married and I thought I knew all his habits. Was I too busy planning the wedding? Was it because he worked shift work so our schedules conflicted and I did not see him much? Did I just ignore all the little things thinking he would change? Did I forget about all the insanity I grew up with thinking it would be different?

Did I see the red flags? Or simply ignore them?

Again, our first major argument was regarding why my husband could not put the roll of toilet paper on the roller attachment! And to make matters worse, he thought I was being irrational! "Come on babe, you're getting upset over nothing. You know I love you," he grinned as he ducked to avoid being hit by a roll of toilet paper I had thrown across the room.

"What the hell is wrong with you? Do you see this?" I shouted for the third time and began demonstrating the object lesson, "Toilet paper gets put on the fuckin' roller and *then* attaches to the toilet paper holder! And put the seat down! Do you get it? YOU'RE NOT A FUCKING BACHELOR ANYMORE!"

Naked and screaming, of course I looked foolish, but I simply didn't understand why he couldn't do this. And then it dawned on me that it was undoubtedly the exact reason why my father couldn't do it either!

As I looked at the toilet paper roller and the package of toilet paper sitting on the sink, I thought to myself, it's happening all over again, and my life is now coming full circle!

After that first fight over the toilet paper, I consulted one of my best friends, who didn't even stop to think about the question. She ranted animatedly about her ex-husband's poor habits and non-existent bathroom etiquette and then finished with, "That fucking son-of-a-bitch, he'd put it on the floor before putting it on the roller!"

Wide eyed, I asked if he ever changed.

"No," she quickly snapped. Then laughing, added, "It's probably the underlying reason why we're divorced!"

My point exactly! I was right! It was true! The inability to put a roll of paper on a roller could actually lead to divorce!

Our married friend immediately chimed in stating proudly, "My husband doesn't do this."

We stared blankly and yell in unison, "Seriously? But why?"

"Because his mother raised him this way!"

Out of fifteen females in the room only one husband would actually put a new roll of toilet paper on the roller when it was empty. I took it as a sign. There was hope for mankind.

As for my husband and I...well...the fragments of our childhoods would start surfacing.

He was an only child and grew up without the arguing and profanity. There was no drinking or smoking; instead, he was immersed in religious education. He said his father took him to many churches to find the "right church," and "right religion." His mother was a purveyor of fine merchandise, as she liked to collect and save things - many from the trash and around the neighborhood.

And between the layers of each of our dysfunctional childhoods, it was going to be a long road.

And our bathroom war was far, far from over...

CHAPTER 8

The Washing Machine

Getting my husband to put the toilet paper on the roller was minor compared to what occurred next.

He was lounging on the couch watching TV when I came storming out of the laundry room, holding one of my wool sweaters, wrinkled and shrunken.

I start yelling. "Are you fucking kidding me, why the *hell* would you put a wool sweater in the washing machine? Who the *fuck* puts a wool sweater in the washer?" My tirade ended with, "What the *hell* is wrong with you? This is hand-made!"

My husband just stared back. He didn't know what to say and by the expressionless look on his face - it was evident once again that he didn't even know what he did wrong!

Infuriated I continued, "This does not go in the machine... look at it...it's ruined... didn't you read the damn tag...there is a reason there is a tag attached to the inside of clothing...what the fuck is the matter with you...don't you know how to sort the damn clothing...you can't put everything in the machine together," I yelled louder. "Just fug-ged-da-boud-it."

He smiled and apologized and said, "I'm sorry honey... I didn't see it...I'll buy you another one."

To him, the solution was all too simple. There was nothing wrong and he'd go out and purchase something else.

Eyes blazing, I threw the sweater across the room and it landed in his lap. "Well then, that would require a trip to Florence, Italy, which would be impossible for *you* because *you* don't have a fucking passport!" I shouted as I retreated to the laundry room, stunned at his inability to see the problem.

The farthest he got was to Cabala's in Pennsylvania. For our first Christmas he bought me several wool sweaters to replace the sweaters he destroyed. Every Christmas since, I receive one or two sweaters.

The laundry conversation persisted for months. Every week my husband ruined some article of my clothing. I begged him to please pay attention when he was doing laundry. I tried to explain about permanent press, delicate cycles, separating colors, and the various water temperatures. The fighting continued and escalated always ending with screaming, shouting, and the slamming of doors.

"You're nuts," he screamed back at me.

"What part of this don't you fucking understand...don't you know how to use the damn washer and dryer...don't you know what setting to use...didn't you ever wash a table cloth...and what about the sheets...they get dirty and need to be washed too...what the hell is wrong with you...towels get washed separately and not with clothing...do you have any idea why we use Woolite and fabric softener...you can't wash everything in hot water... my work pants don't get washed in fucking hot water...the tag says dry clean only...this needs to be sent to the cleaners...why are you using so much damn detergent...the dogs toys and blankets have bacteria and need to be washed too..."

My husband laughed when I talked about washing the dogs bedding. "Are you serious, nobody washes pet bedding and toys? Bacteria on their blankets – you're fucking crazy!" he'd shout

30

back at me before raising the volume on the television signaling he was done with the conversation.

I eventually brought his mother into the argument and blamed her. "Didn't your mother teach you how to do the laundry…didn't you wash clothes in your house…did you have a washing machine in Pennsylvania or did you go down to the creek…you know like the Egyptians, who did their wash in the Nile River?"

He would retort with some pompous comment and our war over the laundry continued as doors slammed and obscenities echoed thru the house. I'm positive the neighbors could hear us.

The lint trap was another matter.

Who would have thought that a square piece of plastic with a fragment of screen attached would be the object of so many arguments?

"Do you know what this is?" I calmly asked as I held a huge wad of lint in my hand.

He looked at me questioningly and muttered, "Dust?"

"No, you fool; it's the *fucking* neighbor's dog! Are you *fucking* kidding me? Do you want to burn the house down? Look at this shit!"

He laughs and thinks I'm funny. "Like you say to me just fuh-ged-da-boud-it. You know I love you don't you?"

I ran my hands through my hair in frustration. My hands cut wildly through the air, as I try to make my point. We are both laughing at how absurd we sounded.

My husband thought he was a comedian, and said, "You look like your swatting bugs!"

I was over the edge because I could not understand what was so difficult about removing the lint trap or why he didn't get it.

So now I'm yelling obscenities as my father did decades before, and I sounded exactly like my mother, who never let my father near the washer or dryer for the same reasons. "Do you even know where the fucking lint trap is located?" My hands whip through my hair as I gesture furiously before throwing the wad of lint across the room. My husband retreats to the shed with promises to remove the lint.

And like my mother, I tape a note above the two machines with instructions on how to use the washer and dryer.

"Lint trap," snapped my girlfriend. Her voice cut through the phone like a razor. She had just found a wad of lint the size of her cat in the lint trap. Her lint trap is one of those long, curled contraptions that her husband thinks is designed this way so it can capture as much lint as possible!

"There was so much lint on that screen that it actually jammed the trap as he was pulling it up. When it wouldn't budge he pushed the trap back into the dryer shoving the entire clump of lint into the machine!"

I couldn't contain my laughter.

"To solve the problem he takes the house vacuum and tries to suck the lint out and somehow in the process the dryer swallows the fuckin' attachment! He spent the rest of the afternoon taking the dryer apart to find the lint and attachment! It's a fuckin' miracle he hasn't set the house on fire."

I was laughing so hard the tears were rolling down my cheeks. "And I thought I had problems," I teased. "My husband won't feel so bad when I tell him this story. What the hell does he think happens to the lint if he doesn't clean the trap?"

"This is even funnier," she states sarcastically. "He thinks that when there is enough lint in the machine, the dryer actually pulls it back down through the hose and out the ventilating cover into the yard where he will later rake it up!"

No, she is not joking.

I was having dinner with my girlfriends who rapidly brought up another issue regarding laundry, the emptying of the pockets.

I smirk amused. "My husband thinks he is innocent when it comes to items in the pants pockets."

Our married girlfriend quickly chimes in. "Gum, candy, cigarettes, food, money, change, paper, writing implements of various colors have made it through all the cycles of the washer and dryer. He has no idea how they got there is his response. I blame everyone, the kids and my husband since I don't know who did it," she finished laughing.

I raised my eyes and burst out laughing. "Last week, my husband held up his work shirt and pants and pointed out huge ink spots on his clothing. He couldn't understand how they got there and refused to wear them. I suggested the common practice of emptying pockets before putting clothes in the machine. The fact that he thinks he had nothing to do with leaving pens in his pockets is funny. The fact that we debate about whose responsibility it is to remove items left in clothing pockets is even funnier."

My single girlfriend says he is lucky he didn't wash his wallet or passport like her boyfriend did. Apparently, this is a problem because he never empties out his pockets.

I agree, spending the day in one of the New Jersey motor vehicle locations or social security office without identification and trying to come up with acceptable documentation can be overwhelming.

We continued to laugh at the insanity of it all.

Over dinner the following evening my husband recalled a story about why laundry is so challenging for him. "Once the laundry machine was broken in our house and I had to go to the laundry mat. I would fill the trash bag with dirty, smelly clothes and leave with the same trash bag filled with now clean clothes."

We are both laughing hysterically. As I am quick to point out how I understand where his laundry habits began and that his behavior now made sense.

"You're not a fucking bachelor anymore," I grinned. "You need to start learning how to do laundry and cleaning out the lint trap."

CHAPTER 9

Read the Manual

Our laundry and lint war continued.

Months went by and the unthinkable happened – my pants were getting too tight. Pregnancy was not even a consideration as I already had a hysterectomy due to my first bought with cancer. I assumed I was gaining weight until testing other clothing I owned, proved that wasn't the issue as everything fit perfectly. Visions of my mother yelling at my father about the laundry popped into my head. I went looking for my husband and found him on the couch. I accused him of washing my pants. We argued and he claimed he had not touched my pants or any of my laundry.

I laugh in disbelief. "So why are these clothes shrinking? Are the dogs doing the fucking laundry when we're not home?"

He shrugged. "It's a possibility. Those dogs are very intelligent," he reminded me as he continued to channel surf with the television remote.

I retreated, vowing to get to the bottom of this.

The truth was eventually revealed early one afternoon. I was home before he was and found clothes in the washer and dryer. As I extracted the laundry from the dryer, I couldn't believe my eyes. Once again, no separation of colors or materials was considered. The whites tumbled out with colored towels, jeans, his work shirts and my favorite, white cotton pants! I held them up to the light. Not only had they magically transformed to a slight hue of blue, but also I could tell from looking at them they had shrunk at least three sizes! Unless I lost twenty pounds I'd never be able to wear them again!

The argument that followed went something like this – "You're fucking unbelievable...why are you touching my clothes... the lint trap is filled with lint...you're going to set the house on fire...why are you washing towels with the pants...how come you refuse to listen...what the hell is the fuckin' problem... you don't regard me...I don't understand what is so fucking difficult..."

And on and on it went.

My husband single-handedly ruined most of my wardrobe during the first year of our marriage. I was tired of crying every time I pulled damaged clothing from the dryer. I don't know when my final outburst came but it was a combination of the high water bill due to washing in hot water, the waste of laundry detergent, the loss of good articles of clothing, and his unwillingness to do the laundry properly!

Exasperated, I held up another article of ruined clothing that resembled something like an old, tie-dyed shirt, "Why can't you read the damn label? The instructions are right on this tag. It explains how the clothing should be washed," I point and shake the material while I am shrieking. "What is so *fucking* hard about this?"

My anger is more apparent when he doesn't answer immediately. My eyes wide in disbelief I shake my head as my hands automatically start pointing to the label. "Why do you think it's there? To test one's eyesight?

My husband smiled and responded as if I'm over reacting again and there is nothing wrong. "Actually I thought the tag was there because they had extra material..."

"Damn it! You don't regard me or my clothing."

"Fuh-ged-da-boud-it…."

The obscenities my father taught me flowed effortlessly before he could even finish his sentence.

More yelling and debating followed…

I slammed the door not wanting to listen to another one of his ridiculous reasons.

Thoroughly disgusted, I met with the girls for lunch one afternoon and brought up the topic, "Who does the laundry in your home?"

Just mentioning one word, "laundry," and these intelligent, educated women turned into vicious, unrecognizable beings. Husbands, and boyfriends, were lucky they were not around during this conversation for they would have been surely seared from the intense heat that blazed from angry eyes.

I quickly discovered I was not suffering alone.

"Absolutely not!" one of my friends shouted back adamantly. She was cooking at the stove and had turned around so fast I thought the spatula she held in her hand was going to fly across the room. Apparently this had been a hot topic in her home.

She gestured angrily as the cooking utensil cut through the air like a machete. "I don't let him touch the laundry! During our first two years together he ruined all of my clothing! I won't let him near the machines!"

"The exact thing happened to me," another repeated. "During the first year of our marriage he destroyed half my wardrobe. He, too, is not allowed near the machine or my clothing," she spat with fire in her eyes.

Now she happened to be on crutches at the time for a broken leg.

"So who is doing the laundry since your leg is in a cast?"

"I hobble or crawl, I don't care how much pain I'm in - he is not getting near that machine or my clothing!"

Again, I felt better knowing I wasn't alone.

The others had similar stories. Items like silk blouses, pants, wool sweaters, jackets, even a leather skirt had been a victim of the laundry war that seemed to exist in households all over. "What about the rest of America?" I muttered.

My one friend summed it up best, "Every woman owns a wool sweater that can fit a small child or can be pulled over a stuffed animal."

We all laughed.

I applauded their solution to end the problem - the boyfriends and husbands were not allowed to touch the laundry or use the machines!

But was it really necessary to start WWIII over laundry? I quickly remembered that my parents did so why not keep the tradition alive!

Now armed with ammunition, I arrived home, feeling confident I was going to put a stop to our laundry war. I stormed into the living room and offered yet another compromise, "YOU'RE NOT A FUCKING BACHELOR ANYMORE! You wash your clothes and I'll wash mine!"

This did not last very long. My clothing still managed to mysteriously get mixed in with the towels. Other shrunken articles were eventually retired to the rag bin to be used for cleaning. And men have the nerve to wonder why we are always out shopping for clothing!

Months later, my prayers were finally answered. A miracle occurred. The old washer broke down and could not be repaired. We were now forced into purchasing new machines. Shopping for a washer and dryer required research and information, so I respectfully phoned my mother!

After a weekend of looking at prices and comparing brands, we eventually became the proud owners of a new energy efficient washer and dryer! These machines were the latest technological upgrade for these important domestic devices.

And those of you who have these new machines know what wonderful inventions they really are. The multitude of settings and ability to wash all types of clothing is a blessing. But using the machines correctly requires reading the instruction manual; something my husband thinks he is exempt from. For him, instruction manuals are just suggestive reading!

He has his own unique way of deciphering an instruction manual.

He starts with the intent look and then the touch of the item when he tackles an installation. I think he believes that somehow the information from the manual will penetrate into his brain as he stares and then opens and closes doors, turns knobs, rotates wires and a variety of different size screws in his hand, like chimpanzees being trained to operate the space station before being launched to the moon!

One afternoon he was assembling an electric snow shovel for my mother. She marveled at how he had all the pieces neatly and strategically arranged on the deck. She couldn't understand why he was picking each piece up, rotating them in his hands and studying each one so intently. Impatient with the lack of progress she made the mistake of asking, "Why can't you just read the manual?"

My thoughts exactly!

"Why the hell can't you just read the FUCKING MANUAL?" I yelled when it came to the installation of the new washer and dryer.

I shoot him my "Alice Look." It's the look Alice (Audrey Meadows) always gave her husband Ralph Kramden (Jackie Gleason) on the classic television show - *The Honeymooners.*

Hands on hips or arms across her chest, Alice would glare at Ralph in silent disbelief as she listened to yet another scheme or plan to accomplish something by cutting corners. After Ralph was done explaining she would continue to stare at him with such incredulity at the nonsensical brainstorm or idea - which in turn would provoke another infuriating outburst from Ralph, who failed miserably in his attempt to explain how beneficial his idea or scheme was going to be.

My arms were folded tightly across my chest. I continued with my "Alice Look" and started again, "Why can't you read the damn instruction manual," I pleaded.

"Just let me look at it," he shouted.

Now I was laughing. "What, the fuck, are you scrutinizing? What, is the machine silently communicating to you, connect a to b…is there some spiritual force from the instruction manual or machine penetrating the directions into your brain…how long are you going to stare at the damn machine?"

"You're lucky to have me," he laughed. "This is a simple process. I really don't need that manual."

"Fuh-ged-da-boud-it! This is ridiculous. You've been fooling around all morning with these machines."

I had enough and called the store.

"The technician will be here within the hour to hook everything up. If you damage this machine because you don't know what you are doing you can wash your damn clothes outside with the fuckin' hose," I snapped.

With the new machines in place the absolute and agreed on compromise over the laundry eventually came to an end. I have the complexity of technology to thank. There were simply too many buttons and settings for him to deal with! And reading the manual to learn the settings was simply too much for my husband. I would do all the laundry and my husband would fold everything.

What ensued next, I really can't blame on my husband. The clothes were still shrinking!

"I swear, honey, I am not touching that machine...I don't even know what buttons to push." My husband stared at the controls as if he is on the deck of a battleship. "Why does everything have to be digital?" he blurted angrily. "If they made things like they used to, I could fix them," he sighed heavily. Rolling his eyes and shaking his head in frustration he added, "You know if we bought the cheaper machines, we probably wouldn't have all these problems."

When I pulled out the instruction manual, it was his cue to leave. "Look at this thing; it's as thick as the Bible. I don't have time to read this," he snapped irritably.

It was my mother who finally figured it out.

She was visiting for the week and one day was helping with the laundry. She wanted to know why I was washing clothes in hot water. "Didn't I teach you anything? You're wasting water," she shouted from the laundry room.

"What the hell are you talking about? I'm washing delicates. The dial is set to cold-cold," I screamed back.

The loud voices bought my husband into the kitchen, who, proceeded to investigate. "Oh honey, you need to come here," he called for me rather smugly.

I held my hand out to feel the water as my husband turned the dial and quickly pulled it back. The water was scorching hot! I immediately blamed him. The tapestry of obscenities was followed by, "If *you* read the directions *you* could have installed the machines and I wouldn't have had those idiots from the store here!"

My husband laughed and told me he loves me and not to worry. That it will be ok.

Minutes later I was on the phone with the appliance retailer. Later, we discovered they had hooked up the hoses incorrectly – hot was cold and cold was hot. Ugh! More ruined clothes.

Over dinner we listened to my mother tell stories about doing laundry in the "olden days," and how she still has the same washer. We laughed at our childishness. "Ok, I get it I'm not a fucking bachelor anymore," he said sarcastically. It was a comment made out of fear…fear of having to spend money on another machine if he broke the new one or actually having to learn to use the machines.

CHAPTER 10

Hot Irons

I started purchasing "wrinkle-free and wash and wear" clothing after my husband's attempts to do laundry; however, wrinkle-free only applies if the article of clothing is removed from the machine and folded or hung up immediately.

One day, I went to work wearing an over-sized shirt and it was extremely wrinkled. It was during radiation treatment for breast cancer at the time. Not only was it easy to take on and off but also it was less irritating on my red-blistered skin. My boss understood but, in a friendly way, suggested I at least iron it!

Although we do own an iron, no ironing is done in our house. We bought it for one purpose, to adhere laminate edging to the shelves my husband built in the bathroom.

I hate to iron and so does my husband.

My husband claims he did iron when he was single.

"Yeah, right," I responded cynically. "Now that's funny. I'd love to hear all about your ironing experiences. Tell me *exactly* where you did your ironing," my voice dripped with sarcasm.

"On the kitchen table!"

I turned my head, eyebrows raised, and gave him the "Alice Look." My arms immediately folded across my chest. I tilted my head and laughed smugly.

"You're kidding me, right? What, in between the piles and piles of unopened mail and other fucking crap? Get serious. Come to think of it, I never saw an iron in your apartment. And if you had an iron, where did you keep it?" I persisted chuckling.

"Why should I expose *you* to something that *you* wouldn't do," he snapped, knowing that it was senseless to continue the conversation because he never owned an iron.

"You're right, I hate to iron it's a fact," I maintained as I retreated to the kitchen.

I heard him bellowing, "What didn't your mother teach you to iron…at least I know how…what the hell is so hard about it anyway…"

I thought about it. The more I reflected, I began to realize why I don't iron and immediately blamed my mother!

Now my mother…she ironed *everything*. The laundry basket was *always* full. The ironing board was *always* out, and she was constantly ironing something. Socks, underwear, sheets, every article of clothing and piece of fabric that was in our house was ironed. My mother of course was a stay at home mom for many years. She had time for this chore.

So why do I blame my mother for my lack of ironing skill, ability… or whatever you want to call it. It was something we were simply *not* permitted to do! And once in college, who had time for that menial task?

Eventually out in the working world my suits all went to the cleaners. I was single and could afford it. Thanks to the economic constraints my husband and I have been subjected to, trips to the cleaners are rare these days. I am deeply indebted to the person who invented wash and wear, wrinkle-free clothing!

My mother blames the school system for my incapability to iron. Instead of semester after semester of sewing, I enrolled in woodshop!

"What the *hell* are you going to do with that?" She argued, as she reluctantly signed the permission slip allowing me to register.

I reflect on the breadboards my brothers and I made which are still proudly displayed on the kitchen wall in her home, or the wooden gumball machines that are covered with decades of dust in the living room. I call my mother to inquire about them.

I am momentarily transported back to the 1970's kitchen, with the dark cabinets, round table, and Formica counter tops listening to my mother who wastes no time getting right to the nucleus of my issue.

"What the *hell* do you want with that stuff? I should never have let you take wood shop; if you took sewing you would know how to sew and iron and there wouldn't be a basket of clothing in your living room. What the hell do you need another bread board for?"

She's right. Why the hell do I need another breadboard?

CHAPTER 11

The Laundry Basket

Who is to blame for the laundry conflicts between men and women? My girlfriends and I were discussing this at work one day. One was teaching her sons to do laundry for three reasons. First, because once they are off to college and eventually living on their own, they are not going to be bringing their clothing home for her to wash, iron, or fold! Second, she doesn't want them to get married and think they are exempt from household chores and that washing should be a woman's job. Finally, if they wind up divorced, they will not be bringing their laundry back home for her to do!

Talk about long range planning and having all angles covered!

My other friend offered some thought provoking comments. While admitting she didn't like anyone touching the machine, she taught her children to be self-sufficient. "I want my kids to be able to help their spouses and not be a hindrance. I also didn't want them to turn out like *my* mother. My father did *absolutely* nothing. My mother did everything. She was taught to serve my father. I wasn't going to raise my children that way. We're a unit we all work as a team."

I applauded her attitude and readily agreed. My father was also part of the 'do absolutely nothing club.' It was always get me this…get me that…do this…laundry, cooking, cleaning were expected and things men did not do.

My other friend laughed and stated, "When we were married, that fuckin' bastard husband of mine didn't do anything in the house and my son is just like him because that's what he witnessed when he was growing up. He won't even fold his own clothes," she spat.

Folding clothes is what my husband agreed to do. Not only can he do this well, but he also excels at it!

My husband tells me I can't fold clothes and he is right! I totally agree. I hate folding clothes. I also missed this lesson from my mom. Not only could she iron, but she also knew how to fold. Sheets, towels, shirts, pants were always perfect, not a crease or wrinkle. Every article of clothing and piece of fabric was stacked or folded neatly in drawers or closets. My husband and I own a few sets of sheets and I still can't get them like my mom does, perfectly crisp and tight – like they are coming fresh out of the package.

I don't have time to sit and fluff and remove every crease and make flawless folds. My husband does this perfectly! There are two reasons for this: the first, he is obsessive compulsive and the second, he worked in retail and spent much time working in soft lines or the clothing section. He knows how to fold clothing!

So how could there be any more problems regarding laundry? I do the laundry, he folds. It was a good compromise. What could possibly go wrong?

It all centered on a plastic 18"x20" inch laundry basket! It's amazing that so many issues between husbands and wives arise from something as trivial as a plastic laundry basket full of clothing. Ironically it's one thing I discovered that could get my husband off the couch!

The plastic, blue laundry basket has become another piece of furniture in our living room that is utilized solely by my husband. Sometimes he uses it as a footrest. Sometimes he takes off his filthy clothes and throws them on top of it or dirty towels fly out of the bathroom and expertly land in the basket. The laundry basket is not empty of course – it is full of clean clothes! The youngest dog has a pallet in every room of the house but he favors the laundry basket too and, on occasion, can be found cuddling up on the clean clothing!

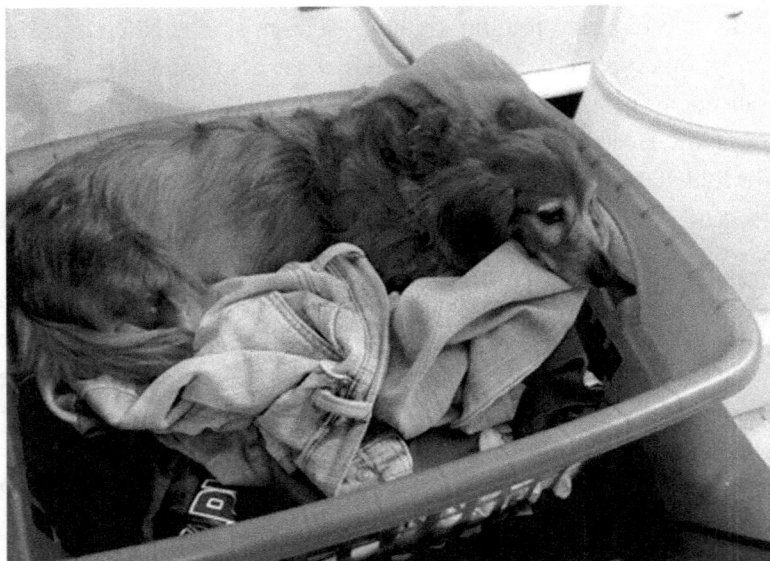

Joey sleeping on clean laundry

The laundry basket is also like a way station or halfway point. It is where crucial, executive decisions are made about where the laundry is going.

This is where he decides what is dirty enough to actually go to the laundry room! It is settled by the smell test. Smelling each article of clothing solves where the clothing will end up – in the laundry room to be washed, to remain in the laundry basket with the rest of the clean clothing or on the chair to be worn again!

The laundry basket always seems to be filled with clothing. My husband could be watching television with the basket sitting next to him, piled high with clean clothes, for days or even weeks, which *is* the reason why I went to work with a wrinkled blouse as it had been sitting in the basket for weeks!

I solve problems with such ease at work but when I come home, I debate about toilet paper, how to wash clothes, and a laundry basket that continually sits in the middle of our living room. I could take the clothes out and put them and the basket away, but I have already done this and I refuse to do it anymore!

My roll with the laundry basket is to fill it with clean laundry and move it around the living room to where my husband is sitting, hoping he will fold the clothes.

A co-worker was reading my manuscript. She called and wanted to know if the laundry basket is still in the living room. I laughed hysterically. I took a picture of the blue laundry basket sitting in front of the couch with my iPhone and hit send.

I didn't grow up like this, or did I?

My brother is quick to refresh my memory. Laughing, he provides a few highlights. "The laundry basket sat in the living room, and mom was always after someone to take it upstairs. When it finally made it to the second floor it sat next to the ironing board and was continuously subjected to a host of profanity. It was moved, kicked and yelled at for being in the way. Don't you remember the incident when dad tripped over it and it wound up back at the bottom of the stairs, or the countless times he threw the entire basket full of clean clothing down the stairs?"

We laughed at the insanity of it all.

However he was right. It was all coming back to me - like a bad nightmare. The laundry basket was always sitting at the top or bottom of the stairs waiting to be carried down or up if it was filled with dirty or clean clothes. Or it sat by the back door waiting for someone to carry it to the basement to wash or back up two more flights of stairs to resume its spot next to the ironing board. We all walked by it perhaps because somehow we subconsciously identified it as a piece of furniture!

Nevertheless, no matter where it sat it always wound up at the bottom of one of the staircases, most of the time kicked or thrown by my father in his fits of anger.

I am very grateful for our ranch-style home, which has no stairs!

One day, it finally got to me. I couldn't stand the mess and the overflowing clothing on the floor so I started folding. To my surprise, my husband looked over, and like lava spewing from a dormant volcano, jumped up off the couch and grabbed his shirt out of my hands and started re-folding it! His face was getting redder and redder, indicating his blood pressure had skyrocketed.

He started yelling, "Don't touch that... don't fold my fucking socks that way...look what you did to the underwear...how could you fold a t-shirt like this...what's wrong with you...don't touch my shit..."

I grinned in disbelief. More obscenities... more laughing at our infantile behavior

And on and on it went.

It is interesting to watch my husband fold the laundry. The entire process is taken to a whole other level in our home.

Like some ancient ritual, piece-by-piece of clothing is taken out of the basket and given a quick, brisk shake. Then, like a fine piece of ancient parchment, the article is gently laid across his chest. His hand gradually runs across the fabric, smoothing out every wrinkle and crease. Next, comes what my girlfriend refers to as the "chin tuck." The chin comes down to hold the clothing in the center and the right arm brings the clothing across the chest followed by the left arm. It's amazing the perfect little package he creates. The entire process is similar to the sign of the cross one might make during prayer services!

I am not sure if this is obsessive compulsive, or plain insanity. My girlfriend says it's downright disturbing! She and I were discussing laundry and folding, as her boyfriend is just as neurotic. So much so that he folds clothes the exact same way! I was shocked. I didn't believe it. Apparently neither could she. Only she had taken it a step further and had videotaped him folding his clothes on her cell phone. It was hilarious. He was just as, if not more, obsessive than my husband.

Thoroughly amused I hand her the cell phone. "You should put that on YouTube."

Later we started comparing notes with some of the other girls at lunch and what we found even funnier is that we all did the same thing after the clothes were folded – we purposely messed them up! My husband could be folding shirts, underwear, or socks and I will walk by and jokingly knock his little, neat pile over. I shrug, "If you would just regard me."

He laughs and tells me I'm evil.

I give him the "Alice Look" and tell him he should be medicated.

"You're right," he readily agrees.

The neatly, folded clothing will *then* sit for days or weeks in the laundry basket. When I get sick of looking at the basket in the middle of the floor, I reach in and grab a pair of my husband's underwear – this is usually done while he is sitting on the couch watching television.

Somehow the third, invisible eye he has that is hidden on his body, detects this action causing him to immediately forget about the TV show and he jumps off the couch and follows me into the bedroom.

"What are you doing...where are you going...give me those clothes...you're not putting them in my draws...you don't know where they go...I'll do that..."

Now I'll admit, when I'm busy working, cleaning, cooking, gardening, doing laundry, filling the toilet paper holder - you get the picture – organizing clothing in the drawers is the last thing I have time for! My husband has his own unique system of obsessive-compulsive categorizing. It more disconcerting than the folding!

Clearly he had forgotten the, oh so important, "put the shit away" clause that was imbedded somewhere in our laundry contract!

I hand him his underwear and grin. "You're not a fucking bachelor anymore. The deal was I wash and you fold. After you fold the clothes you have to put them away. I am sick of looking at that laundry basket. I work too and you need to help out because I can't do everything. YOU'RE NOT A FUCKING BACHELOR ANYMORE!"

CHAPTER 12

The Convenience Store

Growing up, the convenience store was at the bottom of the hill, in a small strip shopping mall next to the Grand Union supermarket. It's where my father went to get the newspaper, coffee, cigarettes, and lottery tickets. The name of the establishment eludes me. I could easily look it up or ask my mother but I won't for the awful memories it evokes. But what I will say is this - when my father said he was "Going to the bottom of the hill" – the translation was – he was taking another trip to the convenience store for cigarettes and he would probably stop by the liquor store that was located *conveniently* next door!

Besides cigarettes and liquor, he was forever coming home with some sort of trinket, gadget, or "great buy" or some unusual merchandise from his precious convenience store. Some of the things he bought resembled items sold by a vendor at an outdoor flea market. One day it was a dish, another it was a cup or glass. He actually bought utensils for the outdoor grill for my husband and me there. His reason for purchasing these items was always the same - "It was a great deal."

My mother, and I would look at him like he was a fool. How foolish could he be to actually spend money on such cheaply made things? It contradicted everything he stood for and disciplined us against. Didn't he know everything cost *more* money in the convenience store? The stuff that he thought he was getting for such a great deal could be purchased for half the price at the Caldor or K-Mart, which was located in the *convenient* shopping plaza's just up the hill.

My brothers and I knew this – so why didn't he, we'd wonder. And why didn't he consult my mother since she was the one who did the shopping!

Anyone who is acquainted with my mother is well aware that she is not your ordinary shopper. She doesn't stop at random stores and grab anything off the shelf. No, my mother took shopping to a higher level. This was a gift she possessed and excelled at. What made her an extraordinary shopper was first she understood the concept of comparison-shopping. Second, she did her homework. Something she was taught by her parents who dragged her to store after store, as the goal was to get the best merchandise for the best price. "Effects of living through WWII, learning to ration and what was passed on to them from their parents living through the depression," that's the way it was my mother stated.

She knew the stores, read the circulars, researched items and made sure she always obtained quality merchandise at the best rate. Whether it was for clothing, food, household products, toys, or appliances, my mother was suited and equipped for this role. Sam Walton would have been proud of her. She would have made great contributions to any of the big-box retailers. All this was long before the computer and Internet. At the age of seventy-six her buying competency continues as she navigates through her iPad so effortlessly it would make Apple founder Steve Jobs proud!

Now my father – knew absolutely nothing about buying anything except for cigarettes, coffee, beer, and the newspaper. And again, being a creature of habit, it was always at the convenience store at the bottom of the hill.

His world really came crashing in one year when tragedy struck. The convenience store caught on fire and burnt down! Now he had to find another place to buy his newspaper, coffee, and cigarettes! This was long before Dunkin' Donuts, Wawa, and 7-11's decorated the corners of every neighborhood.

He could have just purchased the newspaper and coffee in numerous other establishments nearby, but some of them didn't sell coffee and lottery tickets. The rest of the equation had to include a liquor store.

As a child I didn't understand what was more important the liquor, coffee, or cigarettes. As an adult, well, the answer was all too clear.

In any event, to solve his problem he drove across town just so he could buy everything in one place! And when I say across town, I mean way across town, up three major hills and right to the border of the neighboring town!

Who the *hell* drives to the other side of town to get the newspaper and coffee? The argument between my parents would commence every time he did this.

My mother would express what I was silently thinking, a waste of fuel and money. She gave *him* the "Alice Look" and the bickering began.

The dialogue went something like this, "You're such a fool... who drives to the other side of town to get the newspaper...you complain about the high gas prices and this is what you do...what a waste of gas...you actually bought this piece of garbage...how could you spend our hard earned money on this...what the hell is wrong with you...you don't buy grilling utensils at a convenience store...and why are you drinking so much coffee...you are going to get sick...why waste money on coffee when I make it every day...why are you wasting so much money on cigarettes...your killing me and the children with that smoke....you don't want to know what your lungs are going to look like....."

And on and on it went, day after day after day.

Over time the script became standard but oscillated between the similar phrases and intertwined with the usual tasteless vulgarities when my father responded.

My mother, who was reading my notes, looks up at me astonished and says, "How do you remember all of that?"

"Unfortunately, it's permanently imprinted on my brain like a tattoo," I answer painfully.

As I stated earlier, life was never right in our house if there was no screaming, arguing or loud verbal banter. We actually thought these cycles of violent screaming and quarreling, were normal and occurred in every household. The verbal assault and violence always began with my father. He bullied and provoked my mother purposely and later his own children.

My mother *never* used foul language. She still refuses to believe where I learned such obscenities or why I say the dreaded F...word. "This is why this country is the way it is," she fiercely debated. "Nobody cares about anything." The conversation quickly changes, as I'm quick to remind her about life with my father.

My brothers and I had a secret code name for our parents when they started their verbal battles. I don't recall who actually came up with the nickname that was to follow my parents for decades. We referred to them as the "irrational matter." Matter, that just co-existed, filled with erratic conversation that was sometimes so bizarre it didn't make sense.

For instance, when my mother would complain about the convenience store, smoking, or wasting gas and money my father would retort with a round of hateful obscenities followed by something nonsensical like, "Get lost or drop dead on Broad and Market Street!"

What the *hell* did that mean? Where the *hell* was Broad and Market Street and why would someone what to be lost or dead there? My brothers and I would stare at one another perplexed. We learned early on the consequences for asking for an explanation; instead, we darted up the stairs to our rooms to avoid the wooden spoon or leather strap.

I eventually learned that Broad and Market were actually streets in Newark, New Jersey. It wasn't until I was fifty years old that I actually drove down them! I was in a limo on the way to the airport with my husband and mother when I looked out the window and shouted in disbelief, "Holy shit, this is it? It's the intersection of Broad and Market street! It's the street he was always talking about. Look Mom, you finally got here," I laughed.

My mother shook her head and glanced at me with a melancholy expression at first and then together we burst out laughing uncontrollably. We had both found peace with that harsh memory of long ago.

My husband, who didn't understand what the hell we found so amusing, looked out the window at the boarded up homes and run down properties and starts with his own round of obscenities and wanted to know why the hell the driver is going through such a dangerous part of town. He ended with, "We could have just taken the fuckin' Garden State parkway!"

My mother and I only laughed harder.

CHAPTER 13

Ham and Cheese

The fighting between the "irrational matter," was routine. When the screaming was over, doors slammed from various locations in the house and everyone retreated to their corners and suffered in silence - until it started again. Some of the battles were legendary. The convenience store was one of them; most of the time it started with his drinking or yet another purchase of a pack of cigarettes.

After these purchases, the return dialogue from my father was always the same. In between drags on his non-filtered "cancer sticks" and his fits of coughing, he would yell a litany of colorful expletives.

My mother would laugh at his foolishness. "Yeah, keep on smoking and see where it gets you," she prophesized.

The realities of his three packs of Camel, non-filter cigarettes a day from the convenience store were already present but the harsh consequences would be revealed decades later.

After a few rounds of hateful exchanges my mother would get the last word, "Didn't your mother teach you anything?"

They colorfully blamed one another's parents for their ongoing issues, the house....shopping....smoking....drinking....money....gas...the economy...the car...

And on and on it went.

The root cause for it all was deeply embedded in decades of family history.

Another final expletive and he'd retreat to the TV room in a haze of cigarette smoke.

During these heated exchanges, I would sit there silently and laugh at how ridiculous my father's actions actually were. My mother was right. Purchasing cigarettes was a waste of money and going cause of multitude of illnesses. Shopping? He knew nothing about it. It was a fact. He didn't like going to the mall or to any store. This included grocery shopping. To him, shopping was always better at the convenience store!

SO WHY DO I RESURRECT THESE RIDICULOUS MEMORIES? WHAT IS THE POINT? HOW DOES IT EVEN RELATE TO MY HUSBAND AND OUR MARRIAGE?

Well…

I secretly vowed that when I grew up, none of what transpired between my parents was *never, ever* going to happen to me!

Four decades later this is the same conversation I am having with my husband. One day we were driving and he announced that he is going to stop and pick up some lunchmeat for sandwiches.

I think nothing of it, until he abruptly turns the truck off the road and into a parking lot.

"Why are you stopping here?" I ask. "I thought you said you were going to the store. We don't need gas. What the hell are you stopping at the *fucking* gas station for?"

My husband shrugged and calmly stated, "Calm down babe, I'm just going to pick up some ham and cheese."

"HAM AND CHEESE," I interrupt yelling over Bruce Springsteen's *Born to Run,* which is playing on the radio. I whip around in my seat. I can feel the blood rushing to my face. I am laughing at the absurdity of it and at the same time stare at him in disbelief, screaming, *"WHO THE HELL BUYS LUNCH MEAT AT A FUCKIN GAS STATION...WHAT IS WRONG WITH YOU...YOU CAN'T BE SERIOUS!"*

My husband thinks I'm being unreasonable and begins laughing, which irritates me further.

"This is ridiculous! The Shop Rite is at the *next* light!

He smiles. "Fuh-ged-da-boud-it babe. Why should I drive further? Look we are here. Come, it will be a good experience for you."

I glare at him. My eyes are shooting daggers as I hold the "Alice Look." My annoyance is apparent as I get out of the truck and slam the door. "Somehow I doubt it!"

The Wawa was a buzz of activity. Like radar on a ship, I do a quick scan and suddenly it all made sense – convenience store shopping was imbedded in the genetic composition of men, including my husband!

Ok. Seriously. I know this doesn't include all men, and there are just as many women who are at fault for not spending wisely, but at that particular moment I was in a state of shock because he was actually going to purchase ham and cheese at the gas station and then seeing all those men, just helped solidify my theory.

It was lunchtime and it was men, who were predominately crowded at the deli counter placing orders, arms filled with chips, sodas, and other snacks as they eagerly waited for their sandwiches. My husband threw some rolls in a bag and ordered some ham and cheese, then grabbed the largest bag of chips.

Aghast, I was already silently calculating the cost as I followed him to the drink machine where he grabbed the largest size cup and proceeded to fill it with soda! Once in line he added a pretzel and candy bar. "Do you want something honey?"

"No!" I snapped, fuming.

The minute we were in the truck and the doors closed, I resurrected the argument between my parents about wasting money at the convenience store. The script was the same and the words I grew up hearing over and over and over again, unconsciously flowed easily from my mouth, obscenities included – minus the incomprehensible vulgarities.

"Do you realize you spent over *twenty dollars* on all this fuckin' crap...what the fuck is wrong with you...did you see all those people in there wasting money... did you see what they were buying...some spent over twenty-five dollars or more on lunch...they could have bought it cheaper at the grocery store... don't you have any idea how much damn money you just wasted...who the hell buys a fuckin' quarter pound of ham and cheese at a gas station...I could have gotten a hole pound at the ShopRite cheaper and it would have lasted all week...we could have gone out to a restaurant for the money you just wasted...the damn Shop Rite is down the road...they even make sandwiches which are cheaper than what you just bought..."

My husband interrupts laughing buoyantly, "You're being silly."

I am a realist and deal in facts. My husband knows this but just refuses to admit when I am right. "I will prove it to you when you come to the grocery store with me! Then you will see just how much money you are wasting!"

"The grocery store? Fuh-ged-da-boud-it," He smirks. "Humph. Good luck with that. Now you've really lost it."

More obscenities and joking between us as he assures me he won't be grocery shopping anytime soon.

He concludes with, "Like that's gonna fuckin' happen!"

The conversation continues when we arrive home. He gets the "Alice Look" for the rest of the afternoon.

This was my first indoctrination to the world of convenience store shopping that I vowed was not going to last!

"YOU'RE NOT A FUCKING BACHELOR ANYMORE," echoes through the house as the sliding glass door slams into the worn frame as he heads outside toward his shed, signaling the conversation has ended.

CHAPTER 14

Coffee

Of all the conflicts my husband and I faced the biggest was over a twenty-ounce cup of coffee that, not surprisingly, came from the dreaded fucking convenience store!

I was never a coffee drinker, probably because we were never allowed. I despised coffee and the coffee pot. Some days when my father came home for lunch with his men he would start screaming for me and my mother to prepare lunch and bring it outside for him and his dysfunctional crew. This included the coffee.

"Where the *fuck* is the coffee…what is taking you so long… we don't have all day."

I'd yell at my mother, "What's taking you so long…he's getting mad…"

And sure enough, moments later, he'd march into the house.

The minute that back door slammed my mother would look up. She was horrified and I knew what was coming.

"You're covered in tar…I just cleaned…get out…I'll be right out…don't come in here with those shoes…get out…"

He'd answer with the usual obscenities…added vulgarities… throwing chairs…door slamming…throwing the tissue box and then ending with, some absurd mumbling. This was then followed with, "Go in the fridge and get us some fuckin' beer."

One of my mother's major responsibilities in the house to make sure the coffee pot was always full. My brothers and I were responsible for getting his beer and soda.

That's why I had no interest in coffee. It didn't seem unusual to me not to drink coffee. I even owned a coffee pot, but only used it to boil water for tea. It was a Krups. My mother felt I should have one in case I ever entertained. I even had an unopened can of coffee sitting next to it!

A man I once dated, who lived in my apartment complex, asked if he could come by my apartment for a cup of coffee one afternoon. When he took a sip from the cup I served him I thought he was going to choke.

"What the *hell* is this?" He gasped. "I thought you said you had coffee."

"That's correct. I told you I had coffee. But I never said I knew how to make it!"

I never learned about coffee, how many scoops to use, how much water to put in the pot, coffee brands, or how to prepare it. My husband proudly changed all that!

My husband loves coffee. He drinks coffee like it is water. For him coffee is an all-day affair: two or three cups in the morning, more during work, and more when he comes home. When he isn't making coffee he is buying it -- and buying it, of all places, at the convenience store!

"What do you mean we're stopping...we just got in the car... we are going to be late... you just had coffee at the house not ten minutes ago...if you wanted more why couldn't you put it in a thermos and take it with you...this is just another example of how we are wasting money."

My first real indoctrination to the world of coffee naturally occurred at the convenience store. So here I am back at the Wawa with my husband. The place was always packed. As we entered, I wondered, "Doesn't anyone know how much money they are wasting?"

It was overwhelming. I pretended to look at the selections of chips while I watched the customers from the corners of my eyes - like a swarm of bees coming and going from the coffee bar. My husband was part of the swarm. They all moved about from section to section of the counter with ease, pouring, mixing and stirring. There were so many choices, different pots, and buttons to push.

Drones of young and old came to feast on the nectar. There was no hesitation or stopping. The crowd flowed effortlessly. Everyone seemed to know exactly what he or she was doing. Where did they learn all this and where the hell was the regular coffee, I pondered as I continued to gaze at the spectacle before me?

Seriously, I needed a translator, as I gawked at the rows of coffee pots, neatly labeled robust, Columbian, medium, bold, Arabic, French vanilla, hazelnut, and dark roast, were just a few of the blends.

What the hell was going on? When did America become so obsessed with coffee?

The buzz of stirring and sipping had mesmerized me. People grabbed from stacks of different size cups – everyone seemed to be super-sizing their coffee. Cups, lids, stirrers, caution jackets – each person was assembling their choice of drink like factory workers assembling a car.

Adding milk was an acquired skill. Hands quickly grabbed for the fat free, skim, whole, two percent, or a variety of flavored creamers that rested on ice. A tilt of the wrist or quick splash was the more common technique as opposed to those, who, for whatever reason felt it necessary to raise the carton way above the cup to pour and let the milk splash all over the counter!

Next was the sugar – pure, raw, low calorie, and pseudo sugar in packets of pink, blue, and yellow were neatly separated in bins by color.

Lids in a variety of shapes and sizes fell to the floor as hands snatched for the correct size.

Insulated recyclable carriers were engineering masterpieces as they were filled and expertly carried to the registers. I remain speechless as I watched the coffee frenzy unfold.

It seemed like such a hassle. Why couldn't people just make and drink coffee at home?

Back in the truck my husband laughed and told me he was glad he could expand my horizons. The following week, my husband is excited to take me on a field trip. We drive down the street and arrive at the Wawa.

"Are you kidding me?" I shout, visibly annoyed. The parking lot is so full we circle around the building and wait for someone to pull out before getting a parking spot.

"What are we doing here? You're not getting ham again are you? I just went food shopping!"

My husband smiles and proudly states, "It's *free* coffee day. All coffee is *free* today!" He is grinning from ear to ear, like he won the lottery.

My eyes narrow as I grin in disbelief. "Free coffee...are you fuckin' kidding me? You just had coffee, and we have a full pot at home. You took me here just so you can get a cup of *free* coffee? You can't be serious?"

The convenience store was jam-packed with people – who were primarily crowding around the coffee bar, moving, pouring, mixing and making sure their free cup of coffee was secured. You would have thought these people never had a cup of coffee before. I don't know what was more astonishing: the fact that we went to the convenience store to get *free* coffee or the number of people who were scurrying about just to get a cup of *free* coffee!

I couldn't give him my, *You're not a fucking bachelor anymore* speech, because the coffee was free.

FREE. What is it about the FREE give-a-way - even if you don't need it that makes people feel the need to absolutely have to have it? No matter what you were doing or how far you had to travel you were going to get coffee, because it was FREE.

Getting something for FREE, reminded me of the movie, *A Christmas Story*, released in 1983, is about a nine year old boy, Ralphie and his wish for one Christmas gift, a Red Ryder air gun. It's a glimpse of family life in 1940's, in a small American town and is highlighted with the oaths he learned from his hard-working father.

Ralphie's father wins what he refers to as a "major award," a mannequin leg covered in a fishnet stocking topped with a fringed lamp shade. The "major award" was something that he not only won but was also was FREE. No matter how ridiculous it was his father was determined to keep it. The "leg lamp" has become part of pop culture today and can be found in windows or as a Christmas decoration.

My husband thinks he "won a major award." It's as if he is getting something over on the company because he actually went to get the FREE coffee, even though he didn't need it. What he doesn't realize is that the real winner was Wawa. Once you are in the store saving on coffee, what is to stop you from spending the coffee money on something else?

Not only would he return to Wawa and spend more money, but word travels fast when something is FREE, and he would not only do his part to spread the word about the FREE coffee but here

I am writing about it. Hence, the power of the FREE coffee that would result in many trips to Wawa over the years.

While my *"YOU'RE NOT A FUCKING BACHELOR ANYMORE,"* diatribe was useless on free coffee days, it lingered, silently hovering in the shadows, waiting for the next incident.

CHAPTER 15

Coffee and Money

Inever thought coffee would cause so many arguments during the first year of our marriage. In retrospect it really wasn't about the coffee, it was about the money.

Owning a home was also a bit overwhelming, and one of the realities of life that nobody ever clarifies. All the repairs are now your responsibility. There is no maintenance man to call to fix the leak, the hot water heater, or air conditioning. Repairs will be costly, unless you can afford it or are able to fix them yourself.

For us, money issues would be inevitable.

One of our best female friends bought some suggestive reading for my husband – *The Better Homes and Garden Complete Guide to Home Repair and Improvement.* My mother sent us Martha Stewart's version.

Our first major catastrophe was the toilet. Rotor Rooter lifted the sewer cap, and snaked the lines. The bowl was then lifted off the floor twice before they discovered the problem - tree roots and lots of them. A few hundred dollars later and some special powder to pour down the toilet once a month temporarily solved that problem. Later we would discover the cost of cutting trees down while trying to decide whose idea it was to purchase a house with so many trees on the property. Electrical, plumbing, and air conditioning challenges immediately followed. Money was tight and the repair bills started piling up.

So what did my husband do to add to our financial stress? He insisted on going to the convenience store! Every day on his way to or from work he was purchasing sodas, sandwiches, hot pretzels, snacks, lunch meat, and yes, coffee, coffee, coffee and more coffee! I couldn't believe it!

And like my mother, I unconsciously continued the same arguments I grew up listening to, so feverishly debated by the "irrational matter."

Short on patience, I gave him the "Alice Look."

"Why can't you drink coffee at home before you leave the house…don't you know that everything you buy is cheaper in the supermarket…you're just wasting money…don't you know anything about shopping…. how could you waste money like this… why do you have to drink so much coffee… don't you understand we have bills to pay…didn't your mother teach you anything about shopping…why can't you take your lunch with you… just tell me what you want and I'll buy it at the grocery store it's cheaper… why the *fuck* do you have to drink so much damn coffee…"

And on and on it went…

Now we both worked in retail at the time and comparison-shopping was required weekly. It's what gave our stores the competitive edge. Even if it was a penny we were still required to have the lowest prices.

"What part of that concept did you miss?" I'd ask him when he came home with yet another receipt for food and coffee from the local convenience store.

"But I have to have my coffee."

The "Alice Look" and stance are exaggerated.

I adjust my glasses as I tip my head to one side, grinning, "ok, so answer this, why can't you just take your lunch and a thermos of coffee to work? You're wasting money. I don't understand why you don't get this," I persisted. "IT'S ECONOMICS 101!"

"A Thermos? Are you kidding me! I'm not carrying a thermos to work."

I hold the "Alice Look," arms crossed tightly across my chest. "What? Do you think packing a lunch is only for school children? People do it all the time! I take my lunch. Pick a lunch bag from the closet and I'll pack something for you," I smile as I open the closet door.

His jaw drops. He eyes widen as he stares at me in disbelief, that I would suggest such a thing. "Nobody else takes their lunch. I can buy something at McDonald's and get coffee at the Wawa! That's where everyone goes. Besides I have to have my coffee."

"Are you serious? Does holding a coffee cup from the convenience store translate to some level of "coolness" or that you're "one of the crowd" because you purchased it at the convenience store? You're being absolutely ridiculous. It's a waste of money!" I shouted angrily. "Money that we can't afford to waste!"

He circumvented the issue about the blatant waste of money. "Come on. You don't know what you're missing. Why don't you just try some coffee?"

It took one trip to Dunkin' Donuts and I was converted instantly!

Not only was I converted, but also, I was unconsciously being pulled into the quagmire of the countless episodes between the "irrational matter," over the coffee shop at the bottom of the hill that my father frequented. Only our argument was going to begin at the Dunkin' Donuts and continue on at the Starbucks, Wawa, 7-11, Quick Check, and the thousands of other convenience stores that littered Route 9, Highway 37 in Ocean County and throughout New Jersey, New York, and Pennsylvania that we would frequent!

Soon we were going to Dunkin' Donuts daily. I discovered the iced lattes, coolattas, vanilla bean, macchiatos and other specialties. How could I have possibly gone through decades of my life and missed this delicacy? How did I survive college mid-terms and final exams without ever drinking coffee, I wondered as we sat in the drive-thru for the fifth time that week! And it was at that moment, while we were waiting in the long line at the *convenient* drive-thru for a cup of this wonderful beverage that the CFO in me, the chief financial officer of our household, took over. I started analyzing the cost of our coffee habit.

I rummaged through my purse for a piece of scrap paper and pen. As we moved up a car length I calculated, like a kid counting out change in a candy store to purchase some gum. Even if you were buying a cup of coffee a day it was a lot but my husband like to super-size everything, especially coffee. Ten dollars a day multiple that by seven days a week is seventy dollars a week…multiply by four weeks in a month is two hundred and eighty dollars a month…

Perhaps I made a mistake. I checked my math blocking out the commercial on the radio as we inched forward in line.

I was astonished. "Do you know how much money we spend on coffee a week?" I asked, ill-timed as he rolled down the window.

"No, and who cares, you're not going to stop me from drinking coffee!"

"Believe me I am not *asking* you to stop drinking coffee but…"

The truck moved. We were closer to placing our order. One more car length to go. I felt the mild tap of the brake being applied.

I needed the full facts before I continued my argument. I resumed my calculations before the intercom transmission addressed us with the scripted, "Welcome to Dunkin' Donuts. Can I take your order?"

"Two hundred and eight dollars multiply by twelve months was...three thousand three hundred and sixty dollars!" I proudly supplied the full facts of my argument.

"Don't you dare super-size your order," I shrieked as the truck inched closer to the menu board. "We are spending three thousand dollars a year on coffee."

My husband looks at me perplexed. "Impossible!"

"Well, you do the math."

"You just started drinking coffee, that figure doesn't apply," he attempted to rationalize.

"But it will if we continue spending money buying coffee," I interrupted. As I spoke my voice got louder with every word. The seat belt was digging into my shoulder as I twisted in the seat to face him waving the evidence toward him.

My husband laughed. "That's ludicrous, you added wrong. I just know it!"

"Alright smart-ass, then you go ahead and do the calculations."

My husband flips his hand with a gesture indicating he is dismissing me and the entire argument.

The truck moved and was now in front of the giant menu with a list of options that you can't possibly read the moment you pull up. This could only be achieved if you were perhaps equipped with laser scanning eyes or were some sort of brilliant speed-reader.

The salutation was accompanied by much static. My husband reached over to turn down the volume of the radio, as if this will miraculously clear up the annoying interference.

The faceless employee's voice reeks of impatience as she sighed heavily and repeated the options, and finally the order.

"No," I shouted, "I just want a small."

There was something wrong with the microphone as her voice crackled through the intermittent static. The order is incorrect, which aggravated my husband who immediately blamed the error on the language barrier between him and the heavily accented voice. Instead of admitting his mistake in ordering, because he didn't read the choices correctly, he began arguing with the clearly irritated voice resonating from the board, who is now practically shouting a list of options: whip cream…flat lid or round…cinnamon…sugar… caramel or chocolate syrup…cream or milk…hot or cold…caramel or vanilla latte…"

My husband was livid, the obscenities started and I added to the frustration by offering a dissertation regarding the appalling condition of customer service in America! I finished with, "I'm calling the 1-800 number. We aren't coming here again, and if we just drank coffee at home we wouldn't have to put up with all this nonsense and you wouldn't be so aggravated!"

My husband pounded on the steering wheel with his fist. His outburst continued. "Fuck this," he shrieked. "What the hell is taking them so fucking long…why is it taking so long to pour coffee in a cup…what is so hard about this…why are we still sitting here…and look at this line…what the fuck are they doing in there…its only fucking coffee…"

The obscenities continue.

I add a few of my own expletives, which only thickens the cloud of tension building in the vehicle.

"In case you forgot, it's Saturday and it appears that everyone in Ocean County has either run out of coffee or has an issue with their coffee pot today and has decided to waste money at the convenience store!"

The voice crackles through the intercom, "That will be nine dollars and fifty-eight cents. Proceed and pay at window one."

I throw up my arms in frustration. "You *had* to super-size again! Didn't you hear a word I said? This is what I am talking about. Who spends this much money on coffee? This is it, we aren't coming here anymore!"

During the first two years of our marriage I had spent more time in convenience stores than I had in my entire life!

Coffee competition became fierce in our neighborhood. As more convenience stores opened they all vied for the finest tasting coffee and best prices.

"They're having a sale. It's only ninety-nine cents," my husband reasoned as he entered the house with yet another cup from the local convenience store.

"That's if you buy the small size," I retorted angrily, as I noisily remove pots from the cabinet and slam them on the stove.

I was in the middle of preparing dinner and started the, what the fuck is wrong with everyone and their obsession with coffee conversation? "When did people become so infatuated with coffee? Why is everyone walking around with coffee cups from convenience stores? Everywhere I go people have coffee in their hands. Every time *we* go somewhere we are always stopping to get a cup of coffee!"

My husband smiled lovingly at me as I move about the kitchen and calmly said, "It's only coffee honey. You're getting upset about nothing."

His nonchalant attitude infuriated me.

"Dammit! It's just fuckin ridiculous! If you think you're going to keep up this habit, you're going to have to get a second job," I spat back as I shot him the "Alice Look."

Fast forward decades later – its Sunday, and we are once again waiting in line in the convenient Dunkin' Donuts. We are waiting in line only because someone gave us a gift card. "Where's the gift card? What can we get?"

"Ten large coffees or tea. That's it."

My husband starts complaining. "That's a joke," he smirks.

I turn in my seat and give him the "Alice Look." "You're getting *free* coffee and you're still complaining. You just had two cups before we left the house," I retort angrily as I wave my arms at the line of cars. "Look at this line. We're going to miss the kick off."

It was the last game of the season. The Eagles were planning the Giants. Although our Eagles didn't win the division, it was not only the last game of the regular season but a huge rivalry in the NFC East. The game was a must watch and a must win.

I shake my head in disbelief as I recall our very first trip to Dunkin' Donuts almost twelve years earlier. Nothing had changed.

The truck inches forward. The intermittent static emits from the board as my husband studies it. The unseen voice repeats the order and it's incorrect. "I don't want sugar," I hiss.

More banter between the board and my husband. He doesn't have his glasses and is having difficulty reading the choices.

When we finally reach the window he hands her the gift card and smiles like he is the winner of the lottery. His smile turns to a frown as she hands him the cup. Unbeknownst to my husband they changed the cup size. A large was now the size of the old medium cup.

"Look at this cup size. Do you see what I'm talking about? It's smaller! This is the medium cup. I'll drink all this by the time I pull out of the parking lot. Are you listening to me? Look at this cup!"

I start laughing. "Look at you. Your face is all red. Your blood pressure is going to go up if you don't calm down. You're getting upset over the size of a plastic cup. Perhaps Dunkin' Donuts figured out if they stop giving people the opportunity to super-size they will come back for more coffee."

I look in the bag as we pull out of the drive-thru. "They only gave us one donut."

"Fuckin' idiots," he screams. "What *is* so hard about two coffees and two donuts? I don't understand," he repeats himself as he swings the truck into a parking space, grabs the receipt and slams the door as he exits the vehicle and angrily heads into the store.

I smile at the *inconvenience* of it all!

"I'm putting this in my book," I laugh when he returns.

He angrily puts the truck in reverse and hollers, "Go ahead and call the 1-800 number. I just don't understand what is so hard about taking an order. What is the sense of having a drive thru if you have to go into the store? We're not coming here anymore!"

I don't respond. Instead I am once again laughing at the inconvenience at it all.

A series of home repairs, followed by Hurricane Irene and Hurricane Sandy, was the catalyst that eventually proved to my husband that his coffee habit was too much for our tight budget.

"But I have to have my coffee in the morning. What am I going to do?" He lamented.

I take him into the kitchen and gracefully point to the shiny appliance on the counter top. "Well, let me introduce you to our fucking coffee pot again. Either make it at home and take it with you or go without. YOU'RE NOT A FUCKING BACHELOR ANYMORE!"

CHAPTER 16

Game Day Highlights

The day began with the "Alice Look."

My husband had conveniently forgot his promise to come grocery shopping with me. "Didn't you ever go food shopping with your mother?" I asked after the last convenience store spending spree of ham, rolls, and bags of chips, coffee, and a cheese pretzel.

"Unfortunately, I did and I hated it!" And like a professor teaching his students the procedure for an operation, he recited detail after detail of what it was like to shop with his mother, including names of stores, roads they traveled on, stores in the vicinity, restaurants and places he frequented along the way and then, what happened when they arrived at the store – including how she picked up virtually every product in every aisle!

My mouth hung open, and eyes widened as I stared at him in disbelief. It was as if he was giving a doctoral dissertation!

I'll just provide the condensed version.

"My mother and my grandmother walked around the store for hours with me sitting in the shopping cart…It was like their recreation…they walked mile after mile in store after store…hours up and down the aisles…laps around the store…they stopped to look at *every* item on the shelves…I had no idea what the hell they were looking at…I would eventually agitate my mother so much that she would give me the keys and I would go to the car and listen to the radio…one time I started the car and drove around the parking lot…it was just fucking ridiculous…"

As he recalls memory after memory of riding in shopping carts of stores that have long been put out of business and replaced by big-box retailers, it was easy to see why he despised shopping and preferred the convenience store.

"This is why I hate fucking shopping," he spat as he slammed the refrigerator door in anger.

Just the thought of having to set foot in a grocery store was making him anxious. "I can just go and get my lunch meat at Wawa. This is really unnecessary."

Ugh! Just like my father, my husband's idea of food shopping was at the convenience store.

"Come on babe. You know it's so much faster and simpler. And there will be more time for us to spend together this afternoon," he lamented as he continued trying to appeal to my sympathetic side.

I had finally had enough with the convenience store argument. My breaking point came a week earlier. My eyes widened like a wolf zeroing in on its prey when he entered the house with a cheese pretzel and the all-too-familiar brown, disposable coffee cup, which to me immediately translated to more money wasted.

As the chief financial officer of our household the behavior was inexcusable. I immediately transformed into that creature from another planet and another show for the neighbors was underway. The ear-piercing banter began with, "What the fuck is wrong with you… it's basic economics 101…I just don't understand…the waste of money has got to stop…do you see these bills… damn it, YOU'RE NOT A FUCKING BACHELOR ANYMORE!"

That's when he made his promise to come shopping with me and I was ready to collect.

What was to follow was reminiscent of an afternoon of two teams in the NFL competing on the field.

Overcoming the *why do we have to go today*, we finished breakfast with a plan to start the day. I won the *coin toss* and we pulled out of the snow-covered driveway *en route to the stadium*.

The field trip to the Shop Rite was an entirely new experience for my husband. I should have known better not to take him on a Sunday, but what the hell, he needed to get the full impact of what grocery shopping entailed to understand why he needed to stop going to the convenience store, appreciate the money saving values, and why shopping sometimes takes so damn long! And it's not because we are doing laps up and down the aisles because we have nothing better to do with our time!

The *kickoff* began the moment we pulled into the Shop Rite parking lot.

It's the first and ten.

"Do you think you can park somewhere?" He grumbled, glaring at me as I made several laps around the lot, dodging carriages and pedestrians as I searched for the best spot to improve my entrance and exit strategy. I was like a *running back* looking for the hole. For me it was near one of the cart rails for ease of returning the shopping cart. It was also far enough to avoid the risk of runaway shopping carts smashing into our vehicle.

I successfully avoided a sack.

"Look there's a spot right there," he pointed, waving his hand impatiently.

I ignored him and passed the open parking spot to his amazement.

It's out of bounds.

"What's wrong with you?" He shouted, visibly annoyed and frustrated.

The referee's run to break up the skirmish on the field.

"It's actually too close to the entrance, too much traffic and pedestrians. This truck is not equipped with a camera to display what is behind and you have to watch for people and especially kids who are darting all over the place."

We had no offense – couldn't risk a fumble this early in the game.

Before the sun went down and half time began, I had success-fully squeezed into a spot. My husband was elated: it was as if he completed a *twenty-five yard pass and he was inside the red zone*. The vehicle in park, ignition off, was like the *center snapping the ball*.

He was out of the truck and had the doors shut before I could tell him to grab a quarter from the loose change in the consol.

The penalty flag was thrown.

"A quarter? What the *fuck* for?"

He must have missed this rule in the playbook.

The discussion that followed was like *reviewing a play on the sidelines during a time out.* "It's a deposit. You need it to obtain a shopping cart," I pointed toward the direction of the cart corral.

Quarter in hand, he walked to the cart rail. Now us seasoned shoppers understand the carts sometimes get stuck if jammed together too hard and if that's the case, we just move to the next row and try to extract another cart. Not my husband, he was determined to have the cart that was obviously jammed! I said nothing as the oaths began and watched as he pulled and pushed the cart before finally giving up and moving to the next row.

Un-sportsman like conduct.

"Why the hell are the carts locked up? Whose stupid idea was that? You didn't have to park so far away," he grumbled as we headed toward the entrance.

Encroachment!

I gave him a hug and whispered in his ear, laughing, "Don't worry I won't leave you in the shopping cart! If you like, you can ride in one of the big, plastic carts shaped like a car or truck..."

More laughing and obscenities over inexplicable childhood memories followed.

As we proceeded down the aisles he stopped, and just stared at the merchandise – brand after brand of mayonnaise, pickles, ketchup and salad dressing. And for every item he blindly grabbed for, bottles, unique containers, or something with an alluring advertising strategy, I took it out of the cart and placed it back on the shelf.

Turnover, my ball.

I give him the "Alice Look," pupils as tight as a tourniquet while preparing to explain the problem.

"What? Do you think we are descendants of the Rockefellers or did you inherit some cash that I don't know about? Didn't you even look at the price?"

He shrugged, putting his hands in his pockets. "Not really. If I was in the convenience store I wouldn't have to waste all this time because I wouldn't have so much to choose from," he spat.

"You're lucky to have me," I smiled. "Put that back too, I have a coupon for this one," I pointed to another brand of mayonnaise.

Favoring the right side of the aisle, I stopped to search for the coupon in my plastic file organizer for the corresponding proof. He glanced over to see what I was doing.

Delay of game.

His hands flew through the air in frustration. His eyes were wide-open in disbelief and then he started laughing.

"Are you kidding me? You actually have that divided into categories! Who does that! And you think I'm obsessive! This is just plain insanity!"

I smile proudly. "You think *this* little organizer is bad? You watch as we're shopping. You're going to see women here with laptops, tablets, and notebooks filled with, or scanning or downloading coupons."

"That's ridiculous, nobody does that!"

"Yes, they do," I argued. "It's called being organized and saving money. And depending on the day you shop the coupon is either doubled or tripled." I extend my hand toward him in the middle of the dialogue. "Can you please hold these coupons for the items we're getting?"

Touchdown my game.

The incident that occurred next took place in the pasta aisle. It's one of those stories that develops into a major chapter in the life you and your spouse are creating together. It's one of those stories that you reminisce about at family gatherings or with friends.

"What the *fuck* is wrong now? By the look on your face you'd think I'd committed a crime," he joked.

I was momentarily transported back in time as we argued just like the "irrational matter."

I grabbed the foil package of fettuccine alfredo from the cart repeating the return exercise of setting the item back to its respective place on the shelf. "You can't be serious?" I hissed. The look on my face and tone in my voice reeked of disbelief.

"What do you mean? This is good stuff. I used to eat this all the time," he proudly announced.

"I'm sure it is and I have nothing against the product or company. However, you seem to have forgotten I'm Italian. I cook you the best meals and everything I cook is practically homemade and fresh. My grandmother is not only turning over in her grave she is *jumping* out of it!" I shout, gesturing and waving my hands for emphasis. "Do you actually think I'd make and serve imitation pasta?" I reach for the package on the shelf. "And look at all the sodium! Almost one thousand grams! There is no way I'm buying this," I snap adamantly.

Shoppers nearby were laughing as they listened to our heated debate. Some guy told him he was lucky to have a wife that at least cooked. Another woman told him I was right about the sodium.

The kick is good. Field goal!

"Let's just go. We've already been here too long." He started rubbing his head as we moved up the aisle. "Just get what you want."

We arrived at the deli counter next. It was crowded and busy. "Are you kidding me? Look at all these people waiting. We'll be here all day!"

He gets the "Alice Look" and stance. "You're right. We certainly will be here all day if you don't grab a ticket," I point toward the machine at the end of the counter.

The quarterback gets sacked!

The muscles on his face tightened as his jaw is clenched tighter. He threw up his hands and stomped angrily toward the machine. I don't know what was worse, the crowd or the woman who jumped in front of him and grabbed the ticket first!

It only takes one trip to realize that when your number is called you had better be prepared to give your order.

"One pound of cheese," my husband calls out anxiously.

The girl shakes her head and sighs heavily. "Domestic, imported, yellow or white, thin sliced or thick sliced, name brand or sale item, quarter, half or a pound," she quickly rattled off the choices, annoyed that she had to expand energy reciting the standard cold cut menu.

The red challenge flag is thrown.

Unquestionably the longer you take to decide, the more glares you receive from the employees working behind the counter and the customers waiting in the long line. Needless to say, my husband wasn't making any friends with the frustrated employee or impatiently waiting shoppers. She had already lost him when she opened with domestic or imported. I quickly stepped in and completed the order.

Interception and touchdown. My game.

When it comes time to check out, it never fails, no matter what line I pick, something always goes wrong. The customer in front has issues with coupons...the price is incorrect... the register tape needs to be changed...the employee is talking to other employees or has no sense of urgency as he or she unhurriedly scans the items across the conveyer belt.

My husband was already irritated by the entire experience. Enraged is more like it. He started complaining. "What is taking so long...why did you pick this line...other people are moving and we are still standing here...I'm going to say something if we don't start moving...we are going to miss the kick off...I knew I should have stayed home...this is not going to happen again..."

I ignored him. I was like a general barking out orders regarding the distribution of the merchandise on the conveyer belt.

"When you check out put freezer and cold items together... paper goods are separate...give your club card and coupons to the cashier before she starts scanning items... specify if you want paper or plastic bags...if you have your own bags tell the cashier how many and you'll get a discount...chicken is always kept separate...don't cross-contaminate... detergent or chemicals don't get bagged with the meat...eggs are last..."

And on and on it went.

My husband couldn't keep the pace and he didn't say a word because other men were doing the same thing he was, listening to the wives as they provided directions for the checkout procedure. The only difference was they were pros: they knew the system and helped without complaint.

Then as quickly as it started, the process came to an abrupt halt when the register began emitting electronic beeps. The cashier grabbed the register tape and started scanning it as if she was deciphering some secret code.

"Now what?" growled my husband.

She turned to me with raised eyebrows, her chewing gum snapping loudly while curtly stating, "This coupon says you need to purchase two items in order to receive the sale price!" She smiles jubilantly, as if she just passed the bar exam.

I ignore the adolescent, smart-ass-know-it-all attitude as I quickly scrutinize the merchandise on the conveyor belt. Gravity pulls my head toward my husband. I raise my eyes in question, silently communicating: I know you did something. I know *I* put two items in the cart.

He's guilty. I can tell by the suspicious look on his face.

I give him the "Alice Look."

He stammers. "I…was um…trying to save some money…so I put one back on the shelf. What the hell did we need two for anyway?"

A penalty flag is thrown, again.

The cashier turns on her light. Like a beacon it flashes brightly calling attention to our register and signaling the customer service assistant. He debates with the cashier as to the location of the product and continues with another conversation regarding when she can take her break!

My husband's level of aggravation has magnified! He was horrified that the flashing light had drawn the attention of other shoppers. People are staring. His face was red – indicating his blood pressure is quickly rising.

I immediately silence him with the "Alice Look."

"It's your fault. You shouldn't have returned it to the shelf!" I snapped.

The customer service representative reappears - without the product! He is new and is unable to locate the merchandise.

The customer behind me was now reading a magazine and rolled her eyes at my husband, clearly indicating her annoyance. This further irritated my husband, who in turn shot her a menacing glare and started muttering profanity.

The league will give a fine for unsportsmanlike conduct.

I reminded him he just came from church.

He reminded me that God never had to go grocery shopping and he would forgive him!

I turned back to the impatient cashier. "Don't worry about it, just give me the coupon, I'll use it another time."

My husband jumped to attention. "Oh no, I'll go get it because if I don't I'll never hear the end of it." The obscenities continued as he stalked off to retrieve the item. He received more ugly stares from wives and sympathetic glances from other husbands, who quietly looked on.

"I could be home watching the NFL channel," he let everyone know as he walked away from the register.

He returned and handed the item to the cashier. The customer service assistant disrupts the scanning process to remove money from her register.

My husband frowned and threw up his hands. "Seriously, like they have to do that now, in the middle of ringing up an order?"

The cashier wanted desperately to go on her break. Only now does she have a sense of urgency. We were almost done until she started scanning the coupons. I stared at the monitor intently to verify they were registering and deducting the proper amount. I noticed one is missing. "Do you have the coupon for coffee?"

She looked on the floor and through the coupons and shakes her head as she continued to snap her chewing gum.

My husband gets the "Alice Look" and stance.

His hands flew to his pockets as he began to search.

My hands sliced through the air as I stared at him in disbelief and snapped, "How could you lose that coupon? It was for a dollar off. Didn't you see how much that coffee cost? It's over eight dollars! That was a good coupon!"

He rubbed his temples and then his hands started gesturing angrily as he talked. "I don't know? It was in my pocket. If we got coffee at the convenience store we wouldn't need that coupon. Does it really matter? I've had enough. I want to get out of here," he protested.

If my husband were the quarterback, the coach would have taken him out of the game at this point. Too many fumbles, tackles, and penalties. Fines for misconduct are in progress. The post-game show was going to be entertaining.

The cashier patiently waited while he checked his pockets again. She told him he should have stayed home.

He readily agreed, as he tried to find the opening of a plastic bag so he can finish bagging. His bicep muscles are pronounced as he continues wrestling with the bag. "You're absolutely right. I should have!"

Game over! End of the season, news of a trade to another team was imminent.

The plastic bag ripped at the bottom and the merchandise fell out. More obscenities, as he crumbled the torn bag into a tight ball, throwing it angrily into the cart. He grabbed a paper bag instead.

The chewing gum snapping adolescent, smiled sarcastically as she was happy to be getting rid of us. "You qualify," she stated as she handed me the receipt.

My husband's head shot up sharply. His demeanor changed instantly. He was cheery and smiling. "What, did we win something?"

He acted as if he won tickets to the next Super Bowl. "What do we get?" He asked, his eyes wide with excitement.

I thought about teasing him a bit more...pay back for all the clothing of mine he destroyed.

I took the receipt and thanked the cashier.

"What did we win?" My husband repeated enthusiastically as he pushed the cart toward the exit.

"We get a free ham or turkey because we have enough points."

He frowned. "That's it? After all the money we just spent? What a nightmare. I'm never coming again," he said breathing a sigh of relief once we were in the parking lot. "Ok, you win. I appreciate you. I don't know how you do it."

I grinned knowingly. "You're lucky to have me."

He laughed. "You're lucky that I put up with this!"

To his amazement it still wasn't over. Next was the placement of the bags in the truck. "No, put the eggs in last," I yelled as he started rearranging the bags.

I smiled, "You're not going to leave that cart in front of the truck?"

He scowled. "Who cares where I leave it?"

"Put it back in the cart coral. And get the quarter. I need the quarter. It's toll money for the Parkway."

Even he wasn't going to argue with me about that because anyone living in the state of New Jersey knows how important it is to have change in your car for the tolls on the Garden State Parkway. If you don't have EZ-pass, or there is no attendant at the booth to take your money, you need to have exact change to throw into the bucket or you'll be photographed, sent a fine, and risk having your registration revoked!

"Do you even know how much we spend on tolls a year?"

My husband puts up his hand, signaling he has had enough for one day. "I don't want to hear it," he quietly stated. He then hugged me, and added, "I love you, now let's go home and watch the game."

I give him a quick kiss on the cheek and smile, "Don't think this is your last time coming to the store."

"Seriously," I don't think so," he smirks.

I give him the "Alice Look," and reminded him, "this is what you signed up for." It was a phrase we would playfully throw and repeat at each another in the attempts to remind us that its all part of our marriage commitment.

"This is what you signed up for," I repeated and added, "You're not a Fucking Bachelor Anymore."

CHAPTER 17

Grocery Graduate School

Any couple, who is suffering from the realities of the harsh economic times, will need to think about how they spend and save money. Also, since we had married later in life, at forty, we basically had started out with nothing so money for us was always tight. My husband started complaining about going to the grocery store with me again the following week.

I started to think perhaps it's just me. Was I asking for too much?

So I again asked my girlfriends for their opinions. I began conducting a poll. One friend and colleague summed it up best: "Are you kidding me? Unless it was Christmas Day and there was nothing else open, then I might, just might, go to a convenience store and that is only if I really needed something for cooking!"

I later discovered she had the exact same problem with her boyfriend – not only was he shopping at the local convenience store, but he was also food shopping at the high-end grocery store that just happened to be located, *conveniently,* down the street from his house!

Now don't get me wrong, I am fond of high-end grocery stores, but let's be realistic; if you can't afford it, you don't belong shopping there. My girlfriend was in agreement that men shop anywhere just for the convenience. We blamed it on their mothers for not teaching them.

"You're right. Mothers never prepare them. And they go through life under the assumption that all shopping will be done by their wives. It's not fair that we have to put up with all this crap to make them understand!"

One Saturday afternoon my husband found me clipping coupons. "Where the hell did you get all these coupons?" He questioned, amazed, as he started sifting through the enormous pile.

"My mother sent them. I'm giving some of them to the girls at work. I have one friend who recently moved in with her boyfriend. He also doesn't understand the value of the coupon. Needless to say he was also subjected to the same field trip you were, and because she has children she really needs to look out for the sales. Her boyfriend was lucky to visit a host of grocery stores with a handful of coupons!"

My husband smirked when he heard this. "Ha! He doesn't know what he is in for. You better tell her to tell him he's not a FUCKING BACHELOR ANYMORE!"

Twelve years later grocery shopping usually happens after church on Sundays. First it's to Wal-Mart for the consumables, then to the ShopRite, the pet store and sometimes to the Home Depot. All the stores are conveniently located next to one another as you travel down Route 9. And when the new ShopRite opened in the neighboring town, we made the inconvenient trip.

I like to call this the Destination ShopRite since it's bigger than a super center! There is a Dunkin' Donuts for coffee, a bakery with a multitude of delectable pastries, the aisles are twice as long as a regular store and carry merchandise that you may not normally find in your local grocery store. There are also a variety of food bars to purchase hot food for take-out or you can sit and have lunch. Since it is not conveniently close by, we only shop here when we are in the vicinity.

Anyway, as we shop, my husband looks at the prices and will get the generic product if the regular item is not on sale. He asks if I have coupons, and he now understands the mechanics of the deli counter so I can leave him there while I retrieve merchandise from other aisles to save time. He likes shopping at the Destination ShopRite mostly because he can get coffee and lunch. He also likes the various themed food bars.

He bags quickly and efficiently, always double bagging so we have extra trash bags for the house. He has his routine for cart retrieval and return. On Sundays in the fall, we proudly wear our Philadelphia Eagles football jerseys and trash talk back and forth with the rest of the shoppers and football fanatics, who are also wearing their team shirts. Every aisle is like watching a pre-game show on ESPN as people exchange stats about the season, coaches, players, injuries, point spreads and game predictions. We congratulate unknown shoppers for team victories and sarcastically joke about the defeats. No time is wasted as we move through the store quickly and efficiently in order to arrive home before the one o'clock kick-off starts.

One day since he had kept his temper tantrums to a minimum, I decided to make a nice dinner and directed him into the parking lot of the German Butcher. Anybody that has been to the German Butcher in Forked River is aware of the fantastic cranberry-stuffed chicken, cuts of meat, bread, deserts, and other delicacies they carry.

"Where are we going now? The game is going to start soon."

"I come here sometimes for bread, chicken or meat," I explained as he started to complain. "Don't worry we're not going to miss the kick-off."

I grabbed a ticket while he glared at the crowd of people.

"They are very quick here. Don't worry!" I assured him. "We won't have to wait long. Do you think *I* want to miss the game?"

We spent money on the cranberry and sausage-stuffed chicken breasts and purchased some good cuts of meat and my husband left with a new appreciation for the German Butcher. He was ecstatic with his purchase of fresh beef jerky!

He knows he's NOT A FUCKING BACHELOR ANYMORE!

CHAPTER 18

What's the Point of Having a Kitchen If You're Not Going to Eat in It?

My husband was eating his beef jerky and sausage bread, fresh from the German Butcher in the living room. The dogs, who were hoping to get a taste of the jerky, surround him. His food is piled in a small mound on a dessert dish and is spilling onto the table, crumbs are strewn about the glass top, and the napkins in the kitchen did not make it to his living room picnic. The can of soda did not rest on the coasters that are inches away. Beads of water were dripping down the aluminum forming a small puddle on the wooden tray table positioned nearby.

He wiped his greasy hands on his pants and then on the blanket on the couch. The dogs eagerly waited in the "drop zone" for they know pieces of whatever he is eating will eventually make it to the floor.

The commotion of the dogs scrambling for the food that is now on the floor and my husband yelling at them brought me into the living room.

"Are you fucking kidding me?" I fumed, as I survey the scene. My hands whip through my hair in frustration… "This is ridiculous…YOU'RE NOT A FUCKING BACHELOR anymore!"

As I ran to the kitchen to get paper towels to clean up the mess, I instinctively knew I sounded just like my mother as soon as the words escape my mouth. And the "Why do you have to eat in the living room?" argument, I am all too familiar with, commenced once again.

I grew up eating most meals at the kitchen table. During the holidays or special occasions, my mother removed the china from the china cabinet, which was hand washed and dried. The hand washing of the china always signified something was going to happen in the dining room and the preparations for a meal began. The table was decorated and set with the most formal of place settings: wine, water, champagne glasses, bowls for all the courses, and the silver. One would think the president of the United States was stopping by. Eating in this room on those dishes was for holidays and special events only. Besides the dining room and the kitchen, the only other place to eat in was the TV room.

I NEVER ate in the TV room. It was not an option. Eating in the TV room was reserved for one person in the house and my brothers and I were not on that list. If we didn't sit down to eat at the kitchen table, we didn't eat. In addition, all food on your plate had to be consumed, as there were starving people in the world.

The rules were simple and at an early age my father made sure we understood both them and the consequences – getting your mouth washed out with the soap, beat with the wooden spoon, or getting whipped with his belt. The message was confusing to me, for my father always took his dessert and coffee into the TV room! The crumbs fell to the floor and the coffee never seemed to stay in the cup as he was glued to the television watching his hero, Archie Bunker, on the renowned show, *All in the Family*!

All in the Family, was a sitcom launched in 1971 about a middle-class white family in New York. The show explored economic, social, racial, sexuality, and more controversial issues. It was a progressive conversation at the time.

At least the "irrational matter" was consistent for the script was the same every night. It was a sort of controlled dysfunction. Looking back, I guess there was some level of comfort in knowing exactly what was going to happen every night.

My mother would start. Her questions were simple and easily answered. She would stare at him in disbelief began, "Can't you eat in the kitchen...look at the mess you made...I just cleaned the carpet...can't you clean up after yourself... you just had a beer do you have to have another...do you have to smoke in here...there are ashes all over the carpet...I just cleaned..."

And on and on it went...

The arguing and obscenities from my father ensued. He was fast to react and his entire miserable life spewed out like lava from an erupting volcano. Unfortunately nobody understood the lava was in reality alcohol. It was the cue that my brothers and I understood all too well: it was time to retreat to our rooms where we vowed this was *never* going to happen us!

Fast-forward four decades later, while thankfully there is no alcohol involved my husband prefers to have his meals everywhere but in the kitchen!

"Is this how you were raised? Didn't you have sit down meals with your parents?" I probed as I asked him to please take his plate to the kitchen.

Like my parents he claimed his parents were just as strict and they always ate together in the dining room or kitchen.

My best girlfriend lit a cigarette, laughing buoyantly, before asking, "So what happened? When did his eating habits change? And how did *you* not know *any* of this about him? What signs did *you* miss while you were dating?"

I was shocked when I started thinking about it. "I see your point. Would you believe before we were married we ate in his living room all the time!"

She exhales and laughs. "See, it's not a new habit, so why are you so surprised. Why did you eat in his living room?"

"Well, his kitchen was a mess. Dirty dishes piled in the sink, sticky counter tops, and heaps of mail that hadn't been opened was stacked high on the small round kitchen table. The faint smell of urine from the untrained dog permeated the air." The more I remembered the louder my voice became. "It was disgusting. You couldn't pay me to eat in that kitchen and I certainly wasn't going to cook any meals in there. Eating in the living room was the safer choice for me. It was routine for him."

"Well, there you have it," she stated matter-of-factly. "You can't blame him for something you already knew about!"

She was right, but I saw it differently.

Having my own home, I *now* understood what my mother was always so upset about…she just wanted to keep the house clean. She didn't have the time to be constantly picking up after us. She had invested her hard-earned money in new furniture, and so had we. My father was ruining it, and so was my husband.

So here I am, newly married with a home we purchased with our hard-earned money. We also bought brand new furniture. Unfortunately we live in a flood zone and have survived three floods, escaped the ravages of hurricane Irene and Sandy with minimal damages. Over the years we have had to renovate every room in our house. To save money, my husband and I did most of the work.

We have painted, sanded, spackled, ripped up carpet, installed drywall, laid ceramic tile and flooring, hung doors, cut molding, knocked down walls, and moved furniture from one room to the next more times than I care to count!

I have had to live among piles and piles of our stuff because we don't have garage or any place to store our belongings during all these renovations. I have fought with my husband over design plans, how to cut flooring, reading instruction manuals and have spent more than half of my married life in Home Depot, Lowes and other hardware retailers - and my husband has the unmitigated nerve to argue with me about eating in the fucking living room!

"Damn it," I complain as crumbs fall to the floor. "Can't you at least use a fuckin' tray table? YOU'RE NOT A FUCKING BACHELOR ANYMORE!"

CHAPTER 19

Chips and Dip

Tray tables are reserved for Sunday's beginning in September at the start of the football season and up until the Super Bowl. Again it didn't start out this way – it just happened. I don't know how or when the transformation occurred, but it just did. The grand finale of the NFL season was the Super Bowl. The Super Bowl party was always at our home, which is the smallest and has the least amount of space for all our friends. But the food is always good and plentiful.

Every year my husband and I have the same exact conversation. My husband starts with, "Look at all this food! It's too much. Who is going to eat it all? This is ridiculous. All you have to do is get some chips and dip! Who is wasting money now?"

And every year I respond with, "Chips and dip? Are you kidding me? Seriously, do you think we are going to have all these people here and just offer chips and dip? What the hell is wrong with you? Where were you raised? Didn't your mother teach you anything? What the hell did she serve when you had people over?"

Why do I always make so much food? It's an Italian thing. It's not only how I was raised but it's also in my DNA. To have people over to the house and serve chips and dip – it would be like breaking the commandments of Italian cooking and entertaining!

And every year, after the game is over, my husband hugs me and thanks me for preparing such a great spread!

I smile, give him a quick kiss and tell him, "You're lucky to have me."

My mother was visiting one weekend during the big Eagles vs. Giants game. Anyone who watches football knows about the rivalry between the two teams. She was quietly reading the newspaper when I came in the living room and started opening and organizing the tray tables. "Where do you want your table to the right or left?"

She looked at me with eyebrows raised and pursed lips and as if I was committing a sin, and said, "Are you kidding me? Why are we eating in here?"

"Just fuh-ged-da-boud-it mom."

I ignored what she was really trying to convey which was, I didn't teach you this.

I flashed my mother the "Alice Look." "Mom, it's the big game, where do you want to sit and where do you want your table? I have to get set up before kickoff," I spat, as I quickly moved about the room.

I called the dogs and put their football jerseys and bandanas on. They knew the drill and got settled on their respective pallets because they know food is coming. We already had our jerseys on. I make a mental note to buy an Eagles jersey for my mother for Christmas.

Dishes, napkins, and silverware were set up with snacks and appetizers for everyone. Snacks came out during the commercial breaks. The main course followed during the half-time show. Drinks, dessert, and coffee continued for the post-game show and the other games that followed.

My mother laughed at our banter as the explosive plays and disastrous luck of our opponent unfolded each quarter. The dogs barked as we screamed at the television when a touchdown was scored! She snickered at our foolish behavior, fed the dogs Italian bread, and cheered for the Giants, who eventually lost. Her final comment was, "Well, at least you're not eating on paper plates!"

***

Football season has ended. A Jersey snowstorm, all of six inches, keeps us in for the weekend. My husband spent time catching up on movies.

A scuffle between the dogs interrupts me from my work writing this very chapter. I don't even have to leave my office to know what is going on. The dogs are once again in the proverbial "drop zone," pawing at my husband, who is spread out on the couch sitting with a handful of cookies! The crumbs are scattered across his shirt.

With his mouth filled, my husband is carrying on a conversation with the dogs. They ignore his pleas to stop begging. A can of soda falls to the floor. He immediately blames it on the cattle dog and claims his bushy tail knocked it over.

Images of the "irrational matter" arguing flash through my head. I can feel the heat from the adrenaline rushing through my blood as I dash into the room.

I flash the "Alice Look." And start yelling. "If you weren't eating in the living room none of this would have happened…look at this fuckin' mess…"

My husband smiles and says, "You're being irrational its only soda…"

I cut him off, "Are you fucking kidding me?" I continue yelling, my hands waving furiously through the air. "Do you need a map to locate a dish…I just cleaned…can't you at least get a damn

TV tray.... I'm not cleaning that glass table again… Why can't you eat in the kitchen…Damn it! YOU'RE NOT A FUCKING BACH-ELOR ANYMORE!"

CHAPTER 20

Football Sunday

Football Sunday has become an all-day affair in our home. Our Philadelphia Eagles flag proudly flies in front of the house at the start of the season. A five-foot Christmas tree, stuffed with Eagles ornaments, is put up in September, complete with green and white lights.

Sports channels are immediately sought the minute we wake up and the TV blares throughout the house. A ring tone on my iPhone provides last minute updates, news worthy stories, and scores - all of which I call out like a radio broadcaster throughout the day. Games schedules, channels and times are checked for the entire day.

Menus for game day food are discussed and planned throughout the week. Last minute grocery shopping and any errands happen early Sunday morning and must be completed by kickoff at 1:00pm. Food is plentiful. Nacho's, garlic chicken wings, pizza, chili, burgers, mac and cheese, stuffed potato skins, lasagna, and much more are laid out like a banquet and heavily critiqued. No meals are repeated if they do not receive a high score of delicious from my husband.

Game jerseys, washed during the week, are put on the minute we wake up. A jersey must be clean and reserved for work for NFL Monday. Players getting traded have become a problem because new jerseys are needed for the new season. When DeSean Jackson and LeSean McCoy of the Eagles were traded I was furious. I finally had two nice jerseys to wear and then I had to purchase new jerseys for both my husband and I. The jerseys are not cheap.

None of this happened before I got married. It didn't start out this way – it just happened. When and how, I wish I could recall.

Growing up in North Jersey, you watched the Jets or the Giants. My father never took us to an NFL game so I can't say we were fans. My brothers played football and I was in the marching band in high school and college. Rutgers Football was part of my college years and some games were played at Giants Stadium.

When I moved to Alabama, I taught at University of North Alabama, and I took photographs on the sidelines at the football games, and I routed for them. They were three-time National Champions in their division. It was a great time to be a Lion.

While Alabama did not have an NFL team you still *had* to choose a football team to cheer for. In Alabama there is no choice; you are either an Alabama or Auburn fan. My Alabama sweatshirt still hangs in the back of my closet.

I can honestly say I really had no NFL team affiliation.

There were no expensive NFL jerseys in my closet, no magnets on the refrigerator or car. There was no thought of NFL clothing for the dogs, flags for the house or on the vehicles. There was no NFL Sunday, no cooking, no Super Bowl party planning, or menu planning for games. There were no coffee mugs, cups, snow globes, statues, blankets, or towels with NFL logos. There was no NFL Christmas tree or any ornaments representing any teams for that matter.

I had *absolutely* no NFL team affiliation until I got married.

My husband proudly gave me the *Philadelphia Eagles*.

My husband *never* realized what he was introducing me to when he brought the Eagles into my life. When we moved in together, his NFL paraphernalia consisted of two Christmas Philadelphia Eagles ornaments and two shirts. The combined cost? Probably no more than thirty dollars.

I put his two ornaments on a little tree in the hall the first year we were married. I can recall how I fearfully phoned him at work one night, in tears. I told him there was an incident in the house. One of the dogs ran into the table and one of the Philadelphia Eagle ornaments fell and shattered. I immediately replaced it and the collection of ornaments I purchased grew so much that a new tree was bought every year.

My husband was admiring our tree and I began talking about the Eagles Super Bowl victory in February of 2018, and if I was going to get another Carson Wentz shirt. What sweatshirt did he want next: Foles, Ertz, Blount, Cox, Elliot, Sproles, Jenkins? Who was going to be traded…the quarterback coach…the Eagles garden gnome I'd purchase… if we were going to the game next year…the fan base…

My stream of conscious dialogue was interrupted as I watched him enjoying some leftovers from the game and told him, "You're lucky to have me. And I'm still a bigger fan than you!"

He laughed buoyantly and held up a coffee cup with the Philadelphia Eagles logo on it and pointed to gnomes and other Eagles stuff around the room and said, "You have done nothing but cost me money! To think I only had had two ornaments and two shirts when we met."

I smiled proudly, "I'm still a bigger fan and I predicted we would win the Super Bowl this year…and you didn't believe me…"

"He laughs easily. "Ok, I can't believe how confident you were about your prediction, I'll give you that, but didn't you hear what I just said?"

My eyes twinkly with delight, because I know where he is going with this. "Yes, you had two ornaments and two shirts. The shirt's I inherited because they no longer fit you."

He shook his head in disbelief, "When I look around this house and think about the money you have spent....the money on this stuff...and you talk about me wasting money..."

"This is your team too!"

Laughing, he dismissed me with the wave of his hand and retreated to the kitchen for more coffee.

That evening we are pulling out of the driveway and we both noticed our Philadelphia Eagles flag would need to be replaced. The harsh winter tore the bottom like a piece a paper going through a shredder. It would have been bad luck if we removed and replaced it during the season.

My husband says, "We'll have to get a Super Bowl Championship flag now."

I don't think about the cost, I don't tell him forget about it, or give him the "YOU'RE NOT A FUCKING BACHELOR ANYMORE" speech, I simply agree with him. "Absolutely we will have to replace the flag," and silently wondered how this happened to me. When did the purchase of a flag for a sports team become such a priority in our lives?

CHAPTER 21

Surface Cleaning

My husband is what I refer to as a "surface cleaner." Surface cleaning entails just that – a quick wipe of the table or counter top. Moving items is not necessary as he simply cleans around the blender, mixer, or coffee pot. What is behind or under the bed doesn't matter.

His choice of cleaning products consists of bleach, bleach, and more bleach. He also prefers Pledge or Windex and is a huge fan of End Dust. These are great products and have been around for generations. I have no complaint about any one of them.

They work especially well for surface cleaners for two reasons. The first, one quick swipe and the dust is gone. The second, they have distinctive sterilizing odors. One whiff and you know someone has been cleaning!

Cleaning is a problem in our house. After twelve years we still have been unable to reach an agreeable compromise on this topic.

By the time I get home from work, feed the dogs, cook, clean-up, and throw more laundry in the machine, the last thing I want to do is clean! I don't have time and we have outgrown our small ranch home. I would rather hire a cleaning service or someone to clean. My husband won't entertain the idea of a cleaning service, for he thinks "surface cleaning" is enough.

When we first started dating, if you walked into his apartment you always thought he was cleaning because the odor of bleach or some other cleaning product permeated the air. There was never any clutter in the living room, which consisted of, a couch, coffee table, two end tables, a chair, television, stereo and fireplace. A few photos decorated a wall. The stuffed wildlife was stunning but from an artistic standpoint, should have been flying in the opposite direction of their current positions. The point is that everything always looked neat and orderly. The reality was hidden under the surface of it all.

The bathroom smelled of bleach. A mop occasionally distributed some sort of cleaning product across the kitchen floor. Stacks of mail and bills hid the top of the kitchen table. A sponge distributed bleach across the counters tops intermittently. The furniture looked shiny and clean from the large quantities of End Dust, which over time, had been sprayed across surfaces, as if one was bombing the apartment for some insect infestation.

My husband claims that, in order for a surface to be thoroughly cleaned, the rag *and* surface must be fully and completely saturated with the cleaning product.

I was fooled by the strong odor of a surface cleaner's use of products because the rest of the home looked something like this: The dishwasher was broken and dishes were piled high in the sink. The refrigerator and freezer were filled with expired food. Some of the jars of condiments looked like an experiment in biological germ warfare. The meat in the freezer was…well…let's just say, I wouldn't feed it to my dogs.

But for some reason I didn't really see any of this. What I saw, was - all bachelor men live like this!

One afternoon I decided to peruse the contents of his kitchen cabinets. I looked at him with raised eyebrows as I rubbed my head in disbelief. "Are you kidding me?" The cabinets were filled with canned food, which was not edible due to past expiration dates. "The expiration dates have passed," I gasped as I move the cans around. I was stunned as I examined the labels. "This is a decade old!" I was incredulous. I didn't even have to look at the date because the label on the can was updated years ago. Some of the cans were so old they had rusted on the tops and bottoms.

"This food is not edible," I shouted again. "What the hell have you been saving it for? Are you worried they are going to discontinue SpaghettiOs and spam? What the hell do you eat?"

He shrugged like it wasn't a big deal. "I usually stop at the convenience store or order take-out."

I can't blame him. He didn't lie. He was upfront. He told me he shopped at the convenience store, but I didn't hear that. What I heard was: This was the way bachelor's lived!

"Let's just go out," I suggested.

His vacuuming habits were the same – yes, he "surface vacuumed" too! What is behind the couch or underneath doesn't matter as moving furniture was not necessary; instead, he just vacuumed around everything.

I have to admit, although he "surface vacuums," he does vacuum much better than me. Like ironing, I despise vacuuming and cleaning. Every Saturday morning my father would scream at me about the two things I needed to accomplish – cleaning the bathroom and vacuuming. He seemed to think that knowing how to clean would be beneficial to finding a husband.

The obscenities flowed in between the half sentences. Too vulgar to repeat, I'll provide a cleaner version. "What the hell kind of wife are you going to be if you don't know how to vacuum… after you're done with the living room take that fucking vacuum upstairs…and don't forget about the stairs…no man is going to want to marry a woman who can't clean."

I'd tune him out. The major problem I had with the cleaning process was that I simply saw no point in trying to clean something that needed to be replaced. It was not only impossible but a waste of time.

Unfortunately I can still recall the carpet in our living room; it was mustard gold in color. It was worn not only from simple day-to-day family living but also from the multitude of dogs and cats we owned over the years. We needed new carpet. In was so dilapidated that it felt like we were walking on a bare floor and not carpet. Even the padding underneath was flat. And the floor squeaked as the vacuum passed from section to section. In my opinion, time could have been better spent doing something else.

And the only bathroom in the house was on the second floor and was in need of a makeover. I can still hear my grandmother complaining about it as she slowly began the pilgrimage to the second floor, up the deep-set stairs to use the *only* bathroom in our house!

She was already calling for her son as she steadily made her way back down the fifteen steps, pausing midway to catch her breath. The staircase creaked loudly with each step taken as she continued her descent, crying "fix me!" Even the carpet could not hide the breaks that were hidden beneath.

The only escape for my father was in a glass of scotch as he awaited the inevitable confrontation about the repulsive room from his own mother. We held our breaths as she reached the bottom of the steps and, in front of the rest of the family she scolded her son.

It was an argument that my grandmother started every time she was in our house.

My father never had a good reason as to why he could not add another bathroom or fix the existing one. Only more scotch, cigarettes, incomprehensible excuses, and intolerable language ensued, finally ending with the slamming of doors. Doors and walls didn't escape his wrath as they too suffered damage. While most of the cracks and holes are repaired, I still know *exactly* where they *all* are located. Like ghosts, each one has a story that silently haunts me when I visit my mother.

Crappy carpet, a deteriorating bathroom, and my father always screaming about vacuuming, cleaning, and finding a husband…I was mentally and emotionally damaged. Who wouldn't be?

My husband has a hard time understanding any of it.

And now when my mother visits she is quick to resurrect memories of my past. "Look at all this dog hair… don't you clean anything…the place is a mess…you need new furniture…why is there always something on the counter…what is wrong with you people?"

What is wrong me? Nothing. My husband and I work and like the rest of the world we are just living life. Every day it's something different. There are doctor's appointments, extracurricular activities, auto and home repairs, shopping, errands, laundry and cooking. Dogs need to go to the vet or park. Chasing after the dog hair, cleaning or vacuuming is not high on the priority list.

Don't get me wrong, we are not slobs and clean when we need to. We are just not "domestic engineers" as my mother often refers to herself. There is no cleaning going on in the house while we are working all day.

My mother calls in the evening and wants to know what I'm doing and what all the noise is in the background.

I tell here I'm cleaning fingerprints off the refrigerator and ramble on about items left on the counter, Tupperware, tinfoil balls of trash, and ask why should I put it away?

My mother immediately translated what I said into a lecture about germs. "Who eats without washing their hands…germs on the sink…germs on the stove…germs in the bathroom…"

She highlights the location of all the germs in our house and finishes with, "And those dogs you don't know what germs are on their paws…and they sleep on your bed…you should spray Lysol… you should use vinegar…"

She made it sound like we were living a petri dish of germs and that the entire house is alive and I should be prepared to do battle.

I hang up annoyed.

My husband and the dogs have just passed through my office. I get up and head for the kitchen and grab the Lysol. And, like my mother, I glide from room to room spraying the lemon scent, leaving clouds of the pungent odor behind me.

My husband and the dogs at this time have all settled themselves on the couch. "What the fuck is wrong with you?" he screams as droplets from the spray fall on him. Laughing uncontrollably he grabs a blanket from the back of the couch as he tries to shield himself and the dogs from the pungent mist. "What the fuck? I didn't do anything! Get the hell out of here with that crap!"

"It fucking smells…you and the dogs walked through my office…someone is flatulent…this is fucking ridiculous…it fuckin' smells like a sewer…I'm combatting germs," I scream as I continue to parade through the house spraying.

"Damn it! YOU'RE NOT A FUCKING BACHELOR ANYMORE!"

CHAPTER 22

Vacuum Master

My husband does the vacuuming in our home. Although I've tried to explain, he refuses to understand why I despise the vacuum and I still don't understand why he vacuums around everything. Due to my lack of participation, I have no business commenting, but I do anyway.

"You need to move the furniture," when you vacuum.

"I did." And before I can ask when, he smiles and adds, "I did it when you were in the other room."

He gets the "Alice Look." I give him the hand motion that he taught me – the one hunters use as they silently communicate to one another by putting their two fingers toward their eyes and pointing back and forth to indicate the deer or other wildlife are in the vicinity. I then repeat phrases he learned from his father, who dragged him to church after church, which he now often repeats, and tell him God is watching and his sin will be revealed in the assembly!

He laughs and reminds me that *I'm* lucky to have him.

I shake my head in disbelief and move the couch. I point to crap on the floor. "How do you explain this?"

He scratches the back of his neck, as he considers his answer. "It's just a shadow from the light," he laughs.

I pull out the couch more. "Look, it's a Dorito," I can't imagine how that got there."

I smile anticipating the bullshit response I was going to get.

"The dogs must have had a snack while they were watching television," he smirks.

"Fuh-ged-da-boud-it!"

Another reason cleaning *is* a *huge* challenge in our home is because we have dogs. There is dog hair *everywhere*. No matter where you go in the house there is dog hair. No matter how much we clean the house the dog hair somehow remains. Even when one of them passes on, his dog hair still blows past us like tumbleweed from a ghost town.

The dogs have been instrumental in how we decide on what vacuum to purchase when one breaks. A cattle dog, golden retriever, and longhaired dachshund have made significant contributions to the purchase of new vacuums respectively and our longhaired dachshund, well, my husband assures me has *nothing* to do with any of the tumbleweeds of hair; instead, he blames all the mechanical vacuum failures on my long hair!

It's a fact. I have long hair, but it's a poor excuse for not maintaining the vacuum cleaner.

In twelve years we have spent a small fortune on vacuums. We've tried them all – some of which include - two Bissell's, four Hoover's, two Dirt Devils, two battery-operated vacuums for the kitchen, miscellaneous hand-held vacuums for quick cleaning, a few Swifters, and two shop vacuums!

The Eureka is our current vacuum. I bought it because my mother pointed out that it had the "Good Housekeeping Seal of Approval." The other selling point was a photo of a dog on the front of the box with a sticker that stated something about the best machine for combating pet hair. A photo of a dog and the "Seal of Approval" was all I needed. The price, warranty, or any other information didn't matter. I picked up the box, put it in the shopping cart, and made my way to the checkout line.

"How much did you pay for this?" screamed my husband as my mother and I made our way into the house with our new purchase. "What the hell do we need another vacuum for?" he continued shouting as he examined the large box.

"I can't push that one we have. It's too heavy! Something's wrong with it," I lamented.

"WHAT!" Are you fuckin' kidding me," he hollered. "You don't even use the vacuum. I'm going out to get coffee!"

I get the "Alice Look" for the rest of the day.

It's a great vacuum but like any appliance, it must be maintained to work effectively and efficiently. It has been to the repair shop twice because my husband didn't change the filters, clean the brush, or complete the other routine maintenance that is required.

I shoot him the "Alice Look."

"The manual says it has a HEPPA filter, it needs to be changed."

"What the hell is that?"

My point exactly!

My husband likes to tinker with the vacuum. Because he doesn't do the required maintenance, there is always some type of mechanical problem with every vacuum we have owned. Performing surgery on the vacuums is routine. The surgery begins in the living room without the instruction manual. If he spends more than thirty minutes working on it, he realizes that it's too involved and moves outside to the deck, and when it's critical - it goes to the shed. Once it dies it sits at the curb, waiting for the trash pickup to meet its final death!

However, in our neighborhood, items like vacuums don't last long at the curb as someone, who is collecting metal for scrap, replacement parts, or has the patience for repairs, usually picks them up.

Fast forward – the Eureka has been sick for months. My husband's solution now, "just go out and buy a new fucking vacuum, this thing sucks!" His shouts echo through the house.

Like a tornado, I whip into the bedroom, the vacuum is on the floor, debris from the clog is scattered about the carpet. I start screaming, "There's no money for a new vacuum and why the fuck are you putting the hair and dust on the carpet…why the hell are you taking it apart in the bedroom…"

"Because it will be easy for me to vacuum it up," he interrupts.

I leave the room. There is no reason to respond. No sense in getting myself more stressed out.

By mid-afternoon, the vacuum lies in pieces in my studio. My husband is screaming obscenities at the walls. "Fucking dog hair…damn it…fuh-ged-da-boud-it…this is ridiculous…this is a fucking nightmare…I hate this thing…you need to call your mother…ask her what we should buy!"

It seems he has been able to find the clog and is once again pulling the hair he previously pulled out of the vacuum and then re-vacuumed hours earlier. I bring him the trash bag he yells for.

He has another outburst where he proceeds to blame China as the reason for all the broken vacuums and repairs he has had to make over the years.

The tears are rolling down my face because I am laughing so hard. "Because you can't do the routine maintenance that is required, you're going to blame an entire country?" My voice grows louder. "Because you refuse to read the instruction manual? You're lucky to have me. You're lucky that I put up with this fucking insanity!"

He knows I'm right. He shakes his head in defeat and sighs heavily. "Just get me another garbage bag please. Good thing we have extras from the grocery store."

The permanent home for the vacuum is not the closet but our living room. Because of the large amount of dog hair, it's out all the time. "Why should I waste time putting it in the closet, when we are going to use it every day?" My husband argues. Although its primary parking spot is in the living room, on occasion it visits other areas of the house.

"Why the hell is the vacuum in the hall?" I yelled loudly as I untangled myself from the hose.

"I'm going to use it tomorrow morning," my husband yelled back from the living room.

I enter the living room and I give him the "Alice Look."

"It's Sunday. Three dogs, two people – it's a recipe for an accident, which I almost had. Didn't you hear me trip? Who takes a vacuum out to get ready for use the next day? You're not painting a house…there are no preparations necessary; just plug it into the outlet and use! Please put it back in the living room until you need it."

Days later I am on the phone with my girlfriend.

"What is all that noise?" she asked.

"I am trying to remove the plastic bag my husband has tied to the vacuum cleaner, its filled with the hair and debris he vacuumed up. It's disgusting."

"Why the hell would he hang a bag of dirt in the living room? I thought he has allergies."

"He does. He just recently went to the ear-nose-and-throat doctor and had a round of allergy tests done. Fifty dollars per co-pay and three visits later confirmed he was allergic to just about every type of dust, pollen, and ragweed that exists. Oh yeah, and also cats and dogs!"

Sarcastically she says, "He has allergies and hangs a bag of dust in the living room? No wonder he is always complaining about his nose."

"I know. And would you believe he has the vacuum sitting right next to the couch he sits on and has his coffee in the morning."

We continued to laugh at the absurd behaviors of the men in our life.

Days later my husband wanted to know what happen to the bag he had tied to the vacuum cleaner.

I looked at him incredulously. "Are you kidding me? What the hell were you saving it for?"

"I was waiting until the whole bag was filled before I threw it out."

I threw up my hands in frustration. "Seriously, do you think that once you empty the dust in that plastic bag, it doesn't escape back into the air? Did you forget we have a ceiling fan, which you always have on and that trash bag is practically sitting underneath?"

"The bag is tied! Nothing is going to get out," he shouted.

"I threw it out! I don't understand why it's so difficult to empty the debris from the vacuum container into a bag and take the bag out to the trash...is it too far to walk to the east wing of our house...why must we have a bag of dust perpetually hanging in the middle of the living room?" I was shouting louder than him. I was positive the neighbor next store can hear it all.

"Damn it! YOU'RE NOT A FUCKING BACHELOR ANYMORE!"

CHAPTER 23

Chemical Warfare

We live in a small ranch so you would think it would be easy to keep up with the cleaning. I must admit, it's not. After a day of multi-tasking at work I have had enough. By the time I arrive home, cook, take care of the dogs, and finish other miscellaneous chores, the last thing I want to do is any sort of cleaning, vacuuming included!

In the summer, we spend all our time outside, in the yard, gardening, planting, and enjoying our deck. We don't live "at the shore" but rather "down the shore," as those of us from north Jersey would say. There are a host of recreational activities such as the boardwalk, beach, outdoor concerts, and bike riding that we take part in.

In the fall, the football season begins and life is planned around sixteen weeks of NFL football. Raking leaves, cleaning the vegetable gardens, putting summer furniture away, closing ponds, cleaning gutters, gathering and finally splitting wood for the wood-burning stove *ALL* must happen before the bitter cold arrives.

Consequently, cleaning inside is erratic. Adding to the equation is my husband the surface cleaner, and myself who absolutely abhors housework due to the regimented and abusive cleaning routine I was subjected to as an adolescent! Finally there are the ceiling fans in every room, spreading dog hair, dust and soot from the wood burning stove to every corner of the house!

My husband and I do our best to navigate around our cleaning anxieties, by taking turns with the housework.

When I clean, the house smells of Lysol, preferably lemon fresh scent and surfaces shine. I alternate the scents on occasion but, like my mother, I usually use the traditional lemon scent. She was forever spraying Lysol in the house. Holding her finger on button and releasing the fresh scent in the air, she would chase my father and the cloud of cigarette smoke that perpetually followed him.

My husband doesn't use Lysol at all. He lets me know he cleaned with other products.

I arrived home one evening and was confronted with the smell of bleach. It hit me as I walked through the front door. Chemical warfare ensued while I was at work. My eyes tear and I held my breath. Ugh, the "surface cleaner" was at it again. I immediately headed for the kitchen, muttering obscenities as I cranked open the windows. Even the dogs couldn't stand the smell as they skipped greetings and sprinted to the back door, clearly in need of fresh air.

I stood in the living room waiting for the dogs. Rubbing my temples, I sighed heavily. A headache was eminent. My eyes did a quick scan of the area. It only took a few glances and I could tell you *exactly* what my husband did that day. It was also evident what my Saturday would consist of as he has single-handedly organized it from me.

Fresh pine needles and leaves littered the entrance of the sliding glass doors indicating he brought firewood in from the deck to fill the inside hopper. Like a robot my eyes quickly scanned the living room. A film of ash covered the coffee tables, piano, shelves, credenza, TV, lampshades, books, and photos. It's like some sort of volcanic eruption occurred. I zeroed in on the source – he emptied the ash from the wood-burning stove. I made a mental note to discuss the ash removal when he got home.

The smell of bleach and Pine Sol grew stronger as I neared the bathroom. "Ugh!" I groaned as the pungent odors burned my lungs when I opened the door. There was no window accessible because the bathroom is located between rooms in the center of the house.

I didn't even have to look at the bottles of cleaners to know they are almost empty, but I gave him the benefit of the doubt and check anyway.

"Yup," I mutter, "the directions indicate only a capful is necessary."

For my husband, that's only a suggestion.

I'd like to know where it says half a bottle is needed to clean a 4x8 area. I again wonder what he really learned about cleaning from his mother, the hoarder. His issues probably run deeper than mine.

After some chores, he took a break, and rested his foot on the blue hassock, which is disguised as the laundry basket. His foot brace for his planter fasciitis rests on top of the clean clothing. The only activity the basket had seen all week was that it was moved closer to the couch to help rest his foot.

When he returned home, I thanked my husband for cleaning and told him I appreciated his efforts. I asked him not to use so many chemicals, and I explained how it's not only unnecessary but a waste of product and money. I asked him to sweep up the debris that falls off the logs the next time he fills the wood hopper. I asked him to use the rags to clean and not an entire roll of paper towels. I asked him not to empty the ash with the small shovel. I asked him not to rest his dirty feet on the clean clothing.

He stared at me with a blank look on his face. I am waiting for some sarcastic comment.

Instead, he scratched his head and looked at me suspiciously. "When did you install a camera in the house? How did *you* know what *I* did today?"

The following day my girlfriends and I reminisce about cleaning and who did the housework in their homes while growing up. We laugh about bleach and how it was one of the preferred cleaning products of our mothers. "That's how we learned to clean, we scrubbed and scrubbed with bleach, and nobody cared how much you inhaled. Nobody thought about getting sick, or any other long term effects," my girlfriend laughs.

My other girlfriend admits she has obsessive-compulsive tendencies when it comes to cleaning. I joke that she needs to find a man with similar behaviors. So who does she start dating, a man who turns out to be a slob. He didn't present himself this way when they started dating. The more time he spent time in her home, the more it became apparent he wasn't the neatest person. Lounging on the couch....food on the coffee table...clothes all over....dishes in the sink...her anxiety increased the more she talked about it.

My right hand whipped under my chin gesturing as I spat, "Fuh-ged-da-boud-it."

She immediately understood the meaning of the slang. Translation in this case – get rid of him. Before she could find something nice to say about him, I hold up my hand and signaled for her to stop and immediately provided my advice, "you need to read my book."

Once again, the title was enough. Her face beamed as I delivered highlights before I continued.

"Do you think he is going to change? What do you mean he is sitting home watching TV all day? Is he changing the roll of toilet paper, does he leave the toilet seat up, and what do you mean he doesn't even clean…"

My other girlfriend is nearby and smirks and shakes her head knowingly as I am trying to talk some sense into her. She knows this is not a good relationship for our friend and wishes she would just move on.

"Perhaps if he would just help with the cleaning things would be better," she concludes.

I throw up my hands in frustration.

Later that month talk of cleaning resurfaces.

My mother was coming for the weekend and I asked my husband to vacuum and clean the bathroom while I was at work.

When I arrived home, I found a present – two bags of vacuum dirt and hair in the foyer. Instead of taking them to the trashcan that is next to his car, he left evidence to show he did some housework just in case I didn't believe him. Painfully similar to how an outdoor pet cat would hunt, kill, and deliver a bird or small rodent to its owner!

The smell of Tilex and bleach permeates through the air. The bathroom rugs are on the deck and the bathroom floor was surface cleaned. "Ugh! He didn't do anything. More stuff for me to do," I muttered.

In between writing I stopped to cook, do laundry, fold towels, clean rugs, and mop the bathroom floor! My husband arrived home at midnight and wanted to know why I'm still awake. He surveyed the living room. "Why is the mop out?"

"It's really a new piece of art or rather interactive sculpture that I purchased…it's called, I'm Used for Cleaning Floors!"

"Ha. Ha. Very funny. What, did the toilet overflow? Is that why the mop is out?"

I give him the "Alice Look."

"No, I'm cleaning the floor. It was disgusting and the toilet bowl needed to be scrubbed not just sprayed with cleaner with the hope that by simply spraying the foam chemical over the bowl it will clean the dirt and scum without any further wiping," I retorted as I moved the mop back and forth briskly and shove it in the bucket. Soap film and chemical residue from cleaning products remain in the shower from the over abundant use of cleaner my husband insisted on using over the years.

Apparently the big-eyed, round-shaped army of "Scrubbing Bubbles" from the television commercial with their promises of "No Scrubbing Needed" had put evil thoughts into my husband's head.

The obscenities and hand gestures began. "YOU'RE NOT A FUCKING BACHELOR ANYMORE," I shouted.

CHAPTER 24

Accent Pillows

I enter to the bedroom, hoping I would find a completely made bed with two pillows covered with pillow shams, five decorative pillows in various shapes – square, rectangle, oblong and four more pillows used for sleeping resting atop an extremely expensive comforter. Two stuffed animals should complete the scene that looks like it's right out of the pages of a *Martha Stewart Magazine.*

Instead I am confronted with a pile of pillows that are stacked up on top of the armoire and a heap of blankets, sheets, and pillows on the bed that have not been washed.

I located my husband and give him the "Alice Look" and stance.

"I guess you left the sheets and blankets all jumbled because you were going to strip the bed and take everything to the laundry room to be washed?"

My husband smiled and laughed sarcastically. "You're right those were my intentions."

To avoid having to explain why the bed is not made, he redirected the conversation to a discussion regarding our sleeping habits. He hoped this would somehow detract me from my original focus and make me realize that the pile of sheets on the bed is really my fault.

"If you didn't sleep with so many blankets and pillows…"

Before he can finish the sentence, I snapped back, "What does this have to do with making the bed or washing the sheets?"

"If you didn't wrinkle the fucking sheets and throw the covers all over…"

I interrupt, "Again, what does this have to do with making the bed and cleaning the sheets?"

"If you didn't have all those pillows…"

I smile anticipating the conversation is coming to an end, knowing he has no explanation. "Again, what does this have to do with making the bed?"

Frustrated that he had no rational answer, he threw up his hands in defeat, grabbed the pillow cases and sheets, and headed to the laundry room and proceeded to blame the problem on something else. I hear him shouting, "It would be easier if we didn't have all this stuff…why do we need all this stuff in the house… why do we need all these pillows on the bed…if we didn't have the pillows it would be a lot easier to make the bed…"

After I wash the sheets, my husband insists on making the bed. The obsessive-compulsive behavior takes over and the sheets need to be perfectly tight and adjusted accordingly. Sometimes I help him pull the sheets over the bed, but if he doesn't like how I fold, crease, tuck, or pull, the yelling starts and I'm dismissed from the room. I don't understand why he is so obsessive about the way the bed should be made. He doesn't either. I think back to his mother and often wonder if it's a reaction to her hoarding?

My divorced girlfriend at work explains it best, "their all just fuckin' stupid. Make the bed," she laughs buoyantly. "That will be the day. My ex-husband couldn't do laundry, refused to put a roll of toilet paper on a fuckin' roller, or clean the house. That son-of-a bitch didn't even know where the sheets were located. If I didn't wash the sheets, they would probably never get changed. At least your husband makes the bed."

She's right and I'm grateful for it. My other girlfriend thinks there is no need for all the accent pillows. She thinks it's ridiculous.

The acquisition of these pillows and linens for the bed didn't happen until years later after the first flood in our home.

"We spent a lot of time and money re-doing the bedroom and I wanted it to look nice."

"Why can't we just go back to the old way?" My husband questioned rather seriously.

The old way was a full size bed and furniture that my husband brought into the marriage and claimed was antique.

My mother, the shopper, quickly educated him when he refused to believe me. "One-hundred years or older is considered antique, this isn't even close," she stated confidently as she examined the furniture.

Gesturing toward the dresser I smirked, "This is children's furniture; my brother had this same exact set in his bedroom growing up."

"But this is good furniture, there is nothing wrong with it," he lamented.

"As a matter of fact my best friend's brother had a similar set like this in their house too," I added smugly as I give him the "Alice Look" and continued to remind him why we purchased a new bed.

"You complained you had no room in the full size bed. We were constantly bumping and hitting one another. It was like a war zone – elbows hitting faces and limbs striking one another, nobody could get any sleep. There was no room for both of us. Why the hell do you want to go back to that?" I asked incredulously.

Remodeling the bedroom ended in Bed, Bath and Beyond.

"This is it. This is the last store I'm going into. You'd better find something here," he snapped irritably as we entered the Bed, Bath and Beyond in Manahawkin, New Jersey.

I already knew what I was going to buy. I saw it in the Sunday circular. I just hoped the store had it in stock. If not we'd have to drive to another store. Or I'd call my mother who lived an hour and a half away and I knew she would find it in the store near her. I had just given the old sheets and comforter to the local animal shelter and we needed linens to fit the new mattress.

The color drained from my husband's face as he read the price tag on the comforter set. "You can't be serious…we are not spending three hundred dollars on this…and it doesn't even come with the sheets…"

"Don't worry I have a coupon," I interrupted.

"Coupon!" He shouted. "For what? Twenty percent?" he gestured furiously at the display shaking his head adamantly. "We're not spending money on this."

People nearby were laughing as the exchange continued. One gentleman who was shopping with his wife advised him to buy the comforter. "Get used to it buddy," he laughed. "And wait until you see what happens when she wants to re-decorate in another few years."

"Redecorate!" he shouted. "I can assure you that ain't happening," he snapped back at the customer.

I crossed my arms over my chest and give him the "Alice Look" *and* stance.

My husband groaned. "Don't they have anything cheaper?"

I glared at him. My eyes flashed in anger. "Well, this is what you get for wanting to super-size something else! You wanted a king size bed. And a king size bed needs KING SIZE SHEETS!

We re-did the entire bedroom to fit that bed and furniture in the room and now we need bedding that will fit the king size bed and match the decor! This," I pointed to the display, "is the only thing that matches our color scheme!"

He started rubbing his temples.

"What, did you think we were going to put fucking sleeping bags on the mattress?"

His face lit up, "Now that's and idea. I can get them down from the attic."

I again give him the "Alice Look" and stance.

He threw up his arms, his face twisted in anger. "Do what you want. I just pay rent there anyway!"

I laughed easily and calmly said, "You're lucky to have me," and threw two decorative pillows in the shopping cart.

"Forty dollars for each of these little pillows! What the hell are they for? We don't need this!"

"I just can't have one pillow on the bed, it won't look right. The bed is huge."

"But forty dollars…you give me grief about spending money on a cup of coffee and you're going to spend forty dollars on these two, little pillows?" He shrieked, adding, "You're fuckin' out of your mind!"

"I told you I have coupons."

I was on the phone with my mother by the time we arrived to the aisle where the sheets were located. She was already at the Bed, Bath in Beyond in north Jersey looking at the comforter set and giving her final approval of the purchase. She was going to buy a second set of sheets for us and wanted to make sure the color matched what I was purchasing. She also needed to make sure I purchased the necessary items for the mattress.

My husband's mouth was hanging open.

"Now what's wrong?"

"I'm simply amazed at the speed in which you women move and coordinate."

The outburst from my husband that followed was another one of those stories that becomes a chapter in the family history that you are creating together that is told over and over to family and friends. It's not necessary to repeat, but the highlights are enough for one to understand the scene that had unfolded in aisle after aisle complete with obscenity after obscenity.

It was provoked by the need for Egyptian cotton sheets…800 thread count…extra pillow cases…mattress covers…something to cover the mattress cover…sheet and pillow protectors…summer *and* winter blankets…and finally back to the thread count.

He rubbed his temples as he reluctantly pushed the overflowing shopping cart to the checkout counter. His disgust was apparent as he sighed heavily and held up items for the cashier to scan. "I'm getting a headache…you better have a coupon for all of this…I need a cup of coffee…we're getting coffee when we leave and you better believe *I* will be super-sizing," he complained.

As soon as we're in the parking lot the cell phone rings.

My girlfriend calls to see if we can meet for dinner. My husband snapped a firm, "NO." Then added, "Not unless she's paying for it…after all the money we just spent!"

After she hears his story, she takes my husband's side, "This is ridiculous, something to cover the mattress? For what, are you two expecting early loss of bladder control? Why not just shrink-wrap the whole bed first. Sheet and pillow protectors? What the hell for? Pillows are made to be used, flattened, and not protected. Summer and winter blankets? Just pick one and use it all year long, it's just a blanket."

"Thank you for agreeing with me," yelled my husband into the cell phone as we loaded the packages into the truck.

She continued, "Don't get me wrong, I've been to some stores and have seen some beautiful bedding on display and think to myself, ahh, that's nice, and then I WALK AWAY," she shouted loudly. "I'm on his side. Unless your coupon read the words, "It's Free," I have to agree with him!"

"Fuh-ged-da-boud-it. You just wait until you have your own house," I laughed before hanging up.

Clearly she didn't understand the finer points of bed making and decorating. So I called my mother to inquire and we received a lesson on bed making 101 for the rest of the drive home.

"I learned from my mother…everything was covered… and we took care of our stuff, there was no throwing anything out, and the beds were always made every day…you couldn't leave the house without making the bed…Oh, and the sheets, they were ironed, my mother had a roller iron, and you washed the sheets and drapes…"

"What the hell was that?" I interrupted.

"It was a large contraption that heated up and you sat at it and put the sheets and drapes through…it was in our basement…this is what women did, we were domestic engineers…we stayed home and took care of the house…and the box spring…it was always covered, so it wouldn't get dust or dust mites…you should be do-ing this too…all this talk about bed bugs in the news…and with all of those dogs you two have…they are dirty…you shouldn't have the dogs sleeping in the bedroom…then over the years the materi-al improved…and then years later things became the hypo aller-genic, which you need because your husband says he is allergic… when I went to nursing school we had to make hospital corners and the beds had to be made…sheets had to look sharp and crisp…

and I also watched and learned from all these home shows...like Martha Stewart...this is what the bed should look like."

And on and on it went.

My mother could write an entire book about the history of bed linens and how a bedroom should look!

Even my best girlfriend wouldn't understand.

My husband looked to our best male friend for reinforcement. What *he* got after comparing notes was an explanation on proper bed making techniques from him!

The placement of all the pillows, how the sheets, and comforter should look was reviewed in great detail. My husband was dumfounded and disappointed. His friend had crossed over to the dark side of a domestic responsibility that he considered an incredible waste of time!

My husband shook his head in disgust. "You've turned into Martha Stewart."

"Look," our best male friend explained, "just make the hospital corners and put the fuckin' pillows on the bed. It's a hell of a lot easier. It's not worth arguing over. And it's really not that hard to do. Don't fight it buddy," he laughed.

I chuckled. "You're in good company. Even he knows he's not a *fucking bachelor* anymore."

CHAPTER 25

Just Passing Through...the Bathroom

Every married person or anyone in a relationship living together should have his or her own bathroom! A law should be passed that states at least two bathrooms be constructed in every home.

I am a firm believer in the concept of sharing, and making the best of what you have, but when it comes to this area of the home I am an adamant supporter of separate bathrooms.

Growing up with only one bathroom in the house was a traumatic experience. The only way to the only bathroom in the house was via the staircase. My mother was forever screaming at us to either stop running or stomping our feet so hard because we were ruining the stairs and carpet. It sounded like Herman Munster of the television show *The Munsters was* in the house as feet pounded the old wood as we sprinted up and down the worn staircase. My father screamed threats from the basement office when he had enough of the noise. It really did sound like a herd of cattle as we ran up and down the stairs.

The Munsters was a 1964 sitcom about a family of monsters, vampires, werewolves and Frankenstein living among mortals and thinking nothing was wrong with them. Herman Munster, played by Fred Gwynne was Frankenstein, was seven feet tall wore huge shoes as his feet pounded on the floor or down the staircase in the show sometimes putting a hole right through the floor.

One thing remained constant about our bathroom - it was always occupied. No matter what time during the day, someone *always* was in the bathroom. And if you were even two minutes late getting up for school, the entire morning routine for *everyone* was disrupted. Chaos would erupt as it created total mayhem for everyone else who needed use the bathroom.

This was followed by a lesson in accountability, as the rest of the morning was spent blaming the person who caused everyone to be late or delayed. Bullying was alive and well in our home as he or she was viciously picked on until they departed the house. The ranting resonated from various locations and echoed over the slamming of closets, bedroom doors, and dresser drawers. My father banged on the door and threw things. For some reason the bathroom delays heightened the vulgarities that spewed from the mouth of my father. The script sounded something like this:

"Why can't you get up on time…I have to go to the bathroom…I need to brush my teeth…when the hell are you going to be finished…get the hell out of my way…what the hell did you do to the toothpaste…why can't you put the cap back on…why can't you squeeze the toothpaste from the bottom…why can't you dry your hair in your room…there's no hot water left…who used all the fuckin' hot water again…why can't you do your make-up in the other room…who used the last razor…there is water all over the sink…who left the toilet seat up…why is there no toilet paper… when are you going to be out of the shower…who left their wet towel on the floor…if you were up on time I wouldn't be late…"

As the yelling upstairs escalated my mother would blame my father and the "irrational matter" continued their screaming match in the kitchen. "You know we wouldn't have all this commotion in the morning if you could just install another bathroom in the house!"

She was right. He worked in construction. He built houses. We could never understand why he wouldn't add another bathroom. The shouting continued over the slamming and banging of the kitchen cabinets. He was always looking for matches, cigarettes, and Rolaids. The banging was followed by items, usually the box of tissues sitting on the corner of the counter, which suddenly became air-borne with the quick swipe of the back of his hand. The box of tissues along with stacks of paper and mail soared through the air, hitting doors and walls. Chairs were pushed aside. Like a tornado swirling furiously through the kitchen, nothing in his path was safe.

He'd cut her off with a flurry of obscenities. His head, encased in a shroud of cigarette smoke, would follow him as he made his departure. The back door slammed, and the pick-up truck rumbled out of the driveway heading toward the convenience store for coffee. This was all because someone could not get up in time to use the bathroom!

I vowed that if I ever decided to get married and purchase a home, there would be more than one bathroom in the house.

Living on my own for so long, I must have forgotten the trauma I suffered having to share a bathroom when I was growing up – for the house that my husband and I purchased only has one bathroom!

To make matters worse the bathroom is approximately 6'x10', is located in the center of the house, and accessible by the master bedroom and the living room. There is only room for one person at a time in this bathroom. And due to its location in the center, it is always quicker to cut through the bathroom instead of walking around.

No matter what I'm doing in the bathroom, the dogs, my husband, or both come parading through. And when they're not passing through, my husband always seems to need something that is in the bathroom.

I had a meltdown one morning while I was getting ready for work. It was seven-thirty. I was putting on make-up and fixing my hair. In came my husband with the dogs trailing behind.

"Do you know what I'm going to do with this hot curling iron if you don't get the fuck out of here? This is my time. Why do you need to come in here? What are you doing up? You don't have to be at work until four-o'clock."

I watched my husband's face. I could feel the energy swirling around in his head as he searched for an answer. And as if there is nothing wrong he responded, "I'm letting the dogs out."

The curling iron sliced through the air as I conveyed my irritation. "They ate already and were out twice. What the hell do you think I do in the morning? Why do you think I get up so early?"

My husband gave me a blank look. His mind was trying to think of a better reason as to why he should be in the bathroom.

"I need a tissue."

"Fuh-ged-da-boud-it. Are you fucking kidding me? There is a box on your nightstand."

I refused to move to let him and the dogs pass.

He smiled. "I just wanted to say I love you and I have to pee."

My eyes narrowed and I scowled angrily. "Get the fuck out of here. Go pee in the yard with the dogs," I joked as I ushered everyone out and slammed the door.

Even though we remodeled the bathroom ten years later, it still hasn't stopped my husband and the dogs from using it as a short cut to travel to the other side of the house!

Our house is approximately seventeen hundred square feet. My husband has our house confused with a mansion as he has subliminally added an extra zero to the square footage making it seventeen thousand square feet. He is constantly complaining that it is too far for him to walk around!

Hands on my hips I give him the "Alice Look" and stance. "Are you kidding me? Have you lost your mind?" I storm off and grab the tape measure from the desk.

When you leave the bathroom from one door and enter the living room it is approximately sixteen feet to walk to the kitchen. From the other side you enter the bedroom and it is approximately twenty feet to walk to the kitchen! Heaven help him if we ever purchase a bigger house!

Nonetheless, the conversation regarding the bathroom is always the same.

"Why do you find it necessary to come in here when I'm brushing my teeth," I lament. "You see I'm brushing my teeth… why the hell do you have to shave now…can't you wait until I'm done…we only have one sink…what the fuck is the matter with you?"

My husband looks at me perplexed, shakes his head and simply states, "I don't know!"

I explode and shove him out of the bathroom.

While annoying, I truly believe my husband doesn't know either. It's probably more strange obsessive-compulsive behavior, once again taken to a higher level that I will never understand nor want to.

I ask my best girlfriend why men do this.

Her husband is ten-times more obsessive compulsive than my husband, yet we have learned to live with the same behaviors, sometimes asking why, but understanding that most of the time it's just not worth it. Knowing that I am not suffering alone allows for a certain kinship with others. It's as if we belong to a secret club, and membership is based on the immediate understanding of these strange behaviors without explanation.

We laugh at the insanity of it all. I tell her, "Sometimes the behavior is too bizarre, and it's not worth asking. For instance, why would someone sprinkle half a container of Ajax in the sink and leave it there overnight? The other night he did this again and when I woke up in the morning and went into the kitchen to get fresh coffee, I am hit with the smell of Ajax and not coffee! The Ajax is dried solid to the sink and when I come home from work, it's still there, rock-hard and dried."

"How did you get it out?"

"I didn't. I left it for him to deal with when he came home from work. Would you believe one night I was reading in bed and heard him rummaging under the bathroom sink? I immediately knew he was looking for the Ajax, which I knew we were out of, so what does he do? He takes the Tilex, and sprays it all over the bathroom sink, claiming it works better! Why should I even bother to have a conversation about surface cleaning the sink at midnight?"

I still have great faith that attaching the roll of toilet paper on the roller issue will eventually resolve itself, but we have bigger issues to deal with first.

My husband is an only child and had been a bachelor for so long the concept of sharing space was foreign to him.

"You're not a fucking bachelor anymore!" I'd scream, as I'd find the toilet seat up again."

I must confess that my husband really isn't too bad with this. What changed him? Perhaps it was the time I woke up in the middle of the night and almost fell in the toilet because he left the seat up. The neighbors I'm positive heard our colorful conversation as the epithets flowed freely. My husband was laughing and hiding under the comforter as I was throwing the pillows at him. He claims he doesn't remember the incident.

For many of my other girlfriends leaving the toilet seat up is just as bad as not changing the roll of toilet paper. "Fuh-ged-da-boud-it. That bastard, he didn't give a shit," my divorced friend snapped back. "He didn't do the cleaning, so it didn't matter. He got what was coming to him because when he moved in with his girlfriend, she eventually threw him out for recognizing him for the inconsiderate slob that he was."

***

The next problem or area of opportunity in the bathroom is, once again, *cleaning*. When it's his turn to clean the bathroom his brain immediately shifts to his surface-cleaning mode. The toilet suffers the most, as he doesn't really clean underneath. "Do you see this?" I point to the toilet as I he comes parading through the bathroom with the dogs. It's called cleaning…you have to clean underneath…why can't you do this…this is your mess…it's disgusting…didn't your mother teach you how to clean the bathroom… your lucky to have me…you're not a fucking bachelor anymore…."

My husband and I don't really have knock down drag out fights. Even though we yell a lot, our banter usually turns into laughter. While he can't understand the things I do, I am still continually, amazed at the things he does. So much so that it has become humorous at times. I always tell him, "Your lucky to have me."

He smiles and, returns with the same, "*You're* lucky to have me."

Today, while we are having conversation about cleaning the toilet bowl, he tells me, "You're lucky to have me because if you didn't you wouldn't have all these things to do in the house!

I laugh, not at all surprised at his humor, and remind him that he's not a fucking bachelor anymore and shove a bottle of cleanser into his hands!

CHAPTER 26

Bathroom Storage

If we could afford it, I would hire someone to clean the house. It would solve a lot of our issues. I resurrect the subject during the commercial break of the Dallas - Eagles football game. Dallas was losing so he was in a good mood. "I think we should hire someone to come in and clean the house."

Incredulous is the best way to describe the look he gave me. It was as if I told him we no longer had the NFL channel. "You talk about trying to save money and now you want to waste it? We are not getting a cleaning person," he said. Then he had the nerve to add, "Why don't you just clean one room every night."

The "Alice Look" and stance is immediate. He should have known better to start this argument with me as I quickly remind him why I don't have time to clean. Smiling, this will be one debate I am going to win. "When I get up in the morning before going to work my day usually starts out by letting the dogs out... preparing their food while they bark obnoxiously at the back door...while they eat I am either putting laundry in or taking it out of the machines...then it's back to the dogs...making coffee... getting ready for work...when I arrive home on time – which is only if I don't have to stop at the store - I take care of the dogs, cooking, empty the dishwasher...then it's on the computer to pay bills...you're home during the day watching TV..."

The conversation made a turn for the worse as it suddenly escalated to another issue – "the stuff" in the bathroom.

No matter what size home you purchase there never seems to be enough storage space – especially in the bathroom. I had forgotten my awful childhood memories regarding the lack of space in our bathroom. They were resurrected when we move into our new home with all our "stuff."

Our bathroom has a sink, tub, and toilet. No storage space existed until my husband did some renovating. A vanity and a linen closet were installed. And as soon as the shelves were mounted, I jammed them with our "stuff."

"What is all this?" I heard my husband shouting from the bathroom.

The dogs and I found him with the door to the linen cabinet open and staring. "What the hell is all this?" he demanded, pointing to the "stuff" on the shelves. His voice is loud and challenging. The dogs stuck their noses in the closet and started sniffing. Realizing there were no biscuits, they departed.

"You can't be serious," I stared back, my eyes squinting, wary of why he is even asking.

I give him the "Alice Look."

He threw his hands in the air before exploding, "What the fuck is all this crap?"

I immediately crossed my arms in front of my chest, held the "Alice Look," and calmly stated, "You need to be medicated. I really don't know how else to explain it. But it's the things *you* and *I* use daily!"

Moisturizers, lotions, powders, shampoos, conditioners, nail polish in an assortment of colors, perfume, hair brushes, curling irons, hair dryers, towels, soap, moisturizers, sun-tan lotion, medical supplies, deodorant, cleaning products, towels, wash clothes, and a collection of make-up filled the shelves and drawers.

I remind my husband about the conversation I had with one of my male co-workers about the stuff in the bathroom. "He knows and understands why the cabinets are stuffed with so many feminine products for women. He doesn't need a lot of stuff. I applaud him for his commitment to his spouse. He knows what he signed up for. Why can't you understand this?"

My husband, the only child is still trying to grasp the concept of sharing.

"This is what you signed up for," I laugh as I turned and opened the cabinet above the toilet and pointed. "This cabinet contains all your medical stuff."

"Where are my allergy tablets?" he grumbled.

I continued with the "Alice Look" and calmly stated, "Is there something wrong with your eyesight? You're looking right at them!"

My husband can never find anything in the cabinet or the refrigerator. The item or package could be staring right back at him and he still can't locate it. I just don't know what he is looking at. Somehow a picture of the television remote control is the first thing that pops into my head. My best girlfriend claims they are, "playing possum and that if they pretend to be brain dead someone will come and help them."

Rubbing alcohol, Neosporin, bacitracin, cortisone creams, Band-Aids, ace bandages, peroxide, headache pills, and miscellaneous ointments, are all neatly organized, lined up for him, as he is his own self-prescribed doctor. The cabinet looks like a condensed section of a pharmacy aisle in the store. He has his own unique way of diagnosing or treating his aliments. I call my mother for advice on products to use. My mother, who has been in nursing for over forty years, wants to know where my husband obtained him medical degree?

"Google and Web MD," I laugh.

His herniated disc, polyps, bone spurs, and planter fasciitis always seems to dissipate when he wants to go hunting or fishing. There is no way to manage his pain or aliments. Not one single over-the-counter medication, bandage, brace, or shoe insert has helped him. His pain has become my pain, as the cost of all these remedies is a financial nightmare. Needless to say, his twilight years are not going to be easy. But we continue to purchase product after product with the hope of a cure. And like everything else, he supersizes. For a cut, pouring half a bottle of rubbing alcohol or peroxide on it is routine! One Band-Aid turns into three or a tube of cream is applied as if one were putting suntan lotion on the entire body.

Satisfied that all his supplies are in the cabinet, he started yelling about the drawers in the vanity. "You can't be serious," he laughs. "This is all I get? Three drawers for my stuff?"

"Do the math," I smile lovingly. There are six drawers in the vanity, one side is for you and the other side is for me. That's three drawers each. It's a concept we call sharing. Everything else is in the closet."

He continued to protest. "Three drawers...."

I'd had enough of the ridiculous argument. My irritation was reflected in the tone of my voice, which had just increased two octaves. "Fuh-ged-da-boud-it. Get real, are you joking? You don't have anything to put in them. In case you haven't looked, you are just about bald; you have one hair brush, one bottle of shampoo, hair gel, deodorant, an electric razor, and an assortment of other small items...What the hell do you need with more space? Besides the rest of the stuff is neatly organized in the closet on the shelves!"

He had no more to say. He knew I was right. But from time to time will start the conversation about why he only gets three drawers in the vanity.

My answer varies. Conversations about sharing are difficult when you're talking to someone who is an only child. I offer suggestions as to how he could utilize his space more effectively. Hair products are no longer necessary, and I remind him to throw them out. "What do you think some miracle is going to take place and you're going to wake up with hair?"

He laughs and counters with obscenities. I counter with the "Alice Look" and stance, and remind him that he is hoarding things like his mother and has no need for a hair dryer. "Perhaps I should build you a pyramid like the Egyptian's and you can fill it with your stuff," I joke. "Just remember you're not a fucking bachelor anymore!"

CHAPTER 27

The Toilet Paper Holder is Not Located on the Sink

"What is the point of installing a toilet paper holder next to the toilet if you're not going to put the toilet paper on it?" I asked my girlfriend when I got to work one morning.

Her answer was clear, concise, and quick. "I already had this conversation before we were married. He doesn't do it anymore. He was bad for two years, but I kept exploding every time I saw that roll sitting on the sink."

"Why did he stop?"

She smiled. "He finally realized it's not worth fighting about anymore."

My other girlfriend doesn't have this problem only because her husband is so obsessive-compulsive that the toilet paper is always on the roller! Not only is it on the roller, but also the paper must hang over. "If I put the roll on backwards and the paper is under – then he explodes. Sometimes I do it just to annoy him," she readily admitted.

I giggled, freely admitting I do the same thing.

"I am tired of seeing the roll sitting on the sink. I can't understand how he can open it, wash his hands, and drip water on the sink and the new roll. Before you know it the roll is soaked and can't be used. Then he opens another roll, which also gets placed on the sink. And if I don't put the roll on its holder it will sit there on top of the sink or on top of the roller apparatus until it's empty!"

I continued to complain as we swapped stories.

I smiled wickedly. "But I like your idea. Perhaps that's what I should do – keep putting the toilet paper on backwards."

Two hours later one of my co-workers, who was part of the toilet paper roll conversation, entered my office. She held up her cell phone to show me a photo she just took in the staff bathroom. It was an opened roll of toilet paper sitting on the silver bar, which rested above the empty toilet paper holder! The bar functioned as an adaptive device in case someone needed help getting up!

We laughed at the absurdity of it. "At least they didn't put it on the floor. The bar is the best choice since the sink is nowhere near the toilet!"

I was having lunch with my female co-workers, ages ranging from thirty to sixty years old. Someone started telling us about her boyfriend and how she couldn't understand why the house was such a mess when she came home from work. Issues regarding laundry, cooking habits, and the dreaded toilet paper war were debated.

I knew exactly how they are all feeling and chime in about the manuscript I'm working on. The title was enough. The room erupted in a flurry of more stories. In that moment it was as if I was writing a manifesto of some sort, something that was going to validate the nonsense that goes on in their households. This was going to be the proof they could have as ammunition to prove to their men they were wrong.

That evening I got a text from a co-worker that depicted two empty cardboard rolls from toilet paper on the bathroom windowsill.

I couldn't stop laughing.

My husband entered the room and wanted to know what was so funny.

"I was talking about toilet paper with someone from work."

Knowing where this conversation is heading, he immediately left, guiltily, as he knew the roll was sitting on the sink.

"You're not a fucking bachelor anymore!" I shouted, laughing as the inconsiderate toilet paper changer departed.

My phone buzzed. It's another text message from my co-worker who was asking how I would handle it.

I texted back, "Put it on backwards. It becomes psychological warfare."

***

One weekend I found a brand-new roll of toilet paper in the trashcan. It was partially wet. I immediately sought out my husband.

"Why is there a band new roll of toilet paper stuffed in the trash can? I just bought that package. Why the hell would you waste a role like that and then try to stuff it into the small trashcan. It not only doesn't fit, but tissues are all over the floor. Why the hell would you just leave the tissues there?"

My mother, who was visiting, smirked and added, "Yeah, I was wondering about that."

My husband looks at both of us – the guilt apparent as there is nobody left in the house to accuse – and concocts some ridiculous story about how the roll fell in the toilet, as he was attempting to change the roll…the rest of his account is not worth talking about.

Why is this so hard to do? Have we become so lazy that it is too difficult to replace a roll of toilet paper when it is empty? Does it really take too long to perform this task? I calmly asked my husband about this. When he doesn't respond I ask him again.

"I don't know," he snapped.

I raised my eyebrows in disbelief. "But you have to have some idea."

He ignored me and said, "There is no answer. Just fuh-ged-da-boud-it."

"What? You can't be serious?"

He continued to stare at the television, and shook his head, "It's just what we are programed to do."

I'm the idiot for even having this discussion.

"You're lucky to have me," I retorted.

Tired of the ridiculous conversation, I get up to use the bathroom. The obscenities start. I hear my husband laughing.

"Are you fucking kidding me?" I erupt and come running out of the bathroom. "This is exactly what I'm talking about...this is how the toilet paper gets put on the roller...what the hell is wrong with you...why can't you put the toilet paper on the roller...it's really not that difficult...I don't understand you...it's really very simple...perhaps you don't understand and need me to draw a diagram for you."

My husband laughed harder the more I yelled. I slammed the bathroom door hard, emphasizing my annoyance but not before I reminded him, "Grow up! YOU'RE NOT A FUCKING BACHELOR ANYMORE."

CHAPTER 28

Culinary Wars

Even before we were married, it was clear I would be doing all the cooking, and I was ok with this because I love to cook. My husband's days of foil-packaged, sodium-filled rice, potatoes, pasta, and five-minute microwave meals were over from the moment we had our first date! While he jokes about his eating habits as a bachelor, the canned and packaged food he prepared and consumed, or the convenience store cuisine he relished, he welcomed my delicious home cooking. It was a new world for him.

A new world that he wasn't sure he knew how to exist in. In his defense he wasn't really sure what his role in the kitchen would be as his culinary world was shifting. It would be a long journey – for the both of us.

In the beginning of our marriage, my husband was under the impression that since I was cooking he was exempt from any participation in the kitchen. Instead, he thought his role was to appear for meals, eat, and return to the TV.

Growing up, we were taught two simple things at the dinner table: eat all the food on your plate and help clean up when you were finished eating. I should clarify – the meal was over when my father got up from his chair and lit a cigarette. The conversation was the same every night the minute he swiped the match, held it to the cigarette, and inhaled.

My mother started with, "Why do you have to smoke now? This is disgusting. You're killing us. What's wrong with you?"

I pulled my shirt over my nose before he struck the match.

My father retorted with a round obscenities and blamed Hollywood for his smoking addiction.

Dinner was officially over and, only then, we were allowed to leave the table. Cleaning commenced and everyone helped, except for my father, who cigarette in hand, retreated to the TV room demanding my mother start the coffee, wanting to know what she had for dessert, and when it was going to be served! In his eyes it was always late. I'd silently seethe. We're cleaning up. How the hell could she make coffee when we are still cleaning up?

The kitchen was small. The chairs had to be rotated for access to the refrigerator and then again to open the door to the dishwasher. It was like a bad video game as we'd scurried about trying to clean in the tight space. Most of the time it was only my mother and I doing the cleaning; after all this was woman's work and if I was going to be married one day I'd have to know how to fill a dishwasher!

And right on cue, the obscenities would start again as he bellowed, "Where is the fucking coffee…I work hard all day…get me another beer…and what about dessert…what is taking so long…"

***

My mother would retaliate with, "You'll just have to wait…I work too…if you would help clean up…you could at least start the coffee…you don't do anything around this house…why can't you add another bathroom…I see you were down at that convenience store again…what the hell did you buy this crap for…"

And the war between the "irrational matter" was officially launched.

While I continued to clean up, I tried to ignore their arguing and mutter, "This is certainly not going to happen when I get married!"

Decades later this is how it turned out...

My outburst happened one evening after a meal of broccoli rabe, while I was cleaning the kitchen. "I work just as hard as you! I'll cook dinner and you can help clean up. I think that's a fair compromise. You're not a fucking bachelor anymore!"

My husband reluctantly agreed. And to his credit, he has kept up his part of that bargain. While he has no complaints about the food I cook, he does find fault with how I go about preparing a meal.

His main objection about the kitchen is the number of pots and pans that are required for cooking. I tried to explain. "I like to time everything, so when all the food gets to the table it's hot. The vegetables, sauce, pasta, and bread are cooking at the same time."

I do try to clean as I work, but sometimes that's not possible. By the time the food makes it to the table all the pots and pans are piled in the sink. His solution was that I should cook one thing at a time and clean as I start the next dish! Once the food is cooked it gets put on a plate and left on the counter.

"This isn't a fucking buffet," I erupted one evening. "By the time I'm done cooking, the food would be cold!"

He didn't hear a word I said and continued, "And why does everything have to be in a separate dish? Why can't we just leave it in the pots and take it directly from the stove. Why dirty more dishes?" he complained relentlessly, after another night of scrubbing pots in the sink.

"Because I don't want to eat like a *gavone*!"

"What the hell is that?"

I frowned and realizing I was acquainting him with Italian slang that I had learned from my father. I was acutely aware I mispronounced the word as in my father's world everything was pronounced with a hard *g* sound.

"Tell me what the hell did you just said," he shouted.

"Fuh-ged-da-boud-it," I spat. "It doesn't matter." What is so bad about having a nice, sit down dinner with my husband? Isn't this nice, candles, matching dishes, pleasant music? I refuse to eat out of pots. I wasn't raised like that, and I've waited a long time to have a nice house."

"Ok, ok, ok, but do you have to use so many dishes? It takes me so long to clean up."

"That's why we have a dishwasher. We paid money for it. Why can't you use it? The reason you're spending so much time in the kitchen is because you're washing everything by hand! Why?"

"Because the big pots take up so much room."

"But if you organize all the pots and dishes correctly, they'll all fit in the dishwasher."

There was no rational reason, but just more obsessive-compulsive behavior. And because he didn't grow up with a dish-washer, he was conditioned to and would continue to wash dishes by hand. I shook my head in disbelief as he washed every pot by hand. It's too surreal and I stopped asking why years ago. Besides, this was a good compromise since he didn't cook.

My husband clearly knew nothing about cooking when we met, which explains his love for the convenience store. His idea of cooking was either putting something in the microwave or dumping a package of macaroni and cheese, fettuccine, or rice, into a pot of boiling water and serving it in the pot after five minutes of cooking.

What he got when he married me were meals such as broccoli rabe, fettuccine alfredo, lasagna, garlic shrimp, shrimp scampi, homemade pizza, meatballs, sausage and peppers, jambalaya, a multitude of vegetables, stuffed mushrooms, chicken dishes, homemade roasted tomatoes, a variety of pasta meals, salads, fish, and eggplant parmigiana just to name a few.

After a year or so into our marriage he began taking an interest in cooking. "Can't you just tell me how much to add?"

I honestly couldn't. "It's an Italian thing," I'd respond. "It's a little of this and a little of that. You have to look at the food, taste and smell it…it's like art…like creating a painting."

"Can't you just write the recipe down?"

"There is no recipe. I have to show you."

The "I have to show you conversation" was a daily occurrence. I could have sent him to culinary school for the amount of time we have had these discussions.

"I have to show you…wash your hands…cut the garlic like this…rinse chicken…keep chicken separate…garlic is cut differently for this meal…you don't have to time the pasta exactly as it says on the package…pasta should be al dente not soft and mushy…once the shrimp is washed you have to drain and keep them refrigerated until ready to use…don't use butter but olive oil and not vegetable oil for this meal…cut the tomatoes like this…wrap the fish in foil add seasoning…use the fresh herbs from the garden…the chicken needs to be cleaned and put on a separate dish…now you have to clean the cutting board…"

He didn't hear or process a word I said. This is how my husband likes to cook.

He takes everything out and organizes it in a straight line in the order he will be using it, even if it is not needed yet. A can of vegetables will sit in the sauce pan on the stove, the container of bread crumbs will sit in the Pyrex dish, and the fresh vegetables will be lined up on the counter for cutting in the order according to the directions on the recipe. Sometimes I find it extremely funny and entertaining and I desperately want to know what motivates someone to act in this fashion. My husband has no answers or ideas as to why he does any of it! He believes his behavior is normal.

One evening we were having friends over and he agreed to have most of the meal ready by the time I arrived home from work. I greeted the dogs and checked the food preparations when I noticed a bowl of shrimp sitting on the counter, piled high and deep. The shrimp were not cold and look strange. I could feel my facial muscles contorting. I was on the verge of becoming that irrational creature from another planet again. I already knew what happened but for whatever reason had the need to ask him. Would I feel better hearing the truth?

"Why is the shrimp out? We don't need the shrimp until the pasta is done and the oil is heated. How long has this bowl of shrimp been sitting out?" I asked.

He came over and gave me a quick kiss. "Calm down, honey. I have everything under control. I don't know what you think the problem is."

My hands gestured madly through the air. "How long has this shrimp been out?" I asked again.

"Since I got up this morning," he responded calmly as if there is absolutely nothing wrong and he returned to stirring the sauce.

I could feel the blood rushing to my face. My voice was amplified two octaves.

"What?" I shriek. "Throw it out...do you want people to get sick...I don't understand why you just can't follow the fucking directions I left for you!" I continued shouting more obscenities as

I slammed the freezer door shut after pulling out another bag of shrimp. "You just don't listen to me…I should have just taken the day off…you're lucky I have another bag…and why the hell did you use the entire bag…even with the damn shrimp you have to super-size…what the fuck is wrong with you…"

My husband laughed and thought I was exaggerating as my tirade continued over the importance of maintaining appropriate food temperatures when cooking. He didn't hear a word I said.

He has no problem letting food sit on the counter for hours, eating it, and then returning it to the refrigerator. He has no problem mixing beef and chicken together. He assures me there is nothing wrong. I stopped arguing with him about bacteria, salmonella, and the necessity for accurate food temperatures.

My iPhone beeped, it's a text message from my girlfriend that read, "Here is what transpired this morning."

I stare at it in disbelief. It's a photograph of eggs made in the cardboard container for carrying coffee from the convenience store. I wondered how and why her boyfriend would do something like that. It's not like they don't have a working stove.

Her text continues, "Who the fuck does this? What the fuck is wrong with him?"

I show the photo to my husband, who laughed and said, "Fuh-ged-da-boud-it. And you thought my cooking habits were bad. He's got me beat." He is my husband's hero because there is someone, who in his opinion, has habits that are much worse than his.

Conversation continues on Monday morning about the "egg incident." She also can't understand why her boyfriend leaves food, plastic wrapping, and empty Tupperware containers out on the counter.

"He *must* know my husband," I stated with empathy. "It's the same thing I come home to. A ball of tin foil on the counter from leftover pizza or chicken, napkins, dirty dishes in the microwave, empty juice containers that were obviously too heavy to put in the trash can or carry outside to the recycle can that is just beyond the front door on the way to his car."

My next, major meltdown about the bacteria occurred one Saturday morning.

I woke up to find the dog's food bowls on the counter. The wet dog food had been opened and distributed in the bowls sometime before we went to bed. He topped their meal off with some dry kibbles. The wet food had been out so long that it had dried and was encrusted to the sides of their dishes! My anger is apparent as I furiously slammed cabinet doors and complained about his foolishness. "What the fuck is wrong with you?" I shouted over the barking dogs.

It was just plain laziness, all to avoid having to open the dog food and feed the dogs after they awakened him with their incessant barking. He should have chosen to tolerate the barking dogs instead of dealing with what happened next.

I entered the bedroom. He couldn't see the "Alice Look" and stance as he is hiding under the covers and laughing as I continued ranting, "Who does something like this…their senior dogs…that's why they are up earlier…this is why they bark in the morning… they have to pee…they need to go out…then they want to eat…we can't afford dental work so now they need to eat the moist food… they go nuts over that stuff…that's why they bark…when you're a senior you will have the same problems…and for you it will be worse…what the fuck is wrong with you…you can't let the food sit out all night…you just wasted that dog food…this is just plain laziness…it's like the crap you pull with coffee pot, refrigerator, and dishwasher."

I do give him a lot of credit for cleaning up after dinner and making the coffee. Now that I'm an experienced coffee drinker, I do have something to say about his coffee brewing habits. My girlfriend at work couldn't believe that I didn't drink coffee until I was married. As I was explaining to her my coffee history, I added, "And do you know what my husband did this morning? He mixed two different brands of coffee together. Who mixes Maxwell House Columbian and Starbucks together? I just don't understand his rational. It tastes like fuckin' mud. He can't taste it because he adds half a bottle of flavored creamer to his coffee. Who the hell does that?"

She laughed and said, "What - does he know *my* father?"

I'm stunned as I listened to her story of living in a house with someone who is always mixing two different coffee blends together. It's just plain insanity! Her father even mixes flavored tea bags with regular tea bags. It got so bad she had to go out and purchase her own tea bags and hide them in her room.

We talked more about bad kitchen habits and kitchen appliances.

Our dishwasher was only five years old when it died in January of 2013. Reading the manual, following the trouble shooting directions, watching YouTube, and viewing other testimonials on the Internet only revealed that we needed more help. I called the 1-800 number and a technician was dispatched. One hundred thirty-eight dollars and three cents later the diagnosis was in - the motor seized up from broken glass. My husband called me at work to break the bad news. "The technician can repair it, but the repair is only warrantied for ninety days."

"It's not worth it. We'll buy a new one," I sighed heavily. I knew major appliances would not go on sale until President's Day. The thought of having to wash dishes for a month was devastating.

I came home from work to start dinner and began pulling utensils and dishes from the cabinets. "What the hell?" I shouted as I grabbed the spoons. The obscenities flowed as I wiped the remnants of grease and other food particles from my hand. I removed and examined more dishes and utensils only to find the surface cleaner was at it again! Some things were cleaned and others just rinsed.

"I am not going to make it until President's Day," I cried to my girlfriend. Dirty dishes were still in the dishwasher, piled in the sink, and on the counter. No sooner than I cleaned and dried dishes, I was cooking a meal and would have to start all over again.

My mother did her part to augment our dilemma when she called and told me that Consumer Reports found that one of the best dishwashers was the Bosch, which naturally was not even close to our price range. "The only way we could afford one, is if it was given to us for free," I tell my mother. My disgust is evident as I sigh heavily and tell her I will call her tomorrow that I have dishes to wash!

I think back to the stories my grandmother told me about being raised with nine brothers. As the only female, she literally spent the entire day in the kitchen. There was no electric dishwasher. I could hear her voice in my head, "Once we were done cooking and cleaning the breakfast dishes, we would start all over again for lunch and then dinner."

Ugh. I don't know she did it. I tried to put it all in perspective. I was grumbling about four weeks as opposed to decades.

But living with a surface cleaner can be quite difficult and when a major appliance is broken. Things become more problematic because you must work twice as hard to keep everything clean as the selective obsessive-compulsive behavior continues.

For instance, the refrigerator handle is constantly covered with watermarks, fingerprints, or dried food from hands. The mess inside the refrigerator is even worse. It's like someone had a food fight. My husband always claims it's all from me!

"Really? So these big finger prints somehow match my little fingers," I pointed out as I held my hand up to the prints on the refrigerator door. "Do you know what's in this container?" I held up the lemon-scented anti-bacterial soap. "It's called soap. Use it. You're not a fucking bachelor anymore!"

Our battle continues over the coffee pot and the used coffee grinds. Disinfecting and cleaning the pot have become my responsibility. The used coffee grinds are piled high in a container and spew onto the counter. Instead of dumping the contents into the garden for compost, he will continue throwing the grinds into the canister until it resembles a small mountain. When the grinds start to litter the backsplash, he will stop using the container and dump the coffee grinds into the trashcan. The container full of grinds will remain on the counter until I dump them in the compost!

***

One Sunday we had just arrived home from church and the grocery store. My husband had decided to give me a hand in the kitchen, so I could work on my manuscript. He was making chicken cutlets.

He had to super-size and picked the biggest package of thick chicken cutlets because they were on sale. He feels he can get more pieces of chicken if he slices them himself. I told him he was correct and explained the reason why I don't pound chicken. If on sale, I usually buy the pre-cut, thin-sliced packages because I work and don't have time for pounding and slicing poultry when I get home.

I moved my laptop into the kitchen and don't even have to look up to know what he is doing. My back is to him as I call out directions intermittently.

"Once the chicken is washed don't put it back in the original packaging...you need to put it in a separate dish...use the other cutting board to pound out the chicken...use the poultry scissors to trim...wash your hands...don't touch anything else in the kitchen after you touch the chicken...use your elbow or wrist to turn the water on...don't put that chicken on the cutting board..."

Within five minutes the wooden cutting board is officially contaminated. I will have to buy another one. He doesn't understand why. After he is finished the entire kitchen will have to be wiped down and sanitized. He still doesn't understand why.

"You're not a fucking bachelor anymore! Do you know what salmonella is?"

CHAPTER 29

Appliance Longevity

Since we have been married we have gone through six coffee pots!

My mother is quick to remind me she *still* has the same coffee pot, it's a percolator. It's a relic but still works and makes good coffee. It is at least forty-years-old. My husband I thought she should have a new one so we purchased her a Keurig for Christmas. It's still in the box because she has to make room on the counter for it. Ugh!

"I just don't understand what is wrong with you people! What are you doing to the coffee pots? Why are you going through them so much? I don't understand," she lamented.

I reminded her that manufacturers did not have longevity in mind when they were designing today's appliances. They are not made to last and they didn't have my husband in mind when they were designing them as well!

Our Keurig, a Christmas gift from my brother and sister-in-law, replaced our last coffee pot. Tired of cleaning the pot and the mess of the coffee grinds it looked like it was going to be a fantastic gift. I wasn't sure how this was going to work for us since we drink so much coffee; I thought it may be too expensive to buy the pods, but I figured we'd try it.

After one week my husband started complaining. The convenience of the Keurig is not really a convenience for him as it causes him additional work. He didn't like that he wasn't getting a full cup, even on the largest setting!

This is only because he drinks out of an extra-large mug, more super-sizing behavior. When he adds milk, he has to stick it in the microwave to reheat his coffee! I didn't really want to ask why but I did anyway.

"It's too cold now," he said.

"Then why the hell did you put so much milk in? Or change the temperature setting? If you would just read the directions, it tells you how to change the setting to make the coffee hotter."

No answer.

Again, I don't know why I even asked!

I showed him how to use the additional feature that allows you to continue making coffee from your favorite brands.

He gives *me* the "Alice Look."

"So now you want me to remove one piece of plastic, insert another, and be mindful of the amount of coffee grinds I put in the basket, which even with my glasses I can't see the line...this is all too much fuckin' work!"

I laughed. "Then use the other coffee pot during the week. We'll use the Keurig on the weekends, when I'm here to fill the little basket for you!"

"This pot requires cleaning and the purchase of filters too," I reminded him as I re-read the directions and pointed to the dial that indicates a filter change.

My husband sighed, "More work. It's easier to go to Wawa. And we're almost out of these pods. This is getting too expensive."

"I have a coupon. I'll stop at Bed, Bath and Beyond and pick up that economy pack!"

He grumbled as I grabbed the keys to the truck, "Yeah, well just don't buy anything else while you are there! And you better not stop at Home Goods either. You're not a fucking bachelorette anymore!"

The Keurig has been re-located to the living room. The "Keurig coffee bar," was set up next to the sliding glass door, which exits onto an outside deck. A convenience intended for the ease of grabbing a cup of coffee when outside or when watching television as opposed to walking twenty feet further to the kitchen to brew a pot of coffee!

Our argument about cleaning the coffee pot and now paper towels continued later in the afternoon.

I heard the cabinets opening and the crinkling of paper. I frowned as I headed to the kitchen to investigate what my husband was doing. It seemed there was some sort of coffee accident.

"What the hell is wrong with you?" I ask. "Why is there coffee all over the cabinets…what the hell happened in here…and you have to clean the coffee pot…you're not a fucking bachelor anymore!"

In 2016, the carafe cracked on the bottom. I purchased two one- size-fits-all carafes at two different retail establishments, but they were the wrong size. They had to be returned. We tried to order a carafe online, but it was on back order for at least a month! "Fuh-ged-da-boud-it. Call and fuckin' cancel that order. We're wasting money using the Keurig every day. We're going to get a coffee pot this weekend," my husband demanded.

We made a trip to the Ocean County Mall to purchase a coffee pot at Macy's. Macy's no longer had the huge selection of coffee pots as they did in the past. "Probably because everyone is buying coffee at Wawa," I snapped, irritated. An older model Krups was the affordable choice. It's not too bad but does take up space on the counter. It seemed the easiest to operate, except my husband was having difficulty programing the timer. I handed him the manual. I refused to look at it. We wouldn't have had this problem if he hadn't left the carafe on the hot burner without coffee in the pot. I have no problem pushing the word BREW in the morning.

Perhaps when I win the million-dollar lottery we can go to Wawa every day and not have to worry about having this appliance in the house.

The convenience of the Keurig eventually shut down the use of the Krups, which still sits on the counter in case the Keurig breaks. It was also a direct response to the grocery stores, which began carrying more coffee pod brands and flavors and less containers of coffee grinds. And as time passed, the convenience of the Keurig won. The joke is on me as the cost is outrageous.

I was discussing the cost of the Keurig habit when we returned from the store on Sunday. He likes hazelnut and a variety of mixed brands. I like dark or medium flavors. Hence, the cabinet is stuffed with various brands of coffee pods. My husband shrugged and calmly stated, "when the Keurig dies, we are buying one of those machines that make cappuccino, espresso...."

I settle on the couch with the dogs and think about the inconvenient cost of the convenient appliance and wonder how drinking coffee became so expensive. My husband looks at me and wants to know what is wrong?

We start discussing our coffee habit and how it all began.

"I should just go to Wawa, it would be cheaper," he bursts out laughing.

My eyes twinkle as I smile back. "You're lucky to have me. And you're not a fucking bachelor anymore."

CHAPTER 30

Our Children Have Four Legs

When we were married I already had two children: a golden retriever and an Australian cattle dog. My husband's child was a long hair dachshund. My children had dog licenses, routine visits to the vet, and their vaccinations were current. They were protected from fleas and ticks with the appropriate monthly repellent and they had a notebook containing their medical history complete with all their vet visits, licenses, and vaccine information! Traveling back and forth from Alabama to New Jersey for many years with the dogs was the driving force for this organized canine portfolio, as I had to make sure I had accurate and current records with me in case of an emergency. I also like to be organized.

"I wish every pet owner would keep records like this," veterinary doctors would comment as they viewed their history.

My husband only had *one* piece of paper for the dachshund, and it didn't contain medical information. It simply stated that he was a pure breed with a microchip, only he didn't know the chip identification number!

"Are you kidding me?" I ask, frustrated after unsuccessfully locating any information. "Has he had his rabies shot or any vaccines…do you have any other document's…where is his license… all dogs have to be registered or we will be subject to a fine from the town…has he even been to the vet…and if you're not going to breed him then he needs to be neutered!"

Joey the long-haired dachshund.

My husband's head turned quickly and he glared at me as if I had just told him I had cancelled the entire cable TV packaged. "Neutered!" He shouted aghast. "That's just bullshit. He's an inside dog he doesn't need *any* of that!"

I tuned him out as he pontificated about the removal of his dog's manhood.

So I bought a bigger notebook and added a third section for the dachshund. And to my husband's dismay he compiled quite a medical file over the years.

Getting the dachshund to the vet and up to date on his shots was the first order of business. Months later we packed everyone in the truck and drove to the firehouse and waited in line at the free rabies clinic sponsored by the township.

This is an entirely new adventure for my husband, who had only one dog growing up – a short hair dachshund. I am stunned not just because he owned only one pet, but because he never knew about the free rabies clinics usually sponsored by the town.

Sonny, Heidi, Toby, Winston, Pepsi, Midnight, Chester, and Princeton were just some of the dogs and cats my family had growing up. Oh, yeah, there was also Bill the bird, Fluffy the Guinea Pig, and a multitude of goldfish that always found their way out of the tank and on the plush, midnight blue carpet in the TV room.

Sonny and Heidi were my first dogs. My father gave Heidi away. I was never really sure why. My mother said she had puppies, stole meat off the table, and was difficult to handle. But no matter where he took her she would end up back at our house. One year, on New Year's Day, she was outside barking at the front door!

The ninth life of each cat usually ended somewhere out on the busy county road we lived on. My father would grumble as he trudged down the street with the shovel in his hand while I cried. Nonetheless, we always ended up at the free township clinic with one of the animals when it came time for their shots. It was routine and familiar for me.

My husband continued to argue about the trip for he really didn't understand what the rabies clinic was all about. "It's free," I yelled as I began grabbing the leashes. The action caused the dogs to start barking and dancing around, nudging one another to be first to get the leash attached. "They need to have a rabies shot," I screamed over the cacophony of barking. "It's either this or we pay forty dollars a dog at the vet!"

Realizing it is going to cost money, he grabbed the keys and grumbled, "I'll start the truck."

It seemed everyone in the town who owned a pet was at the free rabies clinic that day. My husband was stunned as he gaped at the line of people and pets that circled the building.

He rubbed his temples and sighed; his disgust apparent as he pounded his fist on the steering wheel. "We have to wait in *that* line," he pointed. "This is ridiculous. We'll be here all day! I could be home working in the yard."

He gets the "Alice Look."

"I can't handle all of them by myself. This is what people do when they have pets! Just grab their travel bowls from the trunk and bring the water. It's hot and you don't want them to get dehydrated, do you?"

Dogs and cats barked, snarled, meowed, howled, and growled as we parked. And the minute we got out of the truck the dachshund started barking and didn't stop until he received his rabies shot.

"People are staring," my husband hissed. "He's an embarrassment."

I picked up the dachshund and hugged him, muttering sweet sentiments in his ear. "My poor, precious baby. Don't listen to him, mama will take care of you."

My husband smirked. "Poor, precious baby," he repeated, his eyebrows furrowed in disbelief. "Those dogs are living the good life! Tell your, poor precious baby to be quiet or he can spend the rest of the afternoon in his cage. He's giving me a headache."

"It's your own fault."

My husband rolled his eyes. "Naturally. Everything is always my fault."

Noise at his feet interrupted his ranting. "What the hell is his problem? These are my new sneakers."

I looked down to see our cattle dog peeing by his foot.

I couldn't help but laugh. "Even he's tired of hearing you talk. I guess it's his way of telling *you* to be quiet."

The woman in front of us told my husband he should have walked the dog before he got in line.

The retriever pulled on this leash wanting to greet every dog that passed. My husband got tangled in the leashes and almost tripped.

The dachshund continued to bark. The dogs around us felt the need to communicate with him and respond. The noise intensified.

My husband threw up his arms. "Can't you make him stop barking? This is just fuckin' ridiculous!"

I answered calmly as I continue to hug the dachshund. "It's your own damn fault. He has no fucking socialization skills because you didn't take him out. Now he has two brothers to play with and we'll take trips to the dog park where he will meet other dogs. I'm sure he will grow out of it."

Actually, I don't know who was worse, the dog barking or my husband who complained the entire time we stood in line.

"I have a headache. We're getting coffee after this!" he snapped. When I didn't respond he added, "Since this clinic is free we can afford coffee."

I didn't argue.

Weeks later we revisit the conversation about the dog's manhood.

"Do we have to neuter him?" My husband objected, after he heard how much it was going to cost.

I gave my husband the "Alice Look" and stance and started yelling, "All he does is hump pillows and blankets! I have had enough. Since you're not breeding him he needs to be neutered!"

My husband had the audacity to start muttering, "Well, you know it's a man thing…he shouldn't have to live like that."

Enraged I stormed out of the room.

In the end, my husband knew I was right as the dog was really out of control.

Neutering would be the beginning of the many expenses the dachshund would incur.

The first major argument was about fleas and ticks. The dachshund's early years were spent in a condo, he went out occasionally, but was not an outside dog.

"And I don't see why you think he needs flea and tick medicine."

"You're kidding me right? You do realize we have a yard?" I asked in disbelief. "He and the other dogs are going to be outside and there are lots of trees and leaves; it's a perfect recipe for the breeding of fleas and ticks."

"This dog never had any fleas or ticks," argued my husband.

"Because he rarely went out!" I snapped back in disbelief, amazed that we were even having this conversation.

The first week we moved into our new home was spent bathing the dachshund in the kitchen sink and picking fleas off him.

"Ok, you're right. So what type of flea stuff does he need?" My husband reluctantly asked while he is drying the dachshund.

"Don't worry. I already had the vet order it. I'm picking it up tomorrow! Like you, he's not a fucking bachelor anymore. I refuse to have him living in squalor!"

We love our dogs. They're our children. When I first met my husband he asked if I had any children.

I immediately responded. "Yes, I have two. I'll show you their pictures."

He laughed when I pulled out photos of my two dogs. I knew he was an animal lover when he showed me his photos. Before you get married, you need to be clear about how your other half feels about animals.

Owning a pet really is like having a child; it's a big responsibility. Like children they need food, clothing, bedding, grooming, treats, toys, dishes, medication, trips to the doctor when they are sick, and exercise. And like any other good mom, my children we're going to have the *best* of everything!

Boudreau, Joey, Napoleon pose for another Christmas card

Three years later, we are back in line at the township's free rabies clinic. The vet was forty minutes late and, to make matters worse, it was raining. I said to my husband, "At least he's not barking. Remember the first time we came, and he wouldn't stop barking?"

Immediately after the words left my mouth, what did the dachshund do? He started barking. My husband and I give each other the "Alice Look."

I smiled proudly. "He's such a smart dog. He understands everything we say. It's amazing isn't it?" I laughed easily.

My husband glared, handed me the cattle dog's leash, and headed next door to the Wawa for coffee.

CHAPTER 31

Affordable Housing

"**W**hy is there a dog cage in the bedroom?" my mother asked. "After all the time you spent decorating the bedroom…that cage looks silly!"

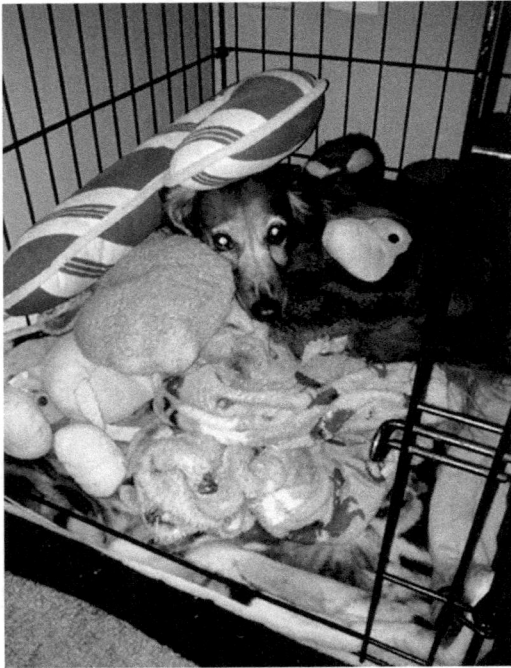

Joey's home base, the cage in the bedroom.

My dogs came into the marriage house broken. The dachshund doesn't understand this concept. Just like a man, he is always marking his territory. He is stubborn; he pees and poops where he wants – most of the time in the house. In his defense, though, he wasn't trained. My husband let him do what he wanted. I have great compassion for the dachshund and vowed that I was going to train him.

I explained the cage to my mother. "We have to lock him in his cage at bed time. If you don't lock the door, he'll creep out in the middle of the night and pee somewhere in the house."

My mother frowned disapprovingly. "But do they all have to sleep in the bedroom? And the germs...do you know about the bacteria they have on their paws...they smell...and you need to clean...you are going to get sick...they are on the bed and there are bugs..."

I ignored her rambling about germs and bacteria. It wasn't worth an argument.

"This is our pack," I explained to my mother. "Where we go they go! They can sleep where they want. We love them and they want to be with us. In the morning, the dachshund whines and cries like a baby because he needs to be let out as he has to pee...I can't hear him in the other room."

You would think after all these years he'd be housebroken. I think, no rather, I know he does it on purpose. He is stubborn and lazy. "Why should he wait for me to let him out? Why should he get his paws wet from the morning dew on the grass," I tell my mother. "And if it snows, we must carry him outside or he won't go out the door. Anytime there is inclement weather, he needs a coat or sweater before he goes out."

"You need a bigger house," was my mother's solution as she is referring to the clutter of dog stuff by the back door and the cages in the bedroom.

I ignored the comment and refused to argue about the size of our home. It always brings up another set of issues dealing with my father and eventually ends with an argument. I sighed heavily still plagued with baggage from long ago and returned to reality. "If that dachshund was loose in the house, he'd pee somewhere."

I could care less about the cage in the bedroom. It was what was in his cage that disturbed me - my husband had only given him *one* small blanket!

"How could you give this precious dog only one blanket? This is the only thing he has to sleep with? It's torn and ratty," I screamed at my husband, as I held up what resembles a rag for washing a car as evidence. "What the hell is wrong with you?"

"This is how we bachelors roll," my husband interrupted, in a fit of laughter.

"Well, you're not fucking bachelors anymore," I retorted sharply.

The following weekend I take my husband on a field trip to the pet store.

"He doesn't need all that," my husband shouted.

"He only has one blanket. He needs more bedding...what if he gets cold...and there is no padding for him...he needs to be comfortable...the poor thing."

"Poor thing," he gasped. "What about my poor wallet! Forty dollars for a bed..."

I cut him off before he can continue. "It's a cuddle fluff...he needs to have something to sit on when we are in the living room, and because he burrows, he can go in or lay on top of it. I refuse to have him live in squalor."

My husband stared in disbelief at the cart full of merchandise for the dog. I glared at my husband daring him to utter another word. "Like you he's not a fucking bachelor anymore!" I spat, as we headed for the register with a cart full of stuff for the dachshund and his cage.

CHAPTER 32

Heavenly Beds

This was the beginning of the purchasing of pet beds. Every room in our home has dog pallets, pillows, or blankets for the dogs. The two big dogs have their own miniature couches that are in the bedroom.

Joey and Boudreau enjoy the comfort of the new Posturepedic bedding

There are two pallets in the kitchen that are covered with two brand-new blankets – Christmas gifts from my mother, who loves animals and agrees they should have these luxuries. In the living room the old comforter from the bed lays across two more pallets my mother bought them for Christmas the year prior. A variety of blankets and pillows are mixed in the mess. As the dogs age, the bedding is upgraded.

"Look at this," I shouted excitedly, as I hold up a dog magazine. "Would you believe they make Posturepedic bedding?"

A firm, "NO," resonates from my husband, who was sprawled on the couch. "Fuckin' fuh-ged-da-boud-it!"

Ten years later, my mother took one look at the cattle dog's bed, grabbed one of her catalogues, and immediately ordered the Posturepedic bed. It has a microfiber cover that can be removed and washed. It came with a pillow in the shape of a bone engraved with his name. The dog can rest his head on the bolster to help with his breathing.

"What the hell is a fuckin' bolster?" my husband asked, as I started removing the giant bed from the packaging.

"His head should be elevated; it helps with his breathing."

His eyes narrowed and reflected annoyance, as he interrupted, "He doesn't fucking need that!"

His complaining continued as he followed me into the living room with the old pallet.

"Where are you going with his old bed? Why can't you just throw it out?"

"I'm throwing the pallet in the living room out and replacing it with his old bed!" The dogs came and investigated. My husband grabbed the vacuum. I'm going to get coffee when I'm done," he snapped. "Nobody else has pet beds all over their home!"

He turned the vacuum on as I started to remind him about the billion-dollar pet industry, the stores, websites, and companies who are dedicated to creating things for the comfort of our pets.

Not only do the dogs have furniture inside but outside as well. For the spring and summer months there are outdoor cushions, so they can sit comfortably on the hot deck. One summer, my mother sent them a raised canvas bed with a canopy to ensure they would not have to sit in the hot sun.

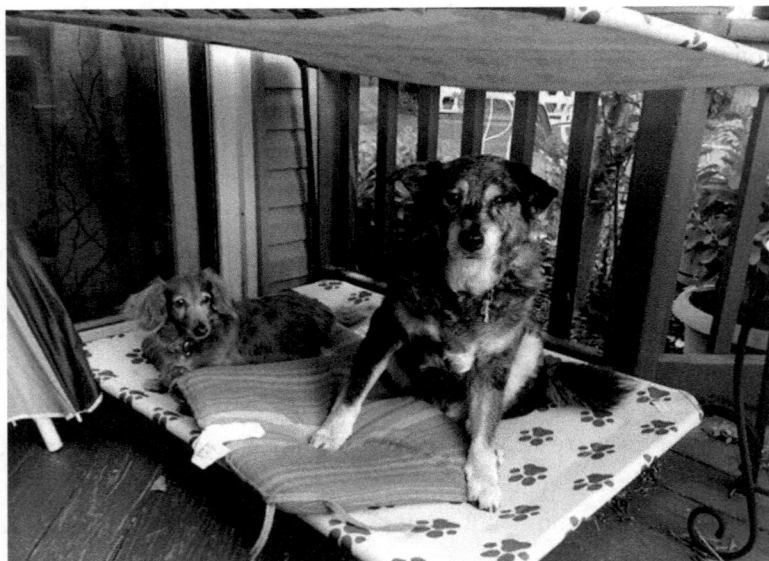

Joey and Boudreau enjoy the great outdoors on the raised canopy bed.

"This is huge," my husband complained. "There is no room for this on the deck. They can go inside if it is too hot for them," he grumbled as he began the assembly process. "This isn't necessary. Now I have to find a place to store it at the end of the summer," he shouted furiously as the assembly process continued. I retreated to the front of the house to get the box out of the trash, so he could look at the picture, as it is clear he isn't going to read the directions.

When we visited my mother, there is also bedding for them upstairs and downstairs. She even purchased a collapsible cage for the dachshund.

"Just something else I have to put together," my husband objected as he stared at the picture on the box and then at the heap of nylon, metal rods, and other miscellaneous parts organized in rows on the carpet. The "assemble in minutes" disclaimer on the package, well, let's just say was not meant to be.

Rather it went something like this: "Who buys this crap…he doesn't need this…it's fuckin' stupid…who made this…there are no directions…"

I was quick to reminded him that he wouldn't have read them anyway, so what did it matter!

My mother does her best to contribute to the dog's well-being, by ensuring they live in style and comfort by not only updating their bedding but their clothing attire as well.

Their wardrobe is quite extensive. One year she brought them reversible coats, one side is flannel and the other is a polyester, water-repellant mix – so they don't come in the house soaking wet from the rain and snow.

My husband hates to admit that he too has made pricey contributions to the canine couture industry. Our dogs have Philadelphia Eagles T-shirts and bandanas, for when we watch the football games. It's the one expense my husband didn't complain about. When we took a trip to the Eagles shop at Lincoln Financial Field in Philadelphia, he bought them dog collars, leashes, and shirts complete with the Eagles logo.

During football season, we proudly wear our Eagles jerseys and cheer the team on. Our exuberance is apparent as we scream at the questionable calls from the referees and good plays. The dachshund and cattle dog match our excitement by barking when we score a touchdown.

There are also sweaters in a variety of colors, and for different seasons. The dachshund has a cute V-neck cardigan for the fall and heavier clothing for the winter. He looks good in green and blue. I took a nice photo of them one year against the snow in their red sweaters, which was later embossed onto coffee cups, a mouse pad, and a decorative plate. It also became our Christmas card that year.

Every Christmas, I make a greeting card depicting the dogs. Everyone looks forward to the scenes I pose them in. In bed, at the dinner table, as the three wise men in the manger, with the Christmas lights, outdoor decorations, in the pile of leaves, in Halloween costumes, in the garden with all the tomatoes…are just some of the few.

Joey posing for another Christmas card.

The cost has become progressively expensive with each year. I thought about forgoing the greeting card in 2011 just like John Grisham wrote about in his book *Skipping Christmas*. Grisham was right - the cost is astronomical. Stamps, envelopes, film processing; more friends equal more cards and more money. After much heated debate, we decided to make only twenty-five cards that year.

Friends and family were disappointed when they hadn't received our annual greeting card. The greeting cards poured in with notes about the dogs and how they were looking forward to their yearly Christmas photo! Weeks later, my husband and I were back at the Wal-Mart waiting in line to use the digital kiosk to make more greeting cards.

My husband was grumbling bitterly, "I don't care who sends us cards next year…this is fucking ridiculous…why can't you just buy a damn box of cards for five dollars and send them…we're not doing this anymore…"

The woman using the kiosk next to us happily showed him the greeting card she was composing with her pets. "Aren't they cute?" She smiled at her beloved pets adoringly then looked at my husband daring him to make some insulting comment about her photo. Other customers glared and gave him the "you should have stayed home look!"

He started chatting with the shoppers about the absurd amount of time and money spent on composing and sending greeting cards.

"Look how cute they look," I interrupted as I pointed to the screen and typed the number fifty into the quantity box.

"Fifty?" His voice was now a loud whisper as he tried not to draw any more attention to himself. The veins in his neck pulsed as the blood surged up through his face. "You can't be serious. We don't even know fifty people."

"Yes, we do. You don't even know who sends us cards or who we send cards to, and if you want to know you could just look at the mail."

I start rattling off the list of names.

He held up his hand in defeat, signaling he did not want to hear anymore. "Just do what you want...I feel a headache coming on...I should have stayed home...I'm going to walk around and we're stopping for coffee at Wawa after your finished!"

"Don't even think about super-sizing that coffee! We can't afford it after all the money we just spent on the greeting cards. YOU'RE NOT A FUCKING BACHELOR ANYMORE," I snapped back.

CHAPTER 33

Who Did This?

We arrive home to our precious children. My outburst occurs ten minutes later.

"Who did this?" I shout.

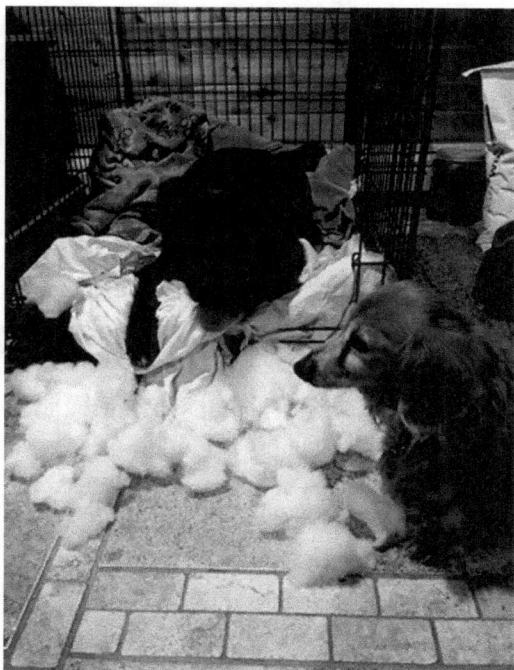

Bentley and Joey take the 5th and admit to nothing.

I hear my husband snickering from the living room. He knows from my tone of voice and the sentence he just heard that it's one of the dogs and not him who is in trouble.

He constantly laughs at me every time I start yelling, "Who did this?"

He thought I was the only one who talked to the dogs this way – that was until I showed him clips from YouTube and Facebook of people who are saying the same sentence to their pets that have managed to get into the garbage, wreck bathrooms, kitchens, and decorate homes with trash, toilet paper, and other material throughout the house. Pet owners across America are all asking their pets, "Who did this?"

I have spent more than a decade running through the interior and exterior of the house asking the same question, "Who did this?"

"Who did this?" I repeat sternly, as I try not to laugh.

The dogs sit and stare at me. I repeat myself again. "Who did this?"

The guilty one dashes to the bedroom.

My conversation continues, as I start to clean up the mess. "What's wrong with you...you just went out...we were only gone for a few minutes..."

"He's not so precious now," laughs my husband, who has now entered the kitchen to see what the problem is.

I throw the paper towels at him and tell him to finish cleaning up the pee. "It's all your fault...you probably didn't let him out before we left...you have to carry him to the grass, he is lazy and refused to walk off the deck into the yard...if he was trained this wouldn't have happened...he needs to go to doggie day care if he continues like this..."

"YOUR'RE NOT A FUCKING BACHELOR ANYMORE," I continue shouting as I head to the laundry room to wash the soiled rug.

CHAPTER 34

Doggie Daycare

My husband claims he will never pay for Doggie Day Care and is not used to boarding pets. When we first started dating, I went skiing for a week and had to board the dogs. He accompanied me to pick up the dogs when I returned. It didn't faze me one bit as I wrote the check and handed it to the receptionist.

"Twelve hundred dollars?" He shouted in disbelief, as I easily handed the check across the counter.

The receptionist glared. I turned to look at him. His face was beet red. The blood had rushed through his neck, face, and to the top of his baldhead as he repeated, "Twelve hundred dollars! Are you kidding me? You could have taken another trip for that much money. Why couldn't your parents just watch them?"

"My father forbids it. The last time they were there I was on a business trip for two weeks. I was only gone for two days when the first incident occurred. The retriever grabbed a whole loaf of Calandra's Italian bread right out of the shopping bag as my mother was carrying bags from the grocery store into the house. My father called me screaming about the dog and how his dinner was ruined because he didn't have any damn Italian bread!"

My husband thought this was absurd, that someone could get so upset over bread. I have since changed all that and have introduced him to some of the finest Italian bread in New Jersey. He now clearly understands the passion between Italians and their fondness for the best and appropriate bread to accompany meals.

While dining at the Il Villaggio, or Calandra's Italian Village in Caldwell New Jersey, one of the Calandra family restaurants with my mother and husband, my husband remarked about how good the bread was. I repeated the story about the dog stealing the bread and the role bread played in our house growing up. I describe the ritual of driving to Newark and waiting in line for freshly baked bread at the bakery with my father. It was before Calandra's grew into the empire it is today.

The trip was never simple. There was never any place to park, the lines were long, but the ride and listening to him ranting obscenities was worth it for the bread was still warm. There was nothing like it.

While we were talking about bread, two little girls ran over to the table happily screaming, "Hey grandma!"

It was my nieces. My mother turned, surprised, and gave them each a hug. "What are you doing here? I thought we weren't going to visit until tomorrow?"

"Daddy sent us down to pick up bread and we saw your car in the parking lot!"

My mother and I started laughing. My husband shook his head in disbelief. I ran out to the car to see the baby. He was two years old, strapped in his car seat, and happily enjoying a Calandra's roll!

The reason my dogs love bread is because an apartment complex I once lived in had a huge duck pond and everyone was always feeding the ducks bread. It was very difficult to walk the dogs because they were always pulling me toward the pond in an attempt to consume as much bread as possible while they were out walking!

When the dogs stole the entire loaf of my father's bread, he refused to deal with them again.

"Don't even think about leaving those fucking dogs with us to watch," my father warned while we were planning our wedding. "It will be a cold day in hell...that fucking retriever growls at me...the cattle dog doesn't listen...and that little one...they're all fucking no good..."

And on and on it went every time he saw the dogs.

The next time the dogs were scheduled for boarding would be during our honeymoon. It cost more, but they had special accommodations - they had the big suite, so they could all be together. The separation anxiety they would suffer was enough and I certainly was not going to allow them to be staring at one another through separate cages.

Fifteen days later we went to pick them up and my husband started his tirade as I was writing out the check and he was scrutinizing the bill.

"What the hell is biohazard waste management...fecal exams...did they need all these shots...fucking dental cleaning...I can't afford to go to the dentist...why do they get to have their teeth cleaned...why did you pay to have them bathed...we could have done that at home..."

I interrupted his ranting as we are loading the dogs into the truck. "I want them fresh and clean. YOU'RE NOT A FUCKING BACHELOR ANYMORE...no smelly dogs in the house!"

Ten years would pass before the dogs would be boarded again. We went to visit my brother in Las Vegas. I spent weeks calling boarding facilities. We settled on Camp Bow Wow mainly because Camp Bow Wow had video cameras that enable you to log on to your iPhone and watch what your pets are doing. "We should have just paid for three more airline tickets," my husband yelled irritably as I turned on the iPhone to get another glimpse of the dogs at Camp Bow Wow.

The trip cost us money even before we departed. Since the dogs hadn't been to a kennel since our wedding they needed a visit to the vet for a round of vaccinations. Stool samples and follow up samples were required because it was discovered that the cattle dog had a worm of some sort, caused by eating the fecal matter left in the yard because my husband did not clean up the poop!

"This is why we don't go on vacation," he complained, after he saw the bill.

We sent them to camp with their beds, blankets, toys, wet and dry food, and treats.

"Do you want them to have a bath before you pick them up?" the friendly attendant asked as we dropped them off.

"NO," snapped my husband before I could open my mouth. "It's costing us enough money…they don't need anything else… there is no reason they had to stay in the big pen," he hissed.

Ignoring his outburst, I give him the "Alice Look" and stance. "They need to be together and I don't want them to suffer from separation anxiety. Besides I have a coupon. I don't want them getting sick or it will be another trip to the vet!"

CHAPTER 35

Realities of Not Having Pet Insurance

Trips to the vet are one thing my husband dreads. His blood pressure skyrockets at the thought. For us, it would become routine; as routine as drinking coffee. We have advances in science and medicine to thank for this. Just as humans are living longer, so are pets. Growing up, when the pet was sick, we went to the vet and the animal was put to sleep. Now, like humans, they are treated for diabetes, cancer, and can even go the dentist.

When we walked into the emergency hospital in Tinton Falls, the rooms were labeled dermatology, allergy, dentistry, oncology, and ophthalmology. As we sat in the waiting room pet owners and their pets were called in to the respective specialty rooms as if it were an emergency room for humans.

My husband stares in disbelief every time we are there. After getting over his initial shock he starts with the expletives over the cost of pet care. This if followed by a short tirade over the insanity of pet owners for taking their pets to the expensive hospital including an irrational list of his own inexplicable reasons for even agreeing to the journey. He then proceeds to the vending area and drinks as much free coffee for every person and pet in the room!

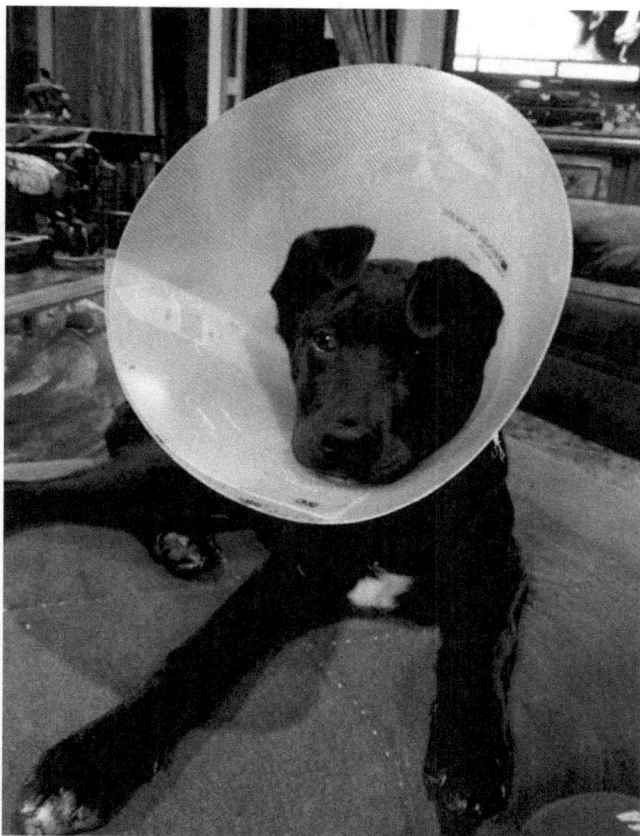

Bentley recovering from surgery.

Our dogs have been to the doctor more times than my husband cares to admit to anyone.

"They go to the vet more than I go to the doctor. Now when I need to see a doctor, I can't because there is no money," he argues.

He is right. Over the years there have been at least ten surgeries between them respectively: abscessed teeth, clogged intestines from eating items that were not meant to be consumed, skirmishes that resulted in casts on paws, and the removal of a variety of lumps and bumps.

In between the major surgeries, there were a host of outpatient procedures that also required emergency trips to the vet, which almost always happen when my husband is at work or in the middle of the night.

I called my husband on his cell phone one evening hysterically crying, "I'm at the vet with the dog...I came home and there was blood on the floor...he needs his ass expressed... it happens to little dogs..."

"What does that mean...expressed...what the hell is wrong with his ass...he shits just fine...what do you mean he needs a fuckin' bland diet..."

I cry more.

The doctor calmly took the cell phone and spoke with my husband. When she was done she handed me the phone and started preparing the medication.

After realizing he was going to be ok, the how much is it going to cost conversation starts.

I wiped the tears from my eyes and the doctor handed me a box of tissues before injecting the dog with an antibiotic. "How much is this going to cost?" My husband snapped.

The doctor could hear him shouting through the cell phone. She smiled politely.

I was furious. "Do you know what it is like to come home and find blood all over the floor...I didn't know what the hell was wrong...I wrapped him in a blanket and rushed up the Parkway...I am stressed out and all you can think about is how much it's going to cost...who cares...my poor, precious baby...what if it was something serious..."

My husband sighed heavily and apologized. "Just pay the damn bill."

The doctor assured me he was going to be ok and reminded me to bring him back next week for a follow up visit.

Unbeknownst to us, anal expression, primarily for the dachshund would become an annual event. In the fall of 2013 the doctor told my husband he should have him checked once a month!

He called me at work to inform me of the results of his visit. "It's still in there…it didn't pop…he gave him pain medicine and an antibiotic…this is a fucking racket these doctors have…how come they don't have a free clinic for ass expression…this is ridiculous…I can do this myself…wait to you see this bill…once a month…that guy is crazy if he thinks I am going to bring this dog to him once a month…"

My husband actually put the dachshund in the shower and ran warm water on his ass, hoping to avoid another trip to the vet.

I was livid. "Is there something wrong with you…I'm making an appointment…my poor precious baby…I don't see a degree on the wall that has DVM after your name…I don't remember you going to veterinary school…look at this poor dog…take him to the vet…"

And on and on it went.

***

$Twelve Hundred Reasons Why You Should Brush Your Dogs Teeth

I am on the phone with my husband again, hysterically crying, our cattle dog was sick.

"He needs to go to the dentist…his face is swollen…he has an abscessed tooth…the local vet doesn't do dental surgery…I am

197

taking him to the dentist across town...my mother gave me her name...she was on the television show the Animal Planet."

"Dentist," he screamed. He was furious. "I can't even go to the dentist...dammit...my teeth are worse than his," he yelled into the phone.

"You don't have an abscessed tooth!" I screamed back.

We went to pick the dog up the following day.

"Twelve hundred dollars," shrieked my husband, as I paid the bill. He glared at the receptionist who took the check as if it was her fault.

I ignored him as I listened to the post-op instructions...bland diet while he recovers...antibiotic schedule...

$Fifteen Hundred Reasons Why Dogs Should Not Assist with Home Repair Projects

It was two o'clock in the morning. The dachshund had been coughing for the last few hours. I jabbed my husband in the arm. "Wake up he's in distress. Something's wrong. Get dressed; we're taking him to the emergency vet!"

"Emergency Vet!" he yelled. "It's two in the morning...I don't believe this...do you know how tired I am...I can't imagine how much this is going to cost..."

"And you think I'm not tired! Who cares how much it will cost," I interjected, screaming. "My precious baby is sick...he has to go to the vet..." And on and on it went as we traveled up the Garden State Parkway. I ignored his shouting as we approached each toll about why I didn't have the toll money ready for him and why I didn't have exact change in the truck. He insisted on having the toll in his hand when we are pulling out of the driveway! I was too upset to comprehend that neurosis. I continued to ignore the obvious comparisons to my father. I desperately wanted to block out memories of tokens and the insanity of it all.

After an x-ray, the dog went immediately into surgery to remove the carpet he decided to eat. Why did he eat the carpet? We were in the middle of remodeling the bedroom due to flooding a present from Mother Nature and the dachshund decided he would chew the carpet we had ripped up and left in the hallway.

My husband was relieved he was ok. Antibiotics...bland diet...return visit to remove the stitches...keep him calm...make sure he wears the plastic cone collar...

The routine was now all too familiar for my husband. It was another thousand-dollar surgery. My husband asked the surgeon if he could get a prescription for an anti-depressant.

I handed the American Express Card to the receptionist. It would become as frequent as attending church on Sundays.

$Three Hundred Reasons Why Husbands Should Keep the Yard Clean

I am on the phone with my husband at work. "The dog is sick...he had diarrhea all over the rug...it looks like black tar...he could be bleeding..."

My husband interrupted me. "Why was the fucking door open...I told you to keep those dogs out of the spare room...the carpet is brand new...I can't believe this...are you sure he is bleeding..."

"I'm taking him to the vet," I sobbed.

"Which one?" he snapped irritably, as he already knows the answer.

"I'm going up to Tinton Falls," I retorted angrily as I wipe the tears from my eyes.

My husband sighed. "I'll call my boss and meet you there."

Two hours later the doctor handed us some pills. "He has the flu...he may have eaten something in the yard..."

That was all I had to hear. I immediately started yelling at my husband, "I told you to cut that fucking berry bush down...I saw him over there the other day...I knew it...he never goes over there...it's all because you didn't cut that fucking weed down...he probably at those fuckin' berries...or that damn weed!"

I handed the American Express card to the receptionist.

$Twelve Hundred Reasons Why Trash Should Never Be Left in the House

We arrived home and my husband is surveying a mess of trash strewn from the kitchen to the living room. "Why are there corn cobs in the living room?"

I already knew the answer and I ran to the kitchen. "I can't believe you left the garbage out," I yelled. "Look at this mess. Oh my god, I told you to take out the trash...there were corn cobs in the trash...we're going to the vet..."

The doctor is bewildered. He removed one cob, but was shocked to know the retriever had already thrown up one of the other cobs! Fifteen hundred dollars is added to MasterCard, for we've reached the limit with the Visa.

The post-op instructions required one of us to stay home and monitor his progress. I called my boss and called out sick.

Except for surgeries, there have been a few times in my life that I have had to actually call out sick from work. My friends and co-workers know this about me. My boss sent me home from work because I came in coughing and sneezing one day. If I have to call out of work it is usually because of our dogs. Over the years our work schedules have changed allowing one of us to be home with the dogs.

There was one particular time when I called out and he was furious.

"He didn't have to have that removed from his eye," my husband declared impatiently as we sit in the waiting room. He sighed heavily as he handed me another tissue and I wiped the tears from my eyes.

"Yes, he did. How the hell did you think he was going to see?"

The following day I called work and called out. "Why are you calling out? The dog is fine," he snapped and shook his head in disgust as he poured another cup of coffee.

I give him the "Alice Look" and stance. "You know this dog... do you actually think he is going to sit here all day quietly without trying to take off that fucking piece of plastic the vet wants him to wear...look he is already trying to use his paw to remove it...what if he gets the stitches out...do you want to go back to the vet...it will cost more money...besides someone needs to give him the antibiotic and you are not going to be here today..."

My husband held up his hand in defeat, signaling for me to stop talking. He hadn't thought about the consequences until I reminded him about the antics of the dog and mentioned the word money. The golden retriever had his own set of rules. When he wanted something he did it. My husband called him Satan. Even he knew, if left alone all day, the dog would have removed the plastic Elizabethan collar and caused more mischief, which would ultimately have resulted in a trip back to the vet.

Shortly after the retriever had recovered, I was back at the vet and on the phone with my husband, sobbing. "It's the dachshund; my precious baby needs to have his ass expressed again."

I pulled the phone away from my ear to avoid the outburst that was to come. Instead my husband sighed and calmly said, "Just make sure you get some of that dog food for the bland diet."

In December of 2009, when our cattle dog exhibited the same symptoms as our golden retriever, Napoleon, who we lost to cancer at the age of ten, I immediately took him to the vet. Not his local vet but back to the twenty-four-hour veterinary hospital, in Tinton Falls or exit 109 off the Parkway. We sped up the Garden State Parkway in the middle of the night. The technician thought I was crazy. She didn't think there was anything wrong with the dog.

The tears were rolling down my cheeks. "He is having trouble breathing. I know he has a tumor," I firmly stated. "Just find it."

She phoned back surprised and apologetic. He was in surgery within hours for a rare adrenal gland tumor. I went every day to see him after work while he was in the critical care unit. We took him for chemo treatments and gave him pills for one year as part of the cancer therapy regime.

The cattle dog is our miracle dog!

My husband wiped the sweat from his forehead and threw up his arms in frustration after the oncologist tells him about the dog's next treatment. He was visibly frustrated when the doctor took the dog back for his medication and dismissed us to the waiting room. "I should have a wing named after me for the all the money we've spent here!"

We waited with groups of other pet owners, who are also dropping their pets off for treatments. The place is packed. He shook his head in amazement at the number of animals coming in and out for chemotherapy. It helped to soften the blow knowing that we were not the only people who were spending money on keeping our pets healthy. Our dachshund came with us for support and was the only dog that barked non-stop the entire time we are there! A technician came over and politely suggested we walk him outside – perhaps that would calm him down.

My husband snickered, "Yeah, good luck with that," and handed me the leash.

"He's an embarrassment," he added, shaking his head.

We had a repeat conversation about the dog's lack of socialization skills during his early development and I took him outside for a quick walk. Later he sat with my husband, who once again made sure he drank enough of the free coffee offered from the vending area. I shot him the "Alice Look" after his fifth cup.

He shot me the "Alice Look," and huffed, "It's the least they could do after all the money we are spending here!"

I'll refrain from discussing the amount of money we spent over the years on the cattle dog in fear of my husband divorcing me. It wasn't really my fault it just happened – surgery, chemo, pills, follow up visits, tests…and more tests.

It's a fact, we have spent a small fortune on our pets, but I know that I am in good company as there are others who have spent more than us caring for these beloved family members.

I am quick to remind my husband that he is not a FUCKING BACHELOR ANYMORE and to just pay the bill.

CHAPTER 36

Going for a Ride

Traveling with the dogs is a major ordeal. Just like children, they feel the need to act up on long trips. On one trip to my mothers, the cattle dog was restless and decided to read. He removed books out of my travel bag. Not finding his choices interesting enough, he proceeded to chew up *The Importance of Michelangelo* and *The Complete Works of Michelangelo*. His displeasure was apparent by the shredded pages strewn about the back of the truck when we stopped at the rest stop!

Laughing while cleaning up the paper my husband said, "He's a fucking cattle dog, a herding dog, why does he want to read about art? I would have thought he'd be more interested in reading a catalogue from Cabela's or a hunting magazine!"

On another trip, the golden retriever, our first born, was jealous my mother was in the front seat. Driving down the Parkway, he continued to push and nudge my arms while I was driving. With the console between me and my mother, he was actually trying to push his way into the front seat. We had to pull over at the Garden State Arts Center, now PNC Bank, and let him out. It still didn't help. He continued his antics all the way to the shore house! That incident was the reason for the two hundred dollar gate we had to purchase for the back seat.

Bentley riding in the truck.

Behind the gate, now at the back of the vehicle, what do all three of them do? Start barking! My husband laughed and turned up the radio. Years later the dogs laugh because the separation gate does not configure to the new truck. It's now in the attic and the dogs are once again in the back seat.

No matter how hard we try to keep the truck clean, it is always full of dog hair.

There are paw and nose prints on the windows and no matter what disinfectant spray we use it still smells. Like children, their toys and travel bowls litter the back seat and trunk.

Traveling with the dogs requires the dachshund's cage, blankets, the cattle dog's Posturepedic bedding, toys, bowls, and food. Once at my mother's all their stuff has to be carried upstairs to the room we sleep in. As the years pass, the cattle dog developed arthritis and could no longer make the climb up the steps. The dachshund was never able to climb the stairs, for they are too deep.

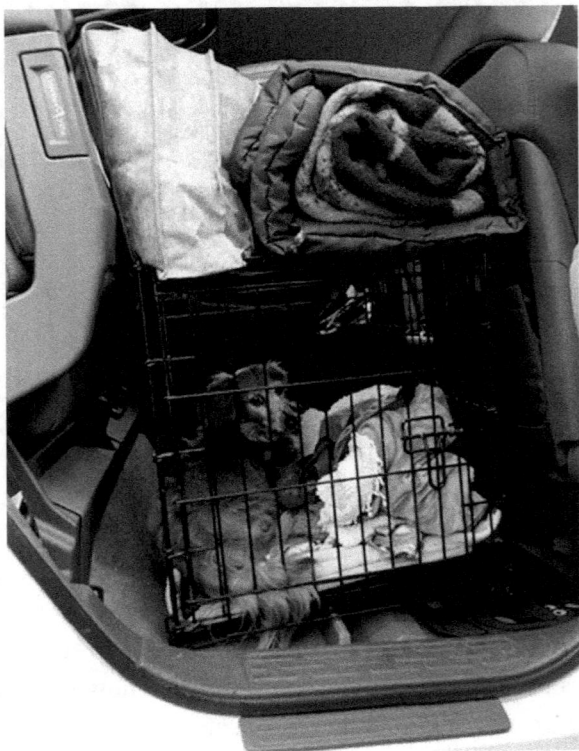

Joey packed for a road trip to grandmas.

On one particular trip we forgot about the dog's arthritis. My husband was annoyed when I reminded him that he'd have to carry the cattle dog to our room at bedtime. "He weighs sixty pounds, are you fucking kidding me? I'm old and I can't make it up these fucking stairs!" He hugs the wall as he cradles the dog in his arms, cursing about why my mother doesn't move out of the big house and that he is going to install an elevator chair for her. I follow with dachshund in my arms.

My mother was yelling at us from the kitchen as we carried the dogs and luggage up the stairs, "Why the hell did you come up here for one day? This is too much!"

I reminded her that we don't have anyone to let the dogs out so they have to come with us and that next time we would sleep on the blow-up air mattress in the living room!

My husband drank several cups of coffee, flavored with the hazelnut creamer my mom purchased especially for him, while making several trips up and down the stairs and through the crowded house as he carried the dog's cage, palettes, toys, blankets, and other stuff out to the truck. He uttered expletives and complained about the entire process and questioned what had happened to his life. My mother makes him more coffee.

I looked at him and he glared at me and said, "Don't say it!"

I ignored him, smiled, and said, "This is what you signed up for and YOU'RE NOT A FUCKING BACHELOR ANYMORE!"

CHAPTER 37

Dog Toys

Another expense my husband likes to complain about is pur-chasing toys for the dogs. He will never understand why they need more toys. We have the same conversation when we were out shopping as I threw another toy into the cart. My husband got the "Alice Look" as he started to complain. He got no support from other pet owners, who glared at his lack of compassion.

"Didn't you have stuff to play with when you were a kid? My children will not be deprived, especially our precious baby...poor thing...I can't believe how cheap you are...what do you want them to do all day...?"

My husband glared and waved his arms irritably at the stuff in the cart and mumbled, "Get a job to pay for all this fucking crap."

The dachshund came into the marriage with one toy. My dogs had a basket full. Before we hit our ten-year anniversary the bas-ket was replaced with a larger one and the collection of toys, well, let's just say we could open a small pet store!

The dachshund was elated when we moved into our first home together and he discovered the basket of stuffed animals. It was like he won the lottery as he played with the animals and left them in every room in the house.

Over the years, the dogs have amassed an impressive collec-tion of toys. Squirrels, hedgehogs, ducks, raccoons, bears, snakes, turtles, mice, fish, cats, crabs, and birds are just a few of the fuzzy animals that are scattered about the house.

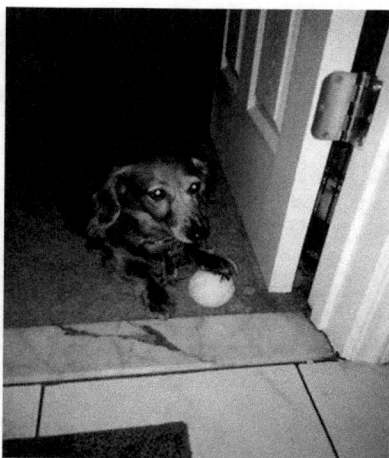

Joey with his favorite dog toy.

If you tell them to get "hedgy" the "monkey" or other toys they will locate them and bring the animal to you. It's funny to watch them run from room to room with various toys in their mouth. If they're not playing with one another they are wrestling with one of us. Like all children, they get more toys at Christmas.

On Christmas morning they sniff around under the tree, wait to be handed presents, and then feverishly begin unwrapping them. My husband and I laugh. He stands by with a trash bag to catch the flying paper. The first Christmas in our house, the dachshund took his present, a hedgehog, and ran to his cage to open it. His socialization skills have improved, and he has learned the concept of sharing and mingling with people.

One year I noticed the dogs Christmas stockings had presents in them and I didn't put them there. I was stunned. After all the complaining my husband did about the basket of dog toys in the living room, he actually went out and bought them more!

Boudreau exhausted after opening Christmas gifts.

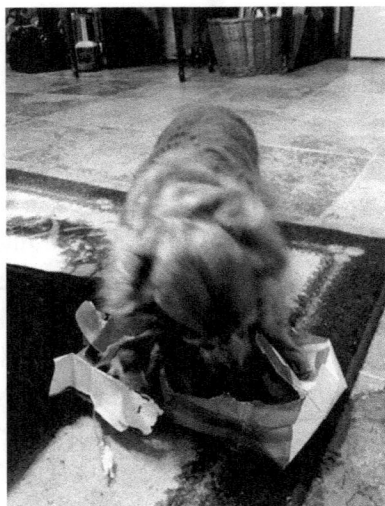

Joey opening Christmas gifts.

Seated on the couch, I turn to him, "You must have been feeling guilty about something to actually have gone out and bought them more toys," I said sarcastically, as I watched the dogs tear open their gifts. My eyes widen. Seated on the couch, I turn and I give him the "Alice Look" and my tone is more accusatory, "You haven't been throwing their toys out again, have you?"

One year he started throwing out their toys thinking I wouldn't notice. I discovered this when I was cleaning and searching for one of the toys. I asked my husband if he saw "hedgy." Suspiciously he muttered a quick "no" and returned to watching TV. I didn't believe him. The following day, I lined up all the toys on the bed, took a picture and e-mailed it to him, with a caption that said, "Cataloguing the children's toys, will know when something is missing!"

While the dogs continued to unwrap their gifts, he stated calmly, "Actually there was nothing wrong with me. I was in Wal-Mart and I saw them. *My* children should have them."

My eyes widen. I understand as the gifts are revealed. The cattle dog received a camouflaged duck and the dachshund got another hedgehog – only this one was also camouflaged. Looking at camouflaged toys will temporarily satisfy his need to go hunting since he, not only doesn't have time, but we can't afford the expense.

More presents are opened revealing biscuits, more toys, and food. Throughout the year, my mother and other friends contribute, by purchasing more toys, treats and food!

Shopping for dog food is like buying a good London broil – no expense is spared. When my husband and I are grocery shopping and he picks food out – most of his choices usually go back to the shelf. When it comes to dog food, they get a variety and the best.

We were shopping in Wal-Mart on a Sunday. "We need dog food," I said as I turned down the aisle.

"Don't we have enough food?"

"No. I mix the wet with the dry – it's easier on their teeth, or they will have to go to the dentist."

My husband waited patiently as I perused the choices of the gourmet canine cuisine. I called out the flavors: porterhouse steak, chicken and rice, filet mignon, beef, salmon, and chicken with lamb. I turned to my husband and held up the chicken with lamb. "Do you think they'll like this?" I was very serious and waited for his response.

He looked at me like I'd lost my mind.

I continued, "Or maybe I'll get them the porter house steak. What do you think?"

"Ha! Why do they get steak three times a week and I only get it once a month, and that's if I'm lucky. Theirs is one hundred percent beef and mine is the fuckin' cow's ass - that cheap crap you buy!"

The male shopper next to me burst into a fit of laughter and agreed as he grabbed some of the canned food from the shelf. He exchanged notes with my husband regarding the exorbitant cost of purchasing canned dog food.

"Do you realize we have been in this aisle for fifteen minutes comparing brands, potential choices and multiplying costs? Sixty cents, seventy cents, just fucking buy something," he hissed in frustration.

I flashed him the "Alice Look."

"I want them to have a variety. How would you like it if you had to eat the same thing every day?"

He has no answer. Instead he snapped, "Ok. Ok. Get what you want."

"You're lucky to have me," I said smiling.

He smiled back and hugged me. "No, you're lucky that I put up with all this!"

Hours later, after the groceries were put away and I was making gravy for the pasta dinner and letting the dogs smell a can of their impending meal. They were barking excitedly at their good fortune. As they barked and pawed at me, I take a closer look at the dog featured on the package. Eye brows raised and mouth open in disbelief, I shouted, "I can't believe this!"

"What now?" my husband hollered from the living room.

"This is all your fault."

He ran into the kitchen and started laughing when I pointed out the problem.

"It's the wrong brand! This happened because you were rushing me!"

Hysterical laughter erupted from my husband. "Do you think they are not going to eat it?"

"That's not the brand they like! It's like they're getting the generic."

"So strap the receipt and the cans to their necks and let them return everything," he continued laughing as he grabbed a soda from the refrigerator, "and remind them, THEY'RE NOT FUCKING BACHELOR'S anymore," he laughed as he retreated to the TV room.

CHAPTER 38

Where Does All the Money Go?

My mother wants to know why we never have any money when we don't have any children.

My husband is all too happy to tell her. "Do you know where all our money goes? I'll tell you – dog food, treats, medications, glucosamine for arthritis, senior dog food, visits to the vet for operations and shots, monthly flea and tick medication, flea repellant, cages, an assortment of leashes and collars, clothing, bedding, products for grooming, including tooth brushes and a host of brushes and combs that all claim to remove the tough under coat of fur! This is what the money is spent on," he yells as he shakes his head and rubs his temples disgusted at the entire conversation and situation. He gives my mother the "Alice Look," and states, "the cost of having pets is astronomical!"

The dogs are running around, growling as they play with their toys.

My mother smiles at the dogs lovingly as she shakes a stuffed animal. The dachshund pulls at the other end growling as he tries to pull it free. "Well, they don't show any signs of slowing down."

She's right. The cattle dog is thirteen and the dachshund is twelve years old. My husband is positive the dogs are going to outlive him. I recall the story of a dachshund that lived until he was nineteen years old! "It was on the news. I think it was a world record."

I grab my iPhone and Google it for proof. "Wow, I was wrong," I said.

My husband smiles as if he won some competition. "I said you were wrong," he smirks.

"It says dachshunds are one of the breeds that live the longest. Rocky, a dachshund, is still living – he's twenty-five! Would you believe it? There is an Australian Cattle dog named Bluey that lived until the age of twenty-nine?" I shout excitedly.

I hand my husband the iPhone for proof. He sighs, defeated. He stares at the dogs now sitting at his feet in disbelief. "Of all dog breeds in the world, we own two breeds that have a long life-span. You can plan on burying me in the flower bed, because you're going to need money for their vet bills!"

"We do save money on grooming," I add smiling.

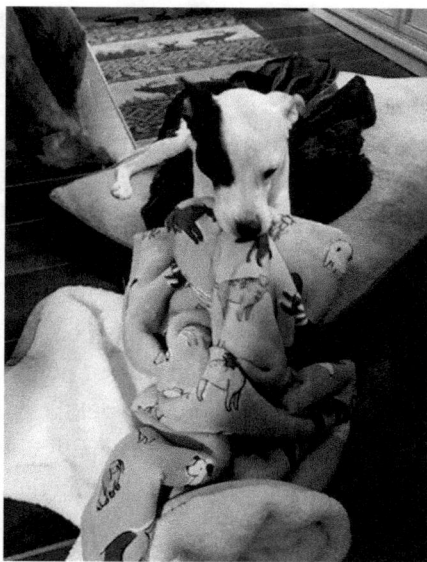

Aaron gets comfortable with his new palette and blankets.

All grooming is done in our home. However, it didn't start out that way. My husband was enraged when we picked them up from the groomer one Saturday afternoon. "Two hundred dollars!"

"Well, we have three dogs," I stuttered as I attempted to justify the expense.

His annoyance was apparent as his eyes narrowed and he peered at me angrily. "As you have clearly pointed out I am not a fucking bachelor anymore, and this is one expense that is going to end right now!"

Ok, he was right. There was no reason why we couldn't wash the dogs at home.

All grooming is done in the yard. They get washed in their small pool with an assortment of shampoos and conditioners to make their fur soft and smell fresh and clean. My husband is in charge of the brushing. He is blatantly annoyed that the dogs have so much fur only because he is practically bald. His inability to grow hair plagues him. The perpetual dog hair in the house is a constant reminder of his baldness.

"If that is the only problem you have to live with, then you should be grateful," I shouted as he began citing reasons why he has no hair. He likes to tell people that I am the cause of his hair loss. Unfortunately for him, I have the pictures, as he was virtually bald when I married him.

"Why can't I grow hair like this?" He complained as he spent hours brushing the cattle dog. Fur flies like tumbleweeds all over the yard. He doesn't even make an attempt to put the hair in a trash bag.

"Dammit! Can't you just put the fur in a fucking trash bag," I shouted as I walked around the yard collecting the hair. "It's flying into the neighbor's yard."

"Fuck those neighbors! It's my yard I'll do as I please!" he retorted impatiently as the brushing continues.

I returned with some cold drinks and the minute I opened the sliding glass doors a wad of the hair blows past my face and into the living room. Exasperated I started yelling. "This is fucking ridiculous! Look at all this hair! Why the hell are you staring at it? Do you think it's going to manifest itself into hair on your head? Just put it in a garbage bag and clean it up! Just face it, you're bald! I married you this way and it's not going to change!"

I dodged the wet towel that was flung toward me.

He smiled, disgusted with the entire conversation, as he knew I was right. "Come help me, I need you to hold him."

I grabbed the towels and continued drying and fluffing. The dogs were calm until they spot the nail clippers.

Nail clipping is like an Olympic event in our home or at the vet. During one visit, the doctor sent a petite blonde technician to clip the cattle dog's nails. The obligatory greeting went well and she led him to the back with extreme confidence.

My husband snickered, "Yeah, this might happen."

Seconds later, a second tech is paged, followed by a third, and forth. They all come out looking like they rolled in dog hair. They had never seen anything like it. "His strength is unbelievable," they acknowledged. The dog looked at everyone innocently, as if nothing ever happened.

"He should be sedated," my husband commented.

Back in the yard, some strange essence overtook my husband as he stood, grinning like some bizarre character from a low budget science fiction film, with the nail clippers in hand. He has silently announced his intentions to the dogs.

The dogs eyeballed the loathsome gadget. Their body stance quickly changed as front paws pounced and set in position – they looked at him and silently communicated, "game on," and take off.

More fur flies…they ran in different directions…my husband started chasing the cattle dog around the yard…the dog was too quick…the games began…the freshly washed dogs were running through the muddy yard…the dachshund took cover deep under the rhododendron bush and started barking…my husband was no match for the agile cattle dog as he leapt over objects and ran through the garden as if he were competing in some agility competition…he stopped and decided to cut sharply to the left…my husband tripped in one of the holes they dug…the obscenities began…the dachshund continued barking…I reached for the camera and take pictures…

When it's over I brought out biscuits for the dogs. My husband, who was now wet and covered in fur and mud, got a cup of coffee.

I give him the "Alice Look" and said, "Don't you think it would be easier if we took them to the groomer?"

He glared and gave me the "Alice Look."

The dogs lay quietly at my feet as I fed them another biscuit.

Our dogs have their own ceramic cookie jar for their treats, and a space in the cabinet above for "distraction toys." As I write, they are eating peanut butter from some oblong, rubber, gadget known as the Kong. It is intended to keep them busy, but our dogs always manage to lick the peanut butter out in less than five minutes. "Don't let the dog's lick you," I yell to my husband, who has a peanut butter allergy.

"Why the fuck did you have to give them that? You know I'm allergic to peanuts."

I slam the sliding glass doors. "It's your damn fault entirely."

My husband stares at me in disbelief as he looks up from his reading. "Oh, this should be good!"

"They are out there eating the fucking dog shit…I asked you to clean up the yard…it's disgusting…I had to give them something."

***

There is also a full complement of dishes. There are bowls for outside in the summer, bowls for travel in the car, bowls at my mom's, bowls for water when we take walks, and their regular bowls in the house. They both have raised dishes to aid with the intake and digestion of their food.

Joey sometimes thinks he is one of the big dogs and tries to eat from the big bowls.

Before we were married, the only bowls the dachshund owned were the traditional attached side-by-side standard stainless-steel bowls. My mother quickly changed that. He now dines from bowls with a beautiful classy French motif, while the cattle dog's matches our Italian-Tuscany designed kitchen. My husband refers to it as the Coliseum. It is elevated on four, seven-inch Doric columns, the frieze is decorated with relief sculpture, two, large bowls are inset into a faux marble design. My mother, the consummate shopper, discovered it on some web site. I believe it cost two hundred and fifty dollars! Traveling with the "Coliseum" is impossible and brings another set of problems. The cattle dog is so accustomed to eating with the elevated dishes that when we visit my mother someone must hold and raise his dish for him while he eats.

My husband complains that, if we didn't have dogs we wouldn't be in debt. He would be able to afford to buy me a Mercedes, a bigger house with more closets, a man cave and a nice pick-up truck for himself. Instead he drives a used Ford Taurus and we live in a small ranch house. When he says he wants to take me out for dinner it's usually to the Chinese buffet down the street. Afterward we find ourselves our en route to the pet store to get senior dog food - dry and wet – the wet to help them chew, glucosamine for their joints, more treats and toys.

"I hope you have a coupon for all this," he stated a bit more calmly as the routine is all too familiar. He rolled his eyes in disgust as he watched the monitor on the cash register as the cost continued to escalate with every item scanned.

I tuned him and the obscenities out as he started his lecture on coupons and how they are for saving money not spending it on something else. "You just saved ten dollars on this bag of dog food and you go ahead and buy ten dollars' worth of wet food and a toy. It makes no fucking sense," he grumbled loudly as he slammed the dog food on the conveyor belt.

The customer behind him smirked and I tried to rationalize the expense - claiming that the dog food is on sale and that if I didn't have the coupon and wanted to buy the wet food it would have been more money?

My husband smiled politely, knowing any more conversation on the topic is futile. He gave me the "Alice Look" and said, "We are going to Dunkin' Donuts after this and I am super-sizing a large iced-caramel latte!"

I swipe the debit card swiftly and forcefully through the card reader. "Yeah, well we just spent all the coffee money on the dogs...plus you have lots of flavors to select from those Keurig cups we have at home!"

Once home, he sat in front of the television and during the commercials found it necessary to re-play the day's events. "I still can't believe it...why do they need all that food...do you see how much money we just spent...this is why we can't go out...this is why I can't go to the dentist...this is why I can't buy fucking coffee at the convenience store!"

"Look at it this way, at least you don't have to have your ass expressed!"

He throws up his hands, gesturing toward me. "Ha. Ha. Very funny! You're a regular comedian," he answered sarcastically. "You better believe that won't be happening to me. You're lucky to have me...no better yet, you're lucky I put up with all this nonsense...you're lucky..."

I got up and headed to the kitchen to make him some more coffee and calmly stated, "Let's face it; you're not a fucking bachelor anymore!"

One dog is cuddled beside him and the other one is at his feet. I smiled as I heard him talking to the dogs, telling them how much he loves them and that he is secretly glad he is not a bachelor anymore. I returned to the room, hand him his coffee grinning, "You're lucky to have me."

He smiled as the dogs nuzzled and licked him and he knows life is good!

Unfortunately, while I was writing this book, Boudreau, our beloved Australian cattle dog passed away on July 5, 2014. Born in Alabama, he was well travelled, loved the dog park, taking trips and made friends everywhere he went. He was a gentle soul who was extremely independent and loved sitting on the bed looking out the window.

Ceiling fans, the air conditioner, and open windows kick up his fur, hidden in corners and under furniture that was not easily reachable with a vacuum, forever reminding us of his presence.

Although not fond of swimming, he learned how in the Tennessee River and was not a fan of the saltwater of the Jersey Shore. He did, however, love to rearrange the environment wherever he went either by digging holes in the yard, or in the sand at the beach, or running through the freshly raked leaves or newly fallen snow.

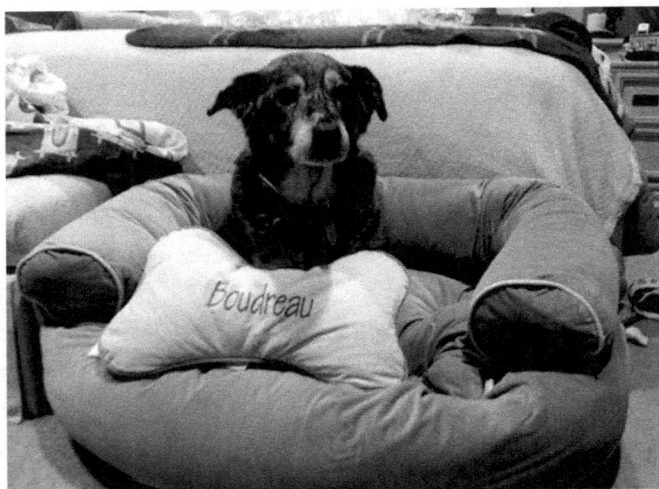

Boudreau enjoying the comfort of his Posturepedic dog palette and engraved pillow.

Boudreau with his new reversible parka for the winter.

He was always on "red alert" for rodents and squirrels that dared trespass into his yard and made sure he checked the perimeter of the yard every night.

He was one of the best dogs we ever had.

He is forever in our hearts and greatly missed…

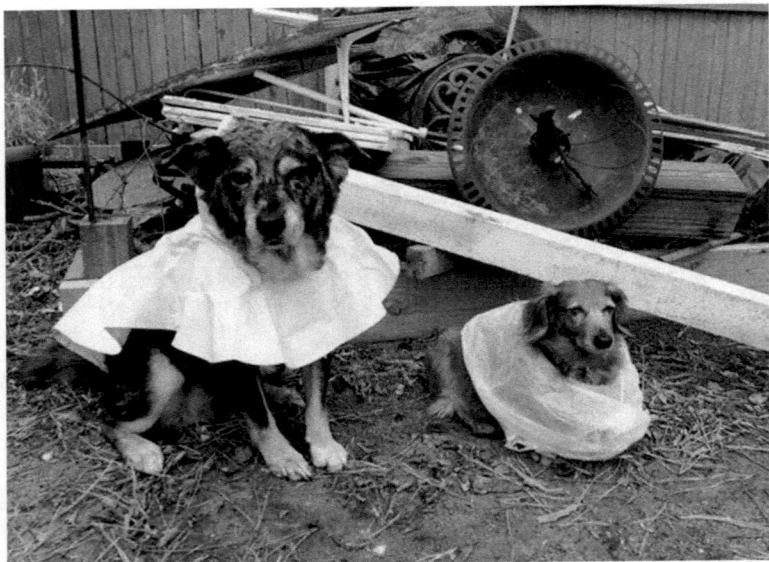

Boudreau and Joey after hurricane Sandy.

CHAPTER 39

Bentley

In January 2015 my girlfriend from work asked if I was ready for another dog. She showed me a picture and I immediately e-mailed it to my husband. When he didn't respond I called him. "Did you look at the picture? My friend knows someone that rescued some dogs from South Carolina."

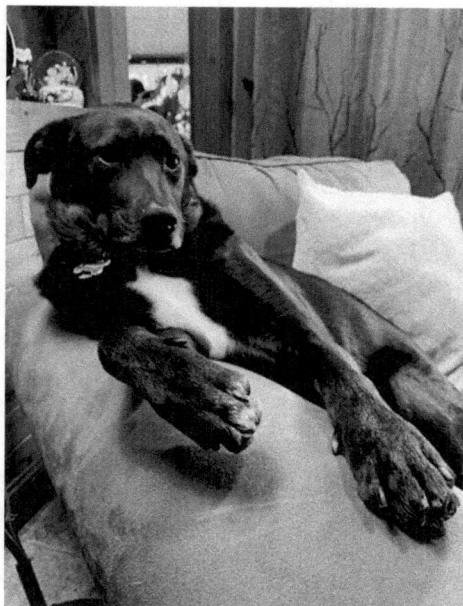

Bentley relaxing on the couch.

"I thought you were sending me a picture of a stuffed animal."

I ignored him and got right to the point. "Can we have him? He is a lab-shepherd mix."

"Yes. Go get him." He didn't think twice. It was a big dog. It's what he wanted for us.

We named him Bentley. This is the first dog we would be raising together from a puppy. We were fifty years old. It was not only one of the coldest winters on record, but it was constantly snowing. Not the best time to be training a new puppy. Not the best time to be training a puppy that had DNA from two, very strong breeds. For me, motherly instinct kicked in and the training began. No matter how cold it was or how late at night, I was determined to have Bentley housebroken.

My husband had forgotten what it was like to raise a puppy. "He just went out," he grumbled, as he attempted to put his little winter coat on him for the fifth time.

"He's a baby; his bladder is forming."

Bentley grew out of his new coats in a week. Within months we made the pilgrimage to the pet store and bought the largest cage, pallet, and complete training kit with coupons for people with new puppies. My husband did not grumble at the expense of the cage but rather its location in the house. "Where the *fuck* are we going to put this? It's huge!" he exclaimed as he pulled the boxes off the shelf for comparison. Customers stared at him as if he were some sort of monster.

"Shhh," I hushed him. "We have plenty of space. I'm going to rearrange the furniture in the living room." He looked at me wide-eyed in horror. Changing the space of an obsessive-compulsive person like my husband can be alarming.

"Don't worry; I'll make sure you know where the couch and TV remote are!"

"We have a lab too, you'll need the big cage," a woman shopping nearby pointed. And added, "He'll also need the big pallet."

The Keurig coffee bar was relocated to the kitchen and furniture was rearranged to accommodate the 42" x 28" wire cage. The giant, red pallet was guaranteed not to rip or tear. Bentley pulled the stuffing out in a few hours. Our attempts to patch it with duct tape failed. When the summer came, I patched it again with the duct tape, so he could be comfortable on the deck. My husband laughed, "Now what are you going to do?"

"I thought if he was older…"

"He's nine months," he interjected. "He's still a puppy. And he doesn't need that anyway. Just throw it out. He's fine with the blankets he has in the cage, besides he spends more time on our bed anyway!"

Bentley not only sleeps on the bed, but the couches as well. My husband can't argue about this because he started the habit by picking him up and putting him on the couch to watch TV with him. Twelve years together and three dogs, which have never jumped or slept on the couches or other furniture and now Bentley is allowed to do both. I don't try to understand his logic. I don't care because the furniture is old and worn. And when my husband complains, I smile and remind him he started the habit the first night we had Bentley.

What my husband does have a problem with is the money we spend on dog food.

"The other dogs didn't eat this brand, why does he need it?"

The dogs now eat limited ingredients dog food. And since the dog food companies no longer make the giant 40-pound huge bags the consumer is forced to the pay for a smaller size bag. I could order it on-line and have it delivered for a cheaper price but ever since our mail carrier threw a package we ordered from NFL.com in our trashcan, thinking I would go check the trash to retrieve our mail, I have absolutely no faith in the mail system!

Bentley sleeping on the couch.

The package was thrown out with the trash and one of the items we ordered was no longer obtainable. When the *hell* did the mail carrier start putting people's mail in the trash! What's the point of having a mailbox! The *"Mail Incident,"* is why I don't have packages delivered to the house anymore.

My husband rarely complains about the dog food and has learned not to ask me to order dog food on-line for fear of me resurrecting the *"mail incident"* and the failure of the postal system and *our* mail carrier, who, claimed she put the mail in the trash because it was raining.

"Seriously," I shout at my husband, who, made the mistake of suggesting I order dog food online again so we didn't have to travel to the pet store. "Is that in their policy manual, put customers mail in trash during inclement weather...they work for the government...what kind of scam is that...that was the only hat that would fit your head and now they don't make it anymore...and the postmaster is at fault for allowing her do this...we need to move... this is bullshit...we should get a PO box...who the hell puts the mail in a trash can...

The longhaired dachshund turned sixteen in January of 2016. "Look how much better he is doing and look how shinny Bentley's coat is," I debate as another argument about the cost of dog food begins.

All in all, my husband's temperament had been pretty mild when it came to the dogs, until what occurred in July of 2016. I refer to it as the "dog tag incident." The dachshund needed a new tag because his was worn; it was so worn you couldn't even see the phone number or address. "What if he gets lost?" I asked my husband.

"He has a fuckin' chip," he replied.

"I don't care. They're getting tags. Besides Bentley doesn't have a tag."

"He has a chip too," my husband debated as we drove down Route 9 toward the pet store.

The dog tags are printed on a laser machine in the store. It requires you to scan your receipt and follow the directions. This wasn't the problem.

The patrons shopping at the time probably heard the outburst from my husband as I paid for two tags and he yelled, "Who the *fuck* pays fourteen fifty for a dog tag? Fourteen fifty are you *fucking* kidding me! What is wrong with you? Now whose wasting money?"

We were shopping in Wal-Mart one Sunday morning and I left my husband with the cart while I went to retrieve some items in another aisle. I returned to find a huge dog pallet in the cart. Shocked, I blurted, "*You* want to buy the dog another palette? This is huge! Where are we going to put it?"

My husband calmly replied, "It's for Bentley's cage. I don't like him sleeping on the plastic. He'll get cold. He needs to be comfortable when were not home."

He was serious.

"The dog has two coats of fur, he is never cold. Besides, he was still a puppy and it wouldn't last. He tore all the blankets, ate the plastic liner for his cage, and the towels I gave him. He doesn't need that. How much it is?" I asked as I started looking for the non-existent price tag, which brings us back to the aisle he found it in.

"Forty dollars," I shouted. "Are you out of your mind?"

He quickly reminded me of the forty-dollar cuddle fluff I insisted on purchasing for the dachshund twelve years prior. "He wasn't a puppy," I exclaim. "And we *still* have the forty-dollar cuddle fluff. So the money was well spent. Bentley is still a puppy. This pallet will be ripped in a day," I spat as we proceeded to the check out.

As predicted, the forty-dollar Posturepedic pallet only lasted a day. Ripped and torn at the seam, it lies next to the couch with his other torn pallet, which gets rotated around the room when we move the furniture. The dogs prefer the couch but still use the pallet. I use one of the pallets for the outside pet canopy in the summer for his comfort.

Bentley was only one year old and had chewed though ten pallets an assortment of towels and blankets. Yet my husband insisted Bentley needs something to sleep on while he was his crate. I told him to tile the bottom. He refused. So, desperate, I ordered a pallet from a website claiming that it was made of the strongest material; Bentley ripped right through the material the following day. The company sent a replacement, which is still packed in the box. We probably won't put it in his cage until he is a senior dog.

Bentley loves to sharpen his teeth and is very destructive. We are constantly purchasing chew toys and bones that claim to be the "strongest" on the market. If I could invent something Bentley could not chew through, I'd be a millionaire.

If you're not careful Bentley will knock you over. When you ask him for his paw, it's like getting punched by a boxer as it flies into your hand or chest. Keeping socks and clothing out of his reach is a chore. He loves going into the laundry room to rummage through the laundry basket.

One of my best girlfriends is mom to a pit-bull mix. We constantly swap photos and laugh about the antics of our fur-babies. Whether it's at the vet, on the bed, playing with toys, or at rest, the lives of these canines are well documented and shared on Facebook and messaged about daily on our iPhones. We talk about them as if they were human. They are part of the family and accompany us wherever we can take them. Bentley even has a pallet in my office. My girlfriend posted a picture of her dog riding in the car on Facebook. I thought nothing of it and texted, "Is he riding in the Mercedes?" She replied, "No, this is when we had the Lexus." I showed the photos to my husband. "See, this dog rides in style."

My husband smirked. "There is no fucking way I would ever let these dogs in a car like that. Are you crazy?"

Bentley in the backyard pool.

My dogs have ridden in every vehicle I have ever owned. I had a golden retriever, Princeton, who rode in the front seat of my 1975 Red Corvette. Boudreau and Napoleon loved the Chevy Blazer and the Jeep.

My girlfriend and I truly believe the dogs are purposely destructive to the men in our lives. The text messages I send to my husband usually begin with, "There was an incident in the house tonight." A photo of the destruction accompanies the text message.

Bentley loves destroying pillows, clothing, pallets, towels, shoes, a deer tail from a hunting trip, or anything that belongs to my husband.

The yard is full of holes and is perpetually muddy. My husband fills the holes only to have Bentley dig them deeper. He runs around like the speed of lightening and can't be caught. My girlfriend and I think he is more than a Shepard and lab mix. I want to have his DNA tested, but my husband forbids it because he feels it is a waste of money. He refuses to speak with the neighbor who told me all about the DNA testing kit available in the pet stores. One of my other girlfriends suggested we enter him in agility contests. If we could afford it, we'd hire the dog whisper or send Bentley for some intensive obedience training. But, nonetheless, we love him and all of his antics.

In December 2016, our dachshund, my little Joey or Jobeher (short for Joey bear) passed away from congestive heart failure. He was just shy of his 17th birthday. It was a hard Christmas for us. I recall commenting to my husband that I still did not understand why God had to take him at Christmas time. While opening a gift I quietly said, "Perhaps God took him because he needed more angels. I wonder if he is a Christmas angel?"

My husband handed me a gift with a card from the dogs. I opened the envelope and cried; it was a Christmas card of dachshunds dressed as angels; a card he purchased before the dog passed.

The following morning, I walked outside and thought about little Jobeher and how I missed him and was hoping he was on his way to the Rainbow Bridge. I asked God to give me a sign. Something. Anything. The sky was clear not a cloud was visible. I went inside and returned with my coffee. Bentley was still running around in the yard. He pounced on the deck like a Clydesdale and sat. He looked toward the sky. I followed his gaze and look up and I see a cloud formation. It was the only one in the sky; it was of a dog running, ears flopping. Call me crazy.

In memory of Joey.

CHAPTER **40**

Aaron

"**B**entley needs a buddy, and if we are going to get another dog we better do it now," my husband reminded me in the summer of 2017.

Bentley would be turning three years old in November and introducing another dog, we already knew from his temperament, was going to be rough. After several trips to the Popcorn Park Zoo Human Society and a successful meet and greet, we adopted Aaron, who was listed as a Border Collie Mix.

This was followed by a trip to my mother's storage unit where we removed Bentley's 48x24 cage and then to Pet Value for toys, a raised dog bowl, bones, tooth- brushes, and bedding.

Chaotic and entertaining is the only way I can describe our lives. Aaron is fast like lightening, and he's impossible to catch as he is running around the yard. He broke through the wooden fence, as if it was invisible, chasing after a chipmunk. He has easily cleared the four-foot deck railing into the garden after the elusive chipmunk and mole. The dog just stands and leaps, it's as if he has springs in his hind legs. I've never seen anything like it. If we could afford it I would enter him in agility contests.

Mix. What does that exactly mean? He has the strength of a Rottweiler and the face of a great dane; some say he's a pit bull, which could be a combination of many strong breeds of dogs, while others say he is a herding dog. I don't care. I love him.

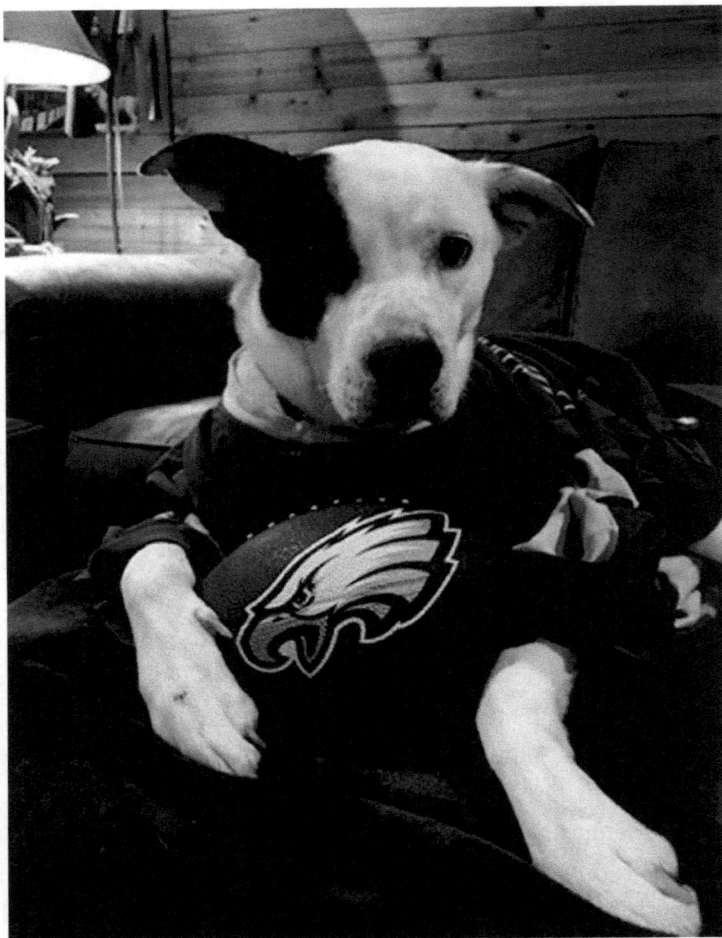

Aaron celebrates Eagles Super bowl victory.

Both dogs playing together are impressive. Their speed and leaping ability are fantastic. They will knock us over if we are not paying attention. The yard is full of holes from digging and is perpetually muddy.

Aaron and Bentley love the couches and there is more dog hair than ever before in our house. The vacuums have been replaced by the Hoover Wind Tunnel and the Shark Navigator.

Like a pack of wolves, both dogs sleep in the bed with us and my husband complains that it is too crowded and hot. Field trips to Pet Value are frequent as they love riding in the truck and going for baths at the newly installed self-service dog wash.

We made the pilgrimage to the free rabies clinic and it was like taking two screaming two-year olds grocery shopping. As seasoned veterans it should have been an easy trip. Aaron howled like some possessed hound dog...impressive but annoying... Bentley behaved as if he never left the house...jumping and barking...a dog barrier will be the next purchase to keep them from trying to get in the front seat of the truck. Angry, irritated, annoyed, either adjectives will describe my husband who gave me the "Alice Look," for the rest of the day.

Two major expensed occurred after Aaron came into our lives.

The first, we are now the proud owners of a white vinyl fence that runs around the property. The second, I took my husband to Lucky's Bed and Biscuit in Manahawkin, New Jersey to inquire about day care and boarding.

After the tour, which included an indoor saltwater pool, I left with a full-color folder with pamphlets on boarding, day care, grooming, and more.

My husband left with a headache after he saw the rates. "Fuhged-da-boud-it," he warned me.

I began filling out the paperwork, made an appointment at the vet for Aaron to have his appropriate shots, and updated his fecal sample.

Aaron enjoys the good life!

My husband complained about the cost. "YOU'RE NOT A FUCKING BACHELOR ANYMORE," I remind him.

A trial stay at Lucky's was eminent.

CHAPTER 41

Did You See the Remote?

Iopened the electric bill and my eyes widened in shock as I read the amount due! The bill had doubled! It didn't take me long to figure out the cause.

The answer was revealed when I came home early one afternoon and found the television on. "What are you guys watching?" I asked the dogs who were lounging on their pallets in the living room sleeping!

My husband was not in the house, the shed, or the yard. I looked out the window and out of the corner of my eye I see him talking to the neighbor down the street! When he came home, I didn't even wait for the door to close before I started shouting.

My anger was obvious, as I flashed him the "Alice Look," and asked, "Why the hell is the fuckin' television on?"

He stared at me expressionlessly. He had absolutely no idea what I was talking about! Which further infuriated me. I saw the television on and nobody was watching it and my brain immediately processed – waste of electricity, higher electric bill, more money, not to mention the wear and tear on the equipment. I don't understand why he does not process this.

I continued the "Alice Look" and stance. "You're not even in the house and the television is on...don't you know what a waste of money this is...do the dogs have a favorite show they like to watch that I don't know about?"

"Now that you mention it, they do," he laughed.

Apparently during the day, they like to watch people hunting alligators, fishing for catfish with their hands in the mud, and catching crabs in Alaska. These are their favorites. "Their educational and entertaining," claimed my husband as he headed into the living room to check on the dogs.

I thought about the consequences I suffered growing up if I left a light on in a room and nobody was in it and leaving the television on with nobody watching was much worse. My husband doesn't know why he leaves the TV on. In my opinion, it's just plain laziness and another inconvenience.

"Why should I turn it off? I come in the house to check on the score of a game or see what is happening on a show, it doesn't make sense to keep turning it on and off," he told me later.

This is followed by how I am missing out on some of the really good TV shows. "Catching catfish…the fishing for crabs… hunting for deer or ducks…storage wars…this is quality TV babe…you really should watch…too bad they didn't have shows like this when we were growing up…"

I tuned him out as I retreat to the kitchen and think about how reality television has become such a part of our every day lives.

I try to recall shows I watched when I was little…Speed Racer, the Flintstones, Scooby Doo, I Dream of Jeannie and Abbott and Costello were some that quickly enter my mind. As I became older I remember racing home from school to watch General Hospital. Distant memories of the family crowing in the den to watch, shows like Happy Days or Lavern and Shirley invade my thoughts. They were amusing and easy to follow. What the hell is so entertaining about sticking your hand in the mud, in a river full of snakes to catch a fish or killing alligators? I just don't get it. My husband watches these shows all the time.

I was curious as to what went on in other homes. What were other boyfriends and husbands watching on TV? I consulted the girls at work. "Do you want to know what my husband watches on TV?" I asked and proceeded to describe the shows. Because I don't know the full names of the programs, I just mention of the words fish, alligator, and snakes and everyone knows what I am talking about.

"Oh my God, mine watches the same stuff."

"So does mine," another one chimed in. "And I can't figure out the attraction?

I agree. It's not like there is a limited selection of programs to watch. There are hundreds of channels, stations, and genres to choose from.

The following day, to be fair, I asked one of the guys at work what he watches on television. He responded quickly without giving it any thought, "The alligator show, you know in the swamps, the river monsters, fishing in the mud for the catfish."

My girlfriend, who heard me ask the same question the prior day, was standing nearby and burst into a fit of laughter. I shook my head in disbelief.

Our male co-worker wanted to know what we found so entertaining.

I wanted to know why he watches these shows and asked him.

His response, "I don't know!"

More insanity!

Just to be fair, I am not criticizing what anyone watches or the programs at all. I just want to know what the attraction is since my husband is unable to explain it.

Some of these reality TV shows look too dangerous for me. As I watch people walking in the river trying to catch a catfish with their hands, I think to myself, "This is why man invented the fishing pole or the imminent dangers - what about snakes?" I have been to the Bayou in Louisiana and there are snakes and alligators everywhere, not to mention insects that could carry our dachshund away. As my husband sits and watches he states, "I would do that!"

I give him the "Alice Look" and stance as I remind him of his fear of snakes.

I think back to what television was like when I was growing up. There were few channels - two, four, five, seven, nine, eleven, and thirteen and CBS, NBC, and ABC were the top networks. We didn't have a television in every room of the house. We had one television and it was in black and white. It wasn't until I was in college that I was able to comprehend the wonders of color television. I was watching General Hospital and couldn't believe the color of clothing, the sets, the hair and make-up. I remember being so shocked at seeing Jackie Zeaman, who played Bobbie Spencer, with red hair. When I'd go home on spring break, I would be thinking about what color hair a person had or clothing as I'd watch the small black and white TV in my mother's kitchen.

The other item we didn't have growing up was a television remote. Someone had to physically get up and change the channels! That responsibility was given to my brothers and me. We were like ping pong balls.

My father would start, "Put it on channel seven!" My brother would get up and change the channel.

Then it was my turn. Not interested in the program, he'd loud-ly bellow, "I'm not watching this. Put the news on. Change it to channel two." I'd sigh heavily and get up and turn it. There would be hell to pay if you didn't comply.

The quarreling began when he wanted the channel changed again. My brother would tell my younger brother that it was his turn. They'd argue. I'd say I just changed it and it was not my turn. The fighting and name-calling progressed rapidly. My father then started with the obscenities and threats of beatings to follow if we didn't stop.

The commotion brought my mother rushing into the room, who said we were watching too much TV and should be in our rooms doing homework! Homework, which we had already completed. She gave a quick whack to the on/off button and the only sound left in the room came from my father and the tornado of obscenities that he projected at all of us. He stood up and the strap crackled as it came whipping off his pants. My brothers and I ran for cover, our legs striking and pounding the rickety steps as we raced up the staircase, seeking escape in the safety of our rooms. We'd hide under our beds or comforters and blankets that were piled on top of us to lessen the strikes from the leather belt.

This was the routine almost every night. And this happened all because we didn't have a fucking remote control! How ludicrous!

Every time I hear someone talking about DYFUSS, I think, "Where the hell were they when I was growing up?"

I call my divorced girlfriend, who is all too familiar with the system. DYFUSS, lawyers, court, child support, visitation, ex-husbands, more lawyers, subpoenas and warrants for jail time are all part of her daily life. It is all so surreal to me. It is rare that a day will pass without a phone call detailing yet another emergency outlining, unpaid child support, missing visitation, warrants for another arrest, calls to lawyers, request to take off to go to court, or back to the lawyer for yet another court appearance. And it's not just her. She is just a fragment of the thousands which this dialogue and behavior is all heavily embedded into the fabric of our daily culture.

No wonder being an attorney is so lucrative. The endless revolving door of problems seem to emerge because we don't know how to communicate or refuse to work together.

My girlfriend stops talking to yell at her children because they are fighting over some zombie-military-type video game they are playing. I ask her if she had a TV remote growing up.

"Nope, my brothers and I were human TV clickers. My father never once got up to change the channel on the television!"

I laugh. I'm ecstatic, happy to know that I did not suffer alone. I think about the whole generation of human TV clickers that exists and the torment we endured for technology.

I can hear her children in the background and their arguing is escalating.

I tell her to get the wooden spoon. We reminisce about how our parents disciplined us with the wooden spoon and belts.

My girlfriend stops talking and tells me to hold on. I hear her yelling threats of a stay in time-out or the video game will be taken away if they don't stop. The youngest is threatening to call DYFUSS!

I shake my head in amazement. My girlfriend shouts, "*Go ahead*," and then gives them a reality check about life in the system, without video games, computers, iPhones, tablets…"

"We didn't have video games to fight about. Perhaps you should just give them the remote," I suggest.

She laughs, "I would if we could find it!"

The one item that gets misplaced the most in our home is the TV remote. It's one of the daily conversations we have in our house. In fact, it's how we start the day. Not hi, good morning, how did you sleep, I love you – instead it's, "Where's the remote?"

The script is the same every day. My husband's lines are first. He starts by yelling from the living room, "Honey, did you see the remote?"

I yell back, "I don't know. You had it last." I answer honestly. He was watching TV last.

"Well, it's not here."

"Did you check the couch?" I know it's probably between the pillows, in the blankets, or on the couch, but he is impatient and is not really looking. Again, I often wonder what he is looking at or perhaps there really is a problem with his eyesight.

"I did, it's not there."

"Did you look under the pillows and blankets? Did you check by the TV?"

"It's not here. I've looked everywhere," he responds, the frustration is apparent as he starts cursing.

I laugh. "Obviously not. Do the dogs have it? Maybe they wanted to watch something and grabbed the remote before you did. Check their pallets."

The accusations start when he can't find it. "You must have taken it!"

"Why the hell would I take it? Let me check my things to do list. Nope, it doesn't say take the TV remote today and hide it from my husband!" My husband becomes more aggravated.

His anxiety level is rising. I can tell by the tone in his voice. I start laughing. "What's the matter are you too lazy to turn on the TV? Is your finger broken and you can't push the button?"

"No! I'd have to stand there and push the button on that box and I'm not fucking doing that," he retorts angrily.

As the dialogue continues our voices get louder and louder with each response.

The obscenities start again. I stop what *I'm* doing because cooking and laundry are not important. I dash into the living room, throw the pillows around, and dig out the remote, which is buried in the couch where he fell asleep last night while watching TV!

More expletives!

"You're lucky to have me!" I snap as I stare at him in disbelief.

He looks at me sheepishly and mutters, "Sorry. I love you babe."

There are only two of us and the dogs. You would think it would be easy to keep track of an object that is two inches in width and eight inches long. Tired of this conversation, I purchased a small wooden box that sits on the coffee table and spins. It holds remotes for the TV and ceiling fan. I even folded up the cable guide and put a pad and pen in the box. Yet my husband can still never seem to locate any of these items.

The remote protrudes proudly from the wood box, like a precious piece of sculpture. It is one of the most important items in the house. The way technology is progressing, it will soon be obsolete. *Alexa*, *Amazon Echo* and other wireless products that I would need the help of a millennial to figure out, have already flooded the market. I couldn't imagine my husband working a television without a remote. While he would love the voice activation, it's when something goes wrong that he would not be able to deal with as it would require reading the instruction manual.

When we are not looking for the television remote, we are trying to figure out how to use it! The cable company mailed their subscribers a nice color booklet detailing all the new features when they upgraded their system. The brochure and cost to mail it is probably the reason why the cable company had to raise their rates!

Inside there is an enlarged photo of the remote, which takes up the entire page! The wonders of this small piece of equipment are highlighted. Its operation is explained in simplistic detail. Like one of the ancient wonders of the world the remote control has a special booklet dedicated to its operation.

I could care less. The new reading material is in the credenza. I don't have time to read it. I just want to know how to turn the TV on and off and change the channels. And I do!

My husband didn't read the new brochure. He doesn't need a manual; therefore, he is always pushing the wrong buttons. He sits in silence because he once again has touched the incorrect button and wants me to come and get rid of the huge wall of snow that crackles across the giant fifty-two-inch screen.

"I think we should leave it as is," I laugh. "It's art. I'll just turn the fucking sound down. We'll call it, *Refusal to Read Instruction Manual.*"

"Can you just fix it without all the fuckin' sarcasm," he demands.

I take the remote. "What the hell were you doing anyway... why do you insist on touching all the damn buttons...what do you mean you wanted to look at the TV guide...do you need glasses... can't you see this...it's the red button that is marked *guide*...how could you miss that...it's red...it's the only *red* button on the damn thing... "

"We should go back to the buying the TV Guide. Those were the good ol' days. It came in the mail and was so much easier," he reminisces.

"So you think the good old days consisted of limited channels, rabbit ears twisted like minimalist sculptures that Alexander Calder would find disturbing, antenna's decorating roof tops, and the TV guide?"

Alexander Calder was a 20th century sculptor who worked in wire. He was a mechanical engineer turned artist and known for his mobiles. Some of his artistic creations were powered by air or motors. Other life size out door pieces were constructed with metal.

"My mother still has one of those old TV antennas on her roof."

I feel my eyes widen in amazement as my husband talks about TV antennas and life in his father's television repair shop and the business of repairing televisions and antennas.

When we went to Pennsylvania to visit his mother, the first thing I noticed looming above, like a giant wire sculpture attached to the roof of her house, was an actual TV antenna.

"What? Is she sending signals to NASA? It's huge!" No other houses in the quiet suburban neighborhood even had a television antenna. "Doesn't she know what cable TV is?"

My husband's lips tightened in annoyance as I continued to ramble on about the ancient technology, cable television, and the reason for the trip – to pick up a ladder and some other items because she was going to finally clean the house!

I take a photo of the antenna on my iPhone and immediately sent it to my girlfriend. Seconds later my phone beeps at the incoming text message, "Where the hell are you? What the *fuck* it that?"

An hour later my husband is in a heated argument with his mother. He stormed back to the truck where he and his best friend start unloading the stuff they had just piled into the truck bed. His mother had changed her mind. She wants the sixty-year-old generator back. The aluminum ladder was next followed by other stuff!

I feel the blood rushing through my limbs, as I fumed with anger. "What the fuck did we come all the way up here for? Why does she need another ladder? She is walking around with a cane, she can barely move. How the hell is she going to operate that old generator?"

My husband slowly turned toward me. The veins in his neck were popping. His face was red and he was rubbing his forehead. I could feel the fury and frustration radiating from his skin. At that moment I knew it was going to be a long ride home and we would be stopping for lots of coffee. "She wants the ladder because you never know when she is going to need to go on the roof! "Fuh-ged-da-boud-it," he snaps. "Put the dogs in the truck and we're leaving!"

I throw up my hands, start gesturing furiously, and began rambling. "Go on the roof! And do what, adjust that fucking antennae? Why can't she just get cable television like everyone else in the neighborhood?"

"I told you my father owned a TV repair shop and there was no way he would ever pay for cable TV. See that house over there," he pointed to the house across the street. "They were the first to get cable on the block and my father was adamant he would not be paying for cable."

I shook my head in disgust about the rejection of progress. My husband once again recalled the few channels he watched growing up. "And if we were lucky we could catch an additional Philly station. If the weather was just right, we moved the antennae."

"Move the fuckin' antennae?" I asked. "This is ridiculous. I can't even believe I am having this conversation with you. What is your mother going to do - go on the roof to deal with the antennae…she is almost eighty years old are you kidding me…go on the roof with her cane…she can barely climb up three steps to enter the house…how is she going do all this…I freely admit my family had issues…hell…I have and uncle who went to jail…but this…this is just plain, fucking insanity…why can't she just get cable TV…does she really think she is going to take out that twenty foot aluminum ladder and climb on the roof…"

CHAPTER 42

Calling the Cable Company

My husband interrupts our reminiscing. "Didn't you get the TV guide in your house? He snaps. We should subscribe."

"Seriously," I laugh. I cross my arms, cock my head to the side and I give him my "Alice Look." "Fuh-ged-da-boud-it! You can't even read the remote, you need glasses, but refuse to go to the eye doctor. How the hell are you going to read the TV Guide? In fact, I don't even know if they make the TV Guide anymore!"

My husband offers a solution. "They should just make the remote control bigger and I wouldn't have these problems."

Unfortunately, the argument about the remote is all too familiar to me. When my father was forced to get cable TV he could not use the remote either. He was always calling for someone to help him fix the TV because he touched something on the remote, or couldn't understand why the VCR had to be set to channel three to view a movie.

Amidst all the yelling, arguing, swearing, and slamming of doors sat the television, like a surreal piece of sculpture. It was the catalyst for the relentless bickering between my parents, the "irrational matter."

I was always amazed how such a simple electronic device could launch such commotion and apprehension in one household.

My father was *always* watching TV. He was a fan of the news, westerns, and history shows. I distinctly can recall the deep voice of the narrator of those war documentaries...

"During the bombing of...the heavy artillery...it was those men that sacrificed their lives..."

War; it was the theme that permeated our house growing up.

We watched other families fight too – on television. Of all the shows he watched, the one he viewed religiously was *All in the Family*. Archie Bunker was his hero. Decades later, when he was forced to get cable, he sat and watched re-runs of every episode.

Keeping with tradition, it should come as no surprise that the television is the source of constant disagreements in our house as well. We had five TV's when we first got married. After we started re-modeling the house, to keep up with technology, they were eventually replaced by one television. It was a fifty-two-inch, flat screen television, which is located in the living room.

One of the five TV's was in the bedroom. To save space we mounted the television to the wall, like they do in the hospital. It seemed like a good idea when my husband suggested it but after a while it looked too institutional. The mirror on the dresser of the new furniture was so big that the TV had to go. My husband was devastated. He did try to re-organize the space to fit a TV but to no avail.

I was happy. No TV in the bedroom equaled no eating in the bed!

He just re-located to the living room and the TV is on constantly.

We don't even have children and the television is on in our house all the time. I watch the news in the morning before I leave for work. My husband gets up, has coffee, and watches TV with the dogs. And if he is outside in the yard or in the shed, the television stays on until he goes to work.

It gets turned off for about two hours until I arrive home and turn it back on to watch the news. In addition to the news, I am a fan of the following shows: Grey's Anatomy, True Blood, Scandal, and Dancing with the Stars. NFL football games are not included in this count. NFL Sunday is the only day the TV should stay on all day.

My husband watches enough television that he can recall the list of channels on the cable lineup without even looking at it. "Can you put the weather on for a minute?" I ask.

He takes the remote and clicks right to the channel. This he is never wrong about. Like a cipher, he finally decoded the remote. The encrypting process occurred while home watching TV.

Then tragedy struck. The new cable channel lineup was printed and mailed to us. There are five columns of channels on both sides of the paper, all color-coded to signify the cable package that you are fortunate enough to be able to afford.

"Why can't we have the NFL package?"

"Because we can't afford it. Or we can cancel the cable and order the dish. And for us we will probably have to have more satellite dishes because of all the damn trees on our property…did you see how ridiculous our neighbors house looks…he has five satellite dishes on his property…it looks terrible…I don't want our house looking we're transmitting to Mars…and who has time to watch seven hundred fuckin' channels anyway?"

My mother made sure my brothers and I did not watch too much television when we were growing up. When she wasn't arguing with my father about the television, she was yelling at us to turn off the TV and do our homework.

In retrospect, I think, what the hell did we have to watch anyway? It's not like there was a lot to view with so few channels and networks. What the hell was she thinking?

And now, when I call her, she is either watching TV or asking me if I saw a certain show. Sometimes she calls or sends me a text message telling me to turn on the television to look at something on a particular program. We laugh as I remind her that *she* is watching *too* much TV!

Television has gotten so complex that anytime there is a problem, my husband, refuses to handle it.

White snow now requires a call to the cable company, so they can trouble shoot the problem. You would think this would be easy. Just thinking about it causes my husband's blood pressure to increase. One afternoon he pushed the wrong button on the remote control. He actually called me at work to ask what he should do.

My boss was aggravated because I answered my cell phone while we were in a meeting, thinking it was an emergency. My only salvation is that she understood all too well because her husband does the same idiotic crap. "Call the cable company the number is right on the channel guide," I hissed into the phone. I am prepared not to have a working television when I get home. My boss further instructed me to complain to the FCC if I don't get satisfaction.

After dinner, I dial the 1-800 number to start the process. After hitting a multitude of prompts and being kept on hold due to "high call volume," which is basically every time you call, I finally got to speak to a live person. My husband will simply hang up and start all over again if he can't understand the person on the other end. We waste more time verifying who I am by confirming, address, phone number, and account information even though I have already spoken and typed the account number when I first made the call.

I repeat firmly and slowly, "It says, 'No Signal,' in the haze of white snow," to the employee on the other end of the line who is lucky if he is making ten dollars an hour.

"Did you unplug this wire…is the cable wire plugged in… turn the TV on… turn the remote off…turn it back on…"

"Yes, yes, yes…all you need to do is shoot the signal, just reboot!" I know what to do and I don't even work for the damn cable company!

I'm aggravated. I have had a long day at work. I am tired and now I'm moving heavy furniture back and forth, so I can reach the wires. I have spent forty minutes on the phone because some entry level customer service representative can't read the instructions on how to trouble shoot the most basic of all cable technical difficulties. I am also pissed at my husband because he is at work and left this for me to handle. While I'm on hold, I send him a text message indicating my annoyance. I end it with, "You're lucky to have me. You're not a fucking bachelor anymore!"

Ten minutes later I send him another text message, "I am still on hold. You're not a fucking bachelor anymore. Stop touching buttons on the remote. I'm not calling the cable company again, next time you have to deal with this!"

Thirty minutes later I send him another text, "You have the NFL package for six months at no charge, courtesy of the cable company for their ineptness to solve the problem in a timely manner." As if he needs *more* television shows to watch!

The sports package invaded our home like locusts. Since it arrived into our home, it has commandeered the television. The day starts with one of the multitude of ESPN channels or the NFL channel; program after program of statistics, reviews of games, team and player controversies, reruns of past and recent games cycle all day long.

When I come home from work and hit the on button for the TV, the last channel watched appears – the NFL channel or ESPN. My husband should be a sports commentator the way he watches the sports package. He watches the sports channels like my father watched the movie *The Godfather*, over and over and over again. So this behavior isn't new to me.

The Godfather, a film released in 1972, followed by Godfather II (1974) and Godfather III (1990) details the life of a New York crime family, mafia bosses and their rise to power. Marlon Brando, Al Pacino, James Caan, Robert DeNiro, Robert Duvall, Kiane Keaton, Talia Shire, and John Cazale are just some of the actors who brought the iconic characters to life.

Ironically, I am not upset by this pattern; instead I am intrigued because he is watching the same games and repeat shows over and over. I asked him about this and he explained that he doesn't want to miss any new updates or news.

"But it's the same stories. This is a repeat," I replied, pointing to the current program.

"I just don't want to miss anything."

I reminded him that if he had an iPhone like me he could just click on the NFL app and have access to the latest updates all day long! I smiled as I grabbed my phone and clicked on the application. I recite news about players, injuries, and team stats that he has *yet* to hear because there is a commercial break on the television. On Sundays I take this a step further by announcing scores while we watch other games. I pull up schedules and other information with the touch of a finger.

Frustrated, at yet another commercial interruption, he yelled, "*Let* me see that fucking thing."

He gets the "Alice Look," as I handed him the device. I knew exactly what was coming next and I waited for him to hand the iPhone back to me. "I can't read this fucking thing...the print is too small."

Using his two hundred-dollar glasses is out of the question. Navigating through three fields on one lens is a problem. I hand him his three-dollar glasses from Wal-Mart and the iPhone and remind him that he's lucky to have me and that he better not get too comfortable with the NFL package because once the promo is over we are not renewing it! "YOU'RE NOT A FUCKING BACHELOR ANYMORE!"

CHAPTER 43

Changing the Oil

I paid over forty dollars for an oil change and my husband was livid.

"You're not fucking single anymore…. you're married and I could have done that…you talk about me wasting money…and why the hell did you have the damn oil changed?"

"The light came on…"

"What light?" He rudely interrupted.

"The light on the dashboard…it came on and read fifteen-percent…what, do you think the truck is going to run without oil… the engine will seize up…I'm not an idiot…so I took it to the dealership because it was due," I shouted.

My husband gave *me* the "Alice Look" and started screaming. He waved his hands through the air as he questioned my apparent insanity. "The dealership charges you more money. Why the *fuck* did you go there?"

I was in the middle of preparing dinner. I stopped cutting the vegetables for the salad and looked up at him. I thought about it, shrugged, and answered calmly, "I don't know, it's what I was taught to do. My father always went to the dealership."

My husband started with the obscenities regarding dealership high prices and my lack of education on automotive repairs while I put the pieces together as to why I went to the dealership for repairs and then explained to my husband.

"Nobody repaired vehicles at my house. If something was wrong with the car my father was immediately back at the dealership. If *any* light that was not required to be on lit up came on the vehicle went straight back to the dealership. If the oil needed to be changed, an appointment was *immediately* made at the dealership. Vehicle maintenance and any major repair work were *always* done at the dealership. I didn't know any other way. My father was fanatical about car maintenance but entrusted someone else to take care of it. The only thing he did do to care for the vehicles was to wash them.

It was ritualistic, like going to church on Sunday, only it happened on Saturday. The day would start at the convenience store. The "irrational matter" was at it again; it was the same dispute over his coffee and cigarette habit. The sound of the screen door slamming signaled he exited the house. He'd throw the garage door open with such force I thought it would exit right through the roof. The obscenities echoed off the walls of the garage. He didn't seem to care that the entire neighborhood could hear him as he prepared for the weekly ritual of washing and waxing vehicles.

My brothers and I would watch him from my brother's bedroom window. His cigarette dangled from his mouth as the smoke drifted to the second floor. We covered our noses with our t-shirts to avoid the foul and bitter smell.

Spackle buckets lined the driveway. Each bucket was filled with sponges, sprays, cleaners, and rags. There were rags for washing, drying, waxing, buffing, and detailing, which were all in separate buckets. The hose would be neatly positioned so he was able to walk around the entire car with ease.

The vehicles were moved around systematically during the washing, drying, and waxing process.

My brothers and I would eventually run outside to help. He let them wash, dry, wax, and use the hose. The minute I appeared he would stop what he was doing. The water stopped spewing from the hose, which he held in one hand, and he'd take a deep drag from his cigarette and just start screaming. Hands cut through the smoke like a raving maniac.

"Get in the house and clean!" You need to fuckin' vacuum… when you're done get up to the bathroom and clean the fucking bathroom. One day you're going to be married…"

Vacuum, cleaning, marriage were the only words in the sentence that were not obscenities!

I'd run inside before he could finish, slamming the door. The tears streamed down my face as I pushed the vacuum angrily around the living room floor.

"That's why I go to the dealership," I finished quietly.

The blood drains from my husband's face as he gains more insight from my dysfunctional childhood.

Three thousand miles later, the truck was on two ramps in our driveway. The car was next, followed by friend's vehicles, and then my mother's beloved Lincoln Continental.

"Does he know what he's doing?" Whispered my mother as she stared at her Lincoln in various stages of repair in our driveway. I shot my mother the "Alice Look," smiled and calmly stated, "He received his degree at Jiffy Lube where he used to work, which qualifies him to be an auto mechanic!"

"Are you kidding me?" She hissed, now irritated.

Tools and tires were strewn about and he was covered in grease. The compressor roared as he removed another tire. "I could have taken it to the dealership," she offered.

"I know, but he doesn't want you to waste money. Don't worry, Mom, it will be ok. He knows what he is doing. Let's go to the Wawa and get him some coffee."

The routine continued as the vehicles reached the three-thousand-mile mark.

During one of the oil changing sessions the CFO in me took over. I added up the cost of oil, filters, and additives and figured, going to the dealership or the convenient oil change retailer down the street, was just about the same price. If you had a coupon it was an added bonus!

My husband had been fooling around with the vehicles all morning and into the afternoon. He had made several trips to the auto parts store for various items, because he ran into a problem with one of the cars. On the way home from one of the trips, he stopped to get more coffee, which he super-sized because he was aggravated. When the day was over, he was covered in grease and there was a big bucket of old oil that he now had to dispose of sitting in the driveway.

I give him the "Alice Look."

I knew I sounded like my mother or this time it was more like Ethel Merman as she is yelling at Dick Shawn, who played her son Sylvester Marcus in the movie *It's a Mad Mad Mad Mad World* when the argument began, but I didn't care. And I didn't care who heard me as I stood screaming in the driveway.

It's a Mad, Mad Mad, Mad World, was a movie released in 1963. People driving on a highway stop to help Jimmy Durante, who is injured and dying. He tells the group that there is a fortune hidden under the big "W." Sid Caesar, Jonathan Winters, Mickey Rooney, Buddy Hackett, Milton Berle leave the scene and secretly decide to try and find the money. Various forms of transportation, meltdowns and frustrations are met as other characters are pulled into the rush to find the money first. Ethel Merman plays the obnoxious, loud-mouth, mother-in-law who convinces her daughter and son-in-law, who were at the scene of the accident in the beginning of the movie to find the money before the others do. Other cast members including Dick Shawn, Jim Backus, Arnold Stang, Jerry Lewis, Buster Keaton and more have roles or cameos as they become involved in the quest for the money as the story unfolds.

"What is wrong with you...look at this mess...this has taken all day...what a waste of time...it's easier just to go somewhere and have the oil changed...and what the hell are you going to do with all that fucking oil...we don't have a container to put it in...how do you think you are going to transport that to the recycling site without spilling it...". The front door slammed behind me. It was too late to go out to eat as planned so I retreated to the kitchen to start dinner. Shortly thereafter I heard yelling followed by more obscenities and ran back to the front door.

In his frustration he had thrown a wrench across the driveway, which skillfully landed in the bucket of oil, which in turn splashed all over the windows and brand-new siding!

My next oil change was at the dealership and it was just as well as the winter months were upon us. And, as predicted, it was a cold winter, too cold to be changing oil in the driveway. I told my husband I'd find a coupon and he could take his car to one of the places up the street that does oil changes. He was out the door before I could give him the coupon. He returned home an hour later and handed me the bill. What followed my husband is reluctant to discuss. If you ask him about it, he'll say he doesn't remember.

I, however, am happy to remind him. I glanced at the bill and immediately turned into the "irrational matter."

"Sixty dollars?" I screamed as I threw the bill on the table. "Fuh-ged-da-boud-it. This is ludicrous! Where the fuck did you go, to the Mercedes dealership? What the hell is wrong with you? Didn't you ask how much it was going to cost, and you have the nerve to yell at me for taking my truck to the dealership? In fact, do you know how much I just paid at the dealership?"

I pulled the receipt from the file cabinet and slammed the drawer. "Twenty-two dollars and I am entitled to a free oil change for my next visit!"

He was sick about the whole incident. It was his fault; he wasn't paying attention, and when he pulled up to the auto place someone just came out and took the car. He didn't ask about the price because he never thought it would cost that much money.

"You're not a fucking bachelor anymore!"

CHAPTER 44

Defeated by Technology

It was the first time I'd ever seen my husband disgusted over the price he paid for a simple oil change. The second time was during my last few visits to the dealership for my routine oil change.

I phoned him while he was at work and I told him all the things that were wrong with the truck, as was written on the *free* multi point inspection report the technician handed to me. "New tires, brake fluid, transmission fluid, tire rotation, Hepa filter, transmission flush, rear differential fluid, new battery…"

He interrupted me before I could finish his deep voice boomed so loudly through the cell phone that everyone in the waiting room could hear him, "Damn it! You don't need any of that! I can do all of it and I'll take care of it this weekend…just get the oil changed… this is how they make money…just get the fucking oil changed and I'll take care of the rest…"

An argument ensues about the battery. I start crying. "But they said my battery is going to die! I'm not going to make it home. What if I get stuck?"

More obscenities from my husband who ends the conversation with, "Fuh-ged-da-boud-it! You're not going to that fucking place anymore. This is the last time. Get that fucking oil changed and come home! You're not a fucking *bachelorette* anymore!"

On the weekend my husband did most of the work himself. Because he was so aggravated with my experience at the dealership he wasn't paying attention and he drained the brand new oil instead of one of the other fluids! More money wasted.

I am once again no longer human as I start screaming in the driveway, "I'm getting rid of the truck...It's too expensive to maintain...you can't just make repairs like you are used too... it's all digital...you have to put it on the lift...I can't believe you drained out all of that fucking that oil..."

He blamed the problem on the manual and lack of detailed directions.

My hands whipped through my hair as I grabbed my head in disbelief. "Manual? Now that's a joke. You're actually reading it? Ugh," I exclaimed as I retreated into the house. The slamming of the front door echoed behind me.

My brother, who lives in Nevada, called to see what we are doing. He tried to console my husband and they reminisced about the 'good old days' when you could actually repair a car. He drives a Mercedes and he hates it because every time something breaks the repair bill is at least one thousand dollars!

Months later, his wife traded the Mercedes car in for a Mercedes SUV! He was livid. All he could think about is the repair bill and the frustration of driving it. There are too many buttons to push and everything is digital.

Further, like my husband, he too is directionally challenged. Getting from point A to B can be stressful if you drive with them. The last thing either of them needs is a vehicle that has all sorts of control buttons!

My husband reminds me that *he* is not a fucking bachelor anymore and that *I* will not be taking the truck back to the dealership!

I crossed my arms and glared. The all too familiar "Alice Look" and stance is instinctive and thanks to my husband is officially programed into the fiber of my being. "Ok, then who is going to repair the new crack that is traveling across the front windshield? I'm not driving around like this; I need to see when I'm driving. What if it cracks and breaks while I'm driving?"

My husband laughs, "Babe, I can assure you it won't happen, and if you hadn't turned on the defroster, you wouldn't have a longer crack. Now you're being ridiculous."

The crack started on the passenger side but during the winter expanded across the entire windshield when I turned on the defroster. Why did I turn it on? To defrost the window! I didn't know it was going to happen. But I needed to see out the window during the storm, so I thought turning on the defroster was the rational thing to do. Apparently not!

Down the shore in New Jersey there is no highway for trucks to travel until you reach exit 98 and pick up I-195 in Belmar or go over the bridge and hop on the Turnpike. As a result, trucks can drive on the southern part of the Garden State Parkway. Why do I even mention this? Because it is the reason why I have had to replace windshields on vehicles. The damage a small pebble can do is costly. The windshield needs to be replaced before I get a ticket. The cost of the windshield for the truck was over five hundred dollars. At least we had insurance.

My husband again reminded me that I would not be taking the truck back to the dealership!

I ignored him and call the insurance company then make arrangements for someone to come and replace the glass while I'm at work. I still needed one hundred dollars to pay the deductible. The glass technician says the crack wasn't too bad and I could have waited to replace the windshield. He gives me a lesson about the thickness and strength of automobile glass.

My husband was livid when I told him and now blamed me for wasting money we don't have!

Three weeks later, on my way to work, another stone hit the new windshield!

Four months later, an impatient driver of a dump truck pulls out of the gas station in front of me, I swerve to avoid an accident, but not before getting hit with pebbles that are pelting the vehicle like hail. I won't even tell my husband about this; it can wait until winter when I turn on the defroster.

The following day my husband enters the house demanding to know what happen to the windshield.

This is a man who can't locate a bottle of ketchup or mayonnaise in the refrigerator, but a nick, smaller than the size of a gnat he can spot! I just don't get it!

"You're not a fucking bachelorette anymore," screams my husband after I tell him what happened. "That doesn't have to be repaired now. And don't even think about going to the dealership," he shouts before retreating to his shed.

Months later, I receive a frantic call from him while I am at work. His car won't start. I tell him to have it towed down the street.

He refused because it will cost money.

Incensed, I snapped, "This is why we have AAA, so you can either call them or ride your bike thirty miles to work."

I don't remember what was wrong and don't care to look at the receipt because I won't understand it all anyway. All I know is that it cost $1,082.99! No sooner was this bill paid off, it was followed by another repair. "Fuckin' state and the damn potholes," ranted my husband as he handed the credit card to the technician. "What the hell are we paying taxes for…why can't they fix that hole."

"If you know it's there why can't you drive around it," I laugh. Secretly I know he can't see it because it *must* be invisible just like when he is looking for something in the refrigerator and it is staring at him in the face.

There would be additional repairs due to pothole damage, age and salt erosion. Which all led to the grand finale, of repair costs all because some part broke and he fixed it by drilling into the catalytic converter.

I scratched my head in disbelief and give him the "Alice Look" and stance. "You're joking, right?"

He proceeded to give me the technical reasons why he made the repair this way and why it would work.

While he was talking, I grabbed my iPhone, googled it, and then proceed to give him the technical reviews as to how ridiculous his repair solution was!

He scowled at the technology in my hand, despising the gadget because there was really nothing he can say at this moment; loathing its ability to provide quick and accurate information at a moment's notice. It is never far from my reach.

I glared back, the sarcasm apparent in my voice, "Who the fuck is going to pay for this repair? We don't have the money for another vehicle. This is ridiculous! Who does shit like this? You better get underneath that car and figure out how to repair it because you're not taking it to the dealership!"

Time and technology were my husband's enemies. The Ford Taurus and Honda Ridgeline both had to go back to the dealership. The digital technology was beyond his capability to repair. I applauded his attempts to repair both. He actually looked at the video and ordered the parts to fix the tailgate of the truck. The tailgate opens two ways: out and down. One of the cables and latches had broken. I was prepared to take the truck to the dealership, but my husband insisted he was going to repair it.

The cable was easy enough, but that latch, it was a different story. It required removing the entire back panel. There were lot of screws and parts. Hours later he came inside looking for a plastic bag for all the parts. He drove to the tire and lube shop down the street, which thankfully a technician was able to repair it.

He returned home defeated. "I'm done. What happened to the cars and trucks you could just go and fix with ease?"

"They're in the junk yards across America," I replied sarcastically.

"You need an engineering degree, just to look at the shit some of these vehicles have." He starts reminiscing about the good old days. "We fixed cars in my driveway it was so easy... and back when I worked at Jiffy Lube..."

I refuse to listen about his glory days of the past. As I got up from the couch I threw a pillow at him. I tell him I love him and he is getting too old to be moving ramps, dragging the compressor and other equipment to the driveway to work on the vehicles. "Just take the cars down the street to get the oil changed." I finished with, "You're lucky to have me. YOU'RE NOT A FUCK-ING BACHELOR ANYMORE. Please stop messing with the vehicles."

CHAPTER 45

Directionally Challenged

My husband put the key into the ignition and the truck engine roared to life. "Can you tell me the directions?"

I gave him the "Alice look." "Seriously, like you're going to remember. Let's go. Why are we still sitting here?"

"Tell me how to get to where we're going," he demanded.

"Fuh-ged-da-boud-it."

I laughed. In 1989 I received a scholarship to study in Italy. I was mailed airline tickets with an itinerary listing the address of my host family and the day and time to report to the University of Perugia. I packed a backpack, was driven to JFK, and flew to Rome. Once in Rome, it was *my* responsibility to get to Perugia. There were no directions, no train schedules, no iPhones with foreign language translating app's. Nobody cared how I arrived as long as it was on time and I was speaking the Italian language. When school ended, I traveled around Europe.

Laughing, I reminded my husband how my sense of direction is so much better than his by recalling this part of my life and finished with, "We're driving to my mother's an hour away, a place you have been many times, and you still want to know which way to go. Don't you see how ridiculous this sounds?"

Knowing he's directionally challenged, I still laughed.

"Ok, Ok, you had your fun; just tell me which road we are fuckin' taking."

"The fuckin' Garden State Parkway. It's the only way from this driveway. It's the only way we ever go. What the fuck is the problem?" I asked.

Instead of tokens, the center console was jammed packed with quarters. He leaned toward the compartment, checked to make sure we had enough change and grabbed two quarters. The toll to get on the Parkway is currently fifty cents. The entrance to the Parkway is four miles from our house. He will hold the money in his hand until we get to the toll.

"Why do you need to have the money in your hand now? We haven't even left the driveway," I snapped; my irritation was all too clear. The single act transported me back to the two-toned, brown paneled station wagon driving with my father. Ugh! More madness. It's the same shit my father did!

What is worse, as the years have passed, I realized that sometimes I automatically reach for the quarters before he even asks and place them into his waiting hand. The behavior is disturbing, and I desperately try to figure out why I do this or how my husband or my father passed this habit, one I have desperately tried to avoid, on to me. Perhaps it really is imbedded into my DNA.

Fifty cents tucked safely in his hand we finally pull out of the driveway. Two short turns to the corner and we are on Route 9. The dogs and all their stuff are jammed into the back seat. Their stuff includes, an over-sized Posturepedic dog pallet, a cage for the dachshund, more pallets, toys, bedding, their food, both dry and wet, and bowls. Our stuff is in the truck bed tied with bungee cords and anything important is in the trunk.

"Tell them to stop jumping, I can't drive," he shouted angrily.

I turned and spoke soothing words to them. "It's ok, precious babies."

The sound of the blinker caused me to twist forward swiftly. My eyes widen in shock as he makes a left turn. Less than thirty seconds on the road and we are stopping.

"Why the *fuck* are we stopping?" I asked. "I already put gas in the truck."

"I need to get coffee," he said easily.

"*Coffee*! You just had *coffee*," I yelled as I banged on the dashboard. The dogs started barking.

"Do you want coffee?" he asked calmly.

I crossed my arms in front of my chest. Glaring, I gave him the "Alice Look." "No," I snapped, shaking my head in disbelief.

When he returned to the truck, he grabbed the quarters and wanted me to repeat the directions.

"Why? You're not going to remember. Just get on the Parkway and I'll tell you once we get near the exit."

The key turned in the ignition. "If I had a Garmin we wouldn't have to go through all this," he retorted.

The dogs resumed barking.

The traffic pattern in New Jersey is always changing, as there is construction everywhere. In fact, I can't remember a time when there hasn't been some sort of construction taking place. Detours, orange cones, or monstrous yellow construction vehicles fill the Parkway, the Turnpike, I-287, Route 280 and other major highways and roads in the state. Construction - it's part of the fabric of New Jersey.

"It's not like this in Pennsylvania. I want my Garmin back," he fumed.

"If you had the Garmin, you would get re-routed and then you'd be lost. Then what?"

He laughed, "That's why I have you."

I reminded him about the time he got lost going to Pennsylvania, where he grew up. Knowing it's not a good subject, I bring it up anyway. "Who gets lost going to a place they grew up?"

He turned the volume on the radio up signaling the conversation is over.

Once my husband knows the directions to get somewhere it is the *only* way he will travel. For example, there are many ways to get to my mother's house, but we will only go the way *he* is familiar with. Like a squirrel, who maps out his territory, my husband refuses to travel a different route. If there is a detour, his anxiety increases. The yelling starts, the dogs begin barking, and once again, I am reminded of those trips in the car on the Garden State Parkway and stuck in traffic as my father screamed at my mother about getting lost, tolls, and other nonsensical stuff.

My mother's voice echoes in my head - *life comes full circle*. Predictions we ignored and still refuse to accept are disturbingly present.

When there is a detour, I immediately grab my iPhone and turn on the Waze App, locate our position, and start giving directions. Pulling over to get directions is out of the question. Reading signs or asking someone for directions is not an option.

"I want my fuckin' Garmin. I want another Garmin for Christmas," he shouted as he followed the detour signs; adding, "I don't even know where we are."

I laughed. "We are still in New Jersey. You're not lost yet."

The obscenities begin...

I thought about the Garmin and wondered how we lost it and where it could be in our seventeen hundred square foot house. I had no idea.

I give him credit. It's not easy driving in New Jersey. Navigating the highways has become more difficult. It is as if you are an actual participant in a giant video game. In addition to the constant construction, detours, signs, relentless potholes, there are more people – more people who are not only driving erratically but are engaging in a host of activities while they are in traffic or driving.

"Look at these fuckin' people," my husband shouted. "They're on the phone, applying make-up, reading, eating, and texting. This is insane!"

Suddenly something hit the windshield. "Fuck! *Another* stone. This fucking road; where the fuck did that stone come from? You see this shit?" He growled as he pointed to the potholes. "This is what our tax dollars are paying for, holes in the fuckin' road!"

The windshield already had three cracks from other stones. "My husband continued his rant. "Fuckin' state."

I suggested he call and complain to the Governor's office. "I work two jobs. I don't have time," he scowled.

This will be the third, no maybe fourth or fifth windshield I will need to replace on the truck.

It started to rain, and I turned on the defroster and heat. In the next instant, the crack in the windshield started expanding from the driver's side to the passenger side.

"Fuck," I screamed. The lines were moving across the window as fast as a spider spinning a web.

"It's your fault. You *had* to turn the heat on," he hollered. "I told you about using that defroster when there are cracks in the windshield."

The windshield now resembled an abstract painting. "That's what people do when they are cold, put the heat on."

The dogs continued barking.

I glance at my husband and start laughing. He is sitting straight up and gripping the steering wheel so tight you can see the whites of his knuckles. His anxiety is mounting and for a minute I see my father and the station wagon. My husband wants to know what is so funny.

"Nothing, I was just thinking about driving in the station wagon with my father and brothers as kids, the traffic, the pile of tokens, there were more toll booths and no cameras."

He is concentrating and doesn't want to hear anymore. Suddenly obscenities and honking horns around us are activated by something unseen ahead.

We reached the Asbury Park toll Plaza and there was a line of cars. Nobody was moving, and we were in the exact change lane. I peered over the dashboard to see if I could see anything.

The truck inches forward.

My husband pounded on the steering wheel. "Fuckin' idiot. Look at this guy, he is getting out of the car and yelling!" Horns started blaring. My husband joined in thinking if he blasted his horn we would start moving faster. "What the fuck does this guy think he is doing?"

More madness.

I stretched my neck and see the guy throwing money at the toll basket and proudly saluting the tollbooth with the Jersey Bird. Ignoring the blaring horns, he returned to his vehicle and sped off.

"Ha, he's on camera. I bet he gets a ticket in the mail," I laughed.

The one hour and thirty-minute trip to my mothers in North Jersey took over two hours due to construction at Exit 144. Like snails, we crawled to exit 145. We could have gotten off at exit 144, but because my husband has never traveled that way before he wasn't going to chance it.

"I grew up around here; I can tell you the way," I argued.

"This is the last time we are traveling on the holidays. If someone wants to visit they can come to our house."

275

"We have dogs, and everyone is allergic," I interrupted.

"I don't give a fuck! Do you not see this fuckin traffic? I must be out of my mind. Look at this shit! Get me the change for the next toll," he shouted.

My cell phone rang. It was my mother she wanted to know where we were and why we were late. I reluctantly explained.

She sighed heavily. "What is wrong with you? Why didn't you just get off at Exit 144 and come up South Orange Avenue? You would have been here already!"

Everyone in New Jersey has a theory on what is the best day and time to leave their house to avoid the traffic on the Garden State Parkway. If you want to get anywhere fast, leaving in the middle of the night probably works best. I wasn't going to suggest that to my husband as he had his own ideas. To get back to south Jersey and beat the traffic my husband's plan was to leave early in the morning. After coffee, breakfast; walking the dogs, changing light bulbs and other stuff for my mother, more coffee and packing the truck, we departed promptly in the middle of the afternoon.

"What the fuck is all this?" He screamed, as we hit the East Orange Toll Plaza. I absently placed the change in his out stretched hand.

"Don't worry it's just the merge," I quietly announced.

"Five or six lanes of traffic attempting to go north or south… this is insanity…why is the exact change light blinking…nobody is moving…look at that bastard, he's cutting across every lane… this is fuckin nuts," he exclaimed.

Visions of my father and the station wagon once again flash through my brain.

Horns blast, and if you dare look at the other irate drivers, hand gestures including the *Jersey Bird* are guaranteed to follow.

"This is one of the joyous times in our life," remarked my husband as he navigated through the cluster of cars all trying to merge into one lane. "Who the fuck designed this? Five lanes merging into one! We don't have shit like this in Pennsylvania."

I'm tired. It's been a long weekend. "Just take your time; at least we are moving."

"You're right, honey, it's moving nicely," he replied sarcastically. A rowdy group of Harleys' won't stand for the poor highway design and created additional lanes in between the cars. They revved their engines behind us as we went through the tunnel. The noise was earsplitting and irritated everyone. The dogs growl and bark loudly and the obscenities from my husband resume.

"Fuckin' jerk!" My husband yelled at the bikes and cars that cut him off. "Fuckin' state! Who the hell authorizes construction on a holiday weekend?"

He's right. Who schedules construction on a holiday weekend? It's absurd. But I grew up here. I'm accustomed to it. I guess it wouldn't be New Jersey without it.

Construction vehicles and materials…orange cones…detour signs…angry motorists…traffic…sitting on the garden State Parkway and crawling at a snail's pace…and God forbid if one person has an accident…the crawl becomes a complete standstill… it's part of the landscape just like the trees that line the sides of the roadways.

When you live in New Jersey you become used to it…daily life is planned around traffic…either going to work or on trip…it is a normal as having a cup of coffee in the morning.

"Don't forget we are going to New York next weekend," I calmly remind him.

"Oh no. You can fuh-ged-da-boud-it," If you think I'm driving back up here. Take the train, bus but I'm not going."

I can't blame him. Driving from south to north Jersey and then into New York city, can be a challenge. I immediately blame E-ZPass. Since its inception an actual person can only be found in the CASH ONLY lane. To get to the CASH ONLY lane you must cut across multiple lanes and you never know what lane is going to be designated as CASH ONLY. Drivers are expected to have exact change or E-ZPass. My husband reminds me to just sign up for E-ZPass. I refuse.

As the CFO of the house I have enough bills and mail to scrutinize and don't need something else to review, wondering if we were overcharged. In addition, the DNA I inherited from my father and grandfather is alive and well. My grandfather would take the back roads before he'd pay the toll and having something like E-ZPass, well the government was watching. I could hear his voice, in broken Italian and English as he expressed worry after worry about life.

I have never cheated the New Jersey toll system. But still get notices in the mail for failure to pay.

"Failure to pay! The tray in my truck is overflowing with quarters, I'm on the Parkway every day, it's how I travel to work," I explain to the customer service representative. "I have no intention of cheating the toll system."

He tells us the technology is perfect and never fails.

"If the state is going to charge for use of the highway, then they should have functioning equipment and someone there to collect the money," my husband tells him during one of my complaint calls. I started taking pictures of the sign not registering THANK YOU after I threw the money into the basket.

If there were people working in the booth, we wouldn't have these problems and my husband wouldn't be cutting across the highway looking for the CASH ONLY booth.

I glanced at my husband and I'm once again transported back in time to driving in the station wagon with my father. Just like my father he is holding the steering wheel tightly with both hands and leaning forward. Red face and bulging veins from his head signified his blood pressure had risen drastically. He was weaving in and out of traffic. It was like he was driving on a racetrack. The tolls are just a pit stop. He started complaining about the tolls.

"Another fuckin' seventy-five cents. This is bullshit," he ranted as he threw the quarters into the basket. When the sign doesn't register PAID THANK YOU, he smashes his palm at the steering wheel and the horn blasts for almost a minute.

"Do you really think blasting the horn will make that sign change," I shouted over the dogs, who, started barking.

His tirade continued as we sped back into traffic. "It's bad enough we live in a state where the taxes are astronomical…we have to pay to commute to work which is another thousand dollars in tolls…just about everything is taxed and now they're talking about adding a tax to gas…we don't have kids and we are living pay check to pay check…I just don't know where the money is going…"

I am not listening. It's the same old story. I grew up listening to my father scream about the same topics. My grandfather, great-grandfather, and generations from decades past all had the same issues in some form or another.

I am not interested in reminding him about medical bills, insurance, car payments, the cable TV bill, cell phones, credit cards, the mortgage, loans, food, dog food, the vet, medication, coffee, or going out to eat. Like a racehorse running around the track, the reasons are crystal clear, and the answers run through my mind easily. The conversation is old and tiring.

"Are you listening to me?" He asks as we approach the next toll.

I smile and calmly stated, "You should pay the toll for the car behind us."

My husband looked at me like I grew ten heads and laughed sarcastically.

"Whaaaat…..have you not heard a fuckin' word I just said. You're fuckin' out of your mind!"

I handed him the toll for two vehicles and smiled. "You have a good life. Pay it forward. Remember the time someone paid my toll? You're not a fucking bachelor anymore, and you can afford it."

And on and on it went…all the way down the Parkway…

CHAPTER 46

Space, Stuff, and Closets

I don't know what is worse: getting married when you're younger when you both have nothing or getting married when you are older when you both have accumulated a multitude of *treasured* items.

I guess there are advantages and disadvantages to both but the only way to solve the argument that will arise about *your* possessions verses *his,* and what things you will be purchasing together and discarding will be to *compromise.*

Planning a wedding was easier then deciding what items of our stuff we were going to keep and what was going to be thrown away. Four TV's, two complete stereo systems, and assortment of furniture, a piano, desk, office supplies, chairs, lamps, kitchen appliances, dishes…and the list went on. We had two or more of everything and neither of us were willing to throw anything away.

My reasoning: my stuff was in better condition and more expensive.

His reasoning: his stuff was just good stuff!

How he thought a couch, which was worn, torn, dilapidated, and stained with years of an assortment of take out cuisine and liquids of unknown origins was still in great condition and clean enough to enter our new home was beyond my comprehension.

Unfortunately, we both suffered permanent damage inflicted by our mothers when it came to the willingness to depart with some of our stuff; his mother, the extreme hoarder, and my mother, an extreme shopper who was also a collector of interesting stuff.

Despite attempts to run away from your past, it seems inescapable, resurfacing at the strangest moments and leaving you to wonder about your own identity. Questions about how it all happened and inner conflicts emerge as you vow not to follow on the same course; nonetheless, it never goes away.

My husband can't stand to watch those television shows about extreme hoarders. It is just too upsetting for him. I don't blame him. It's tragic what a hoarder can do to family members. I feel bad that the scope of the disease is too difficult for him to deal with. It is much easier to forget and retreat into a darker, secluded and safer place; translation, we won't discuss it.

Sometimes I forget this and remind him of his mother's hording tendencies when he arrives home with "great stuff." Stuff he acquired because someone was throwing it out. Trying to convince him we don't need it only starts another conversation, one I have learned is better to avoid.

Clutter is one of my husband's biggest fears. When his mother passed in October of 2015, it was time to face his fear. My husband and I had the pleasure of cleaning out her house.

Once I was over my initial shock, I was determined that we were not going to spend months cleaning. Armed with protective gear, cleansers, and a plan in place, we were done in four days.

Since we don't have a garage or extra storage space, we now have some totes in our hallway with his mother's stuff. My husband's outburst came in January as he complained about the clutter in the house. "You just don't know what this does to me," he shouted as he moved a box in the hallway.

"Really! It's Christmas, the tree is up all the decorations are out, we don't have any closet space," I screamed back at him as I point out various Christmas decorations. Incensed, my rage continued, "What the fuck do you think I am going to do? Start picking through trash, bring it home, and pile it in the house?"

Hands on my hips, I shot him the "Alice Look" and continued laughing because I just don't understand why he doesn't understand my point. "Look, here is your collection of baseball cards, your mother's dishes, her estate paperwork, my artwork, stuff for the taxes, your medical files, Christmas gifts…do you see any trash in the house? Do you see years of moldy food? Do you see newspapers piled to the ceiling?"

He holds up his hands in defeat. "Ok, ok," he laughed. "You're right. I get it. We should look for a bigger house after the holidays."

I summed up my own childhood memories about the overabundance of "stuff," in the house years prior when I was asked to write a magazine article on collectables. I remember chuckling and thinking, no problem this was going to be an easy assignment. The article started out like this:

"A memorable exchange between my parents always has been about the "stuff in the house."

"When are you going to get rid of this stuff?" my father would scream, gesturing toward various piles and cabinets of what he referred to as junk.

"It's not junk," mom retorted.

"Junk, junk, junk…this house is full of junk. Throw it out – you can't use it for anything…" he would continue.

He was referring to Mom's collections of antique dolls, cat and bird figurines, teapots from around the world, cranberry glass, Depression glass, piles of postcards, limited edition plates and an assortment of holiday collectibles.

As I grew older and the house became more cluttered, I vowed that, when I had a place of my own, I was going to live simply."

Fast forward to starting my life with my husband. Here is how my declaration turned out.

My stuff consisted of artwork, teaching lectures and other pedagogical items, a collection of art books that could fill half the wing of the Ocean County library, an electric piano, a computer, over two-hundred owl figurines, baseball cards, coins, canine memorabilia, weight lifting trophies, dishes from Italy, miniature piano figurines and musical items, items from my travels around the world, boxes and boxes of photographs, photography equipment, framed art work, lots of indoor plants, equipment for a variety of recreational activities, an impressive collection of Christmas decorations (collectable items included) and clothing...clothing... and more clothing. I had already moved into our new home and had discarded all my furniture.

His stuff consisted of stereo equipment, recreational items, two holiday ornaments, a bedroom set, a futon, an assortment of mismatched furniture, a weightlifting set, statues of eagles, a deer skin, a variety of stuffed wildlife, and clothing. The rest of it didn't make it near the moving truck.

"Don't even think about putting that dilapidated couch in the truck...throw the food out, its way past the expiration date...we can't eat it...the mattress is going to the dumpster...we'll buy a new one...and what's up with that picture with the dogs smoking cigars and playing cards against a ghastly shade of green...where do you think we are going to put that?"

He smiled excitedly. "This is art, honey. How about in the bedroom?" He joked.

My one girlfriend refers to it as "bachelor art." Don't get me wrong I love all types of art including prints and posters. But, if hung in the right place with the right frame and furniture it would be fine, but our new ranch house did not have a basement, game room, or spare room for this art. Besides, the frame was full of nicks and the picture or rather *poster* was scratched and badly torn.

I ran into one of my colleagues from work on the bike trail one afternoon. She was recently married. I asked how things were going and had she moved into the house with her new husband yet.

Her response, "No, we have too much stuff. There is two of everything and we're having trouble deciding what to keep or rather *he* doesn't want to throw anything out...and then there is this ugly picture of dog's playing cards...where does he think we are going to hang that..."

I couldn't stop laughing.

I told her about our compromise – we bought new furniture, had purchased dishes and silverware, I had all the pots and pans, rotisserie chicken cooker, mixer, and other baking necessities. Recreational items that we were going to use were kept; we designed the living room around the stuffed wildlife.

Every room has been re-done and designed together. We spent countless hours shopping and picking out furniture. The artwork consists mostly of photographs I have taken that represent our life together. Our style is a blend of Italian-Tuscany and log cabin-like. Our friends describe it as warm and cozy.

We kept figurines that blended with our home, gave the rest away and replaced them with different things. A stuffed jack-a-lope greets visitors as they enter the arched doorway into the kitchen. A two-foot moose statue is in the kitchen and utilized as a towel rack. The china, expensive glasses and Capodimonte dishes from Italy are protected in the china cabinet, while a statue of an Italian chef smiles cheerfully from another counter. It's an interesting conversation piece and sort of just blends in with our Italian-Tuscany kitchen. It sounds eclectic, but it flows with the theme.

The deer hide, that was shedding and not well preserved, was replaced by a poster-sized photo of mule deer I took on our honeymoon high up in the Bitterroot Mountains of Montana, while the DVD and cable box rest on a beaver pelt to protect the credenza.

I scaled back on the owl figurines departing with half the collection. Other items were sold, discarded for trash, or given away to friends. It felt good to be rid of it all. Our elation didn't last long. With boxes of junk gone, the open spaces made it too inviting to purchase more stuff.

Our small ranch house is crying for space, ready to explode. Each room filled with what I like to call organized clutter; candles, photographs, nick-knacks, books, art, plants, statues, crafts, painting supplies, and décor for every holiday.

I lament, "If we only had more closet space." My husband agrees. But somehow, we both missed the point. More closet space would only give us a place to store all the stuff. It would be like having an indoor storage bin, only it wouldn't cost a monthly fee!

One of my best girlfriends has a storage unit and is there all the time. She is always going to the storage unit. She is always moving something from the storage unit to some other location or bringing something back to put into the unit. I am amazed at the time she spends going back and forth. It reminds me of a passage from the book *Ciao America* by Beppe Severgnini.

As he learns to navigate through life in the United States he makes funny observations. About moving he writes, *"When you move into an empty house, mattresses, and silverware aren't enough. You need tables, dining chairs, and easy chairs. In fact, you need all those things that Americans take with them in rented U-Haul vans when they move from one state to another. The United States is actually a republic founded on relocation. The whole social order is based on one assumption: people move houses. Presidents move out of the White House, workers go where the work is, and children leave home for college. There are awesome mechanisms in place to facilitate these operations."*

My girlfriend is always at the storage unit. For her, the storage unit is like going grocery shopping. She is always moving furniture, and re-locating someone in the family. She recently informed me that three months after moving her son to a new job out of state, she will now be moving him and *all* his *stuff* right back to New Jersey, because the job didn't work out. I am continually amazed at how much time she spends packing and always think of the passage from Severgnini's book when she tells me she is going to the storage unit or is moving more stuff.

My mother had a storage unit. I referred to it as the "Pyramid" because, in the fashion of the Egyptians, it housed all the stuff from her father's house when he passed away. The amount of money she was spending on the "Pyramid" was ludicrous. Incensed, my father rented a van and, with the help of my longtime friend Brett, we moved all the stuff out of the "Pyramid" and into their house, down to the basement one weekend.

Years later, my husband, my brother, and I moved most of the stuff out of the basement and to the trash. We watched from the windows as parades of cars stopped on the busy county road, and like rats pick through the stuff, hoping to find something…some treasure…something that will keep the tradition of having clutter in the home alive.

My mother forgot about how much money she wasted on "Pyramid #1" and decided to rent "Pyramid #2" decades later. She wasn't sure what she was going to do with furniture and stuff from the house down the shore. In their divorce, my father got the house and the tax burden, and my mother got the stuff in the house.

"Pyramid#2" is bigger and was packed similarly to King Tut's tomb. It was a miracle we could get the metal door closed. Unfortunately "Pyramid #2" was near the home where my husband and I reside. My mother, my husband and I have spent over a decade and in and out of "Pyramid #2." My husband and I are the *"mechanism facilitating"* this operation.

A decade later we are *still* moving stuff from "Pyramid #2" to my mothers. As the years have passed *we* are getting too old to move furniture and I tell my mother to simply stop paying the bill. The lock will get cut off, or better yet, I will give them the key, and perhaps we will see her stuff on that television show where people bid on abandoned or unpaid storage units.

Tired of climbing up and down the pull-down attic stairs in our home, my mother offered us the use of "Pyramid #2."

"Absolutely not," shouted my husband. "We can't afford it and I'm not driving back and forth to get Christmas stuff!"

I give him the "Alice Look." "It's around the corner, not even a quarter of a mile."

"I don't care. Get rid of it…we have too much…throw it out!"

And like my mother and her mother and generations of collectors before me, I refused. Thirty organized Rubbermaid totes of Christmas décor reside in the attic. My husband's two NFL ornaments representing the Philadelphia Eagles football team have morphed into crates of ornaments that can easily decorate an eight-foot tree. Yes, the Eagle ornaments have their own tree too, which we couldn't put out one year because Bentley's cage resided in the spot designated for the "Eagle Christmas tree."

Other boxes contain, not just a manger, but, an *entire* village telling the story of the birth of Christ. Ceramic trees, figurines, and totes of holiday items for every room fill part of the attic. The rest of the attic is packed with luggage and boxes filled with other important objects, like a resume, detailing chapters of each of our lives. Sports memorabilia from our glory days, teaching lectures, art projects, photographs, souvenirs, and other boxes of forgotten objects cram the corners of the small space. Perhaps the Egyptians had the right idea when they detailed their life in hieroglyphics across the walls of tombs, temples, mastabas, and pyramids.

My husband suggested we throw it all out. My solution was to move into a bigger space, which would enable us to not only organize the stuff better, but the stuff would now be more accessible. As the years pass, there will eventually come a time when we would not be able to manage the pull-down stairs to get to the things in the attic.

Weeks later, I ran into my same friend from work on the bike trail; she complained that nothing has changed and she and her new husband were still arguing about their stuff and how they would merge it all.

"I offer her some advice. Perhaps if you consider your space and think about how you can blend your styles and divide the stuff to suit both your needs?"

She is barely listening, too focused on the reality of all the accumulated items. "We have no room for all these TV's…and there is this coffee table that has a broken leg…he has this stupid glove that he used to play softball with…he doesn't even play ball anymore…half the stuff is junk…it's just junk and I can't stand it…I just don't understand why he doesn't want to throw anything out…"

The tears were running down my face from bouts of laughter. I felt her pain, for I knew all too well what she was facing. I gave her a quick summary of our home.

"There is no TV in the bedroom, which is the cause of endless arguments as my husband likes to watch TV in bed. There is nothing wrong with watching TV in bed except he likes to eat in bed too. He isn't the neatest person and we when we re-modeled the bedroom the TV was given away – for there was no room for it.

"We cook in the kitchen and eat there or in the dining room. The spare room is utilized as an office-studio for painting and craft projects. The bulk of our time is spent in the living room. In the spring and summer, we are in the yard. There is no garage, but a large shed out back. The reason we don't have a finished basement or garage is because our criteria when we were looking to purchase a home consisted of *one* thing – a fenced yard for the dogs! Instead of a garage and finished basement, my husband got a modest, unfinished shed! The shed is my husband's man cave!"

My girlfriend shook her head and said her husband didn't have a man cave.

I turned my head and nod knowingly, "Humph, give it a few years and you'll want one for him!"

My other girlfriend readily agrees. Her boyfriend spends more time in his man-cave, a boat, which is parked in their driveway. Trying to resurrect the life this boat once had will cost lots of money. It is doubtful it will ever see water again. When her boyfriend is not in his man cave he is in the house watching CNN, which runs all day long. "How much of the same stories can you fucking watch all day," she ranted one morning.

I understand her issues all too well.

She finally had enough when she arrived home and found the baby watching CNN with him.

"Thank god I'm fucking divorced," laughs my other girl-friend," who walked in during our conversation. "I don't have the patience to put up with that bull-shit anymore, television on all day...no house work getting done... kids can't even watch cartoons anymore...and the news is just as bad..."

Together they both swap stories of bad and inconsiderate behavior regarding the men in their lives. While amused at the insanity in their worlds, I once again am glad I'm not suffering alone. I think to myself, a television for the man cave boat and day care for the baby is imminent.

CHAPTER 47

Man Caves and More Clutter

I believe every man should have a man cave. They need a place for all their mis-matched stuff that doesn't match the décor in the house. They need a place for the stuff that will accumulate over time. My husband's man cave is filled with tools, recreational equipment, deer skulls, an exercise bike, a moldy dartboard, our bikes, a refrigerator, and other items that he assures me will produce great monetary wealth.

"You're not putting that refrigerator in my shed," he argued after we re-modeled the kitchen and the new refrigerator arrived.

"It still works, and we'll need it for the summer. Drinks and food can be kept outside, so you don't have to keep coming in and out of the house. Believe me you'll thank me later."

He reluctantly wheeled it to the back and is glad we have it now. He's talked about installing a TV and phone.

"The only way that will happen is if we meet the host of one of those remodeling shows in Home Depot, who is looking to crash our yard for a makeover…the odds of that happening…well, you can Fuh-ged-da-boud-it!" I snapped.

"Besides, we need to finish the inside of the house, replace fence panels around the yard, and clean up after Hurricane Sandy thundered through before we do anything to that shed!"

Over the years, people have given him more stuff for his man cave. Such as cabinets, wood, carpet, and other things, all which have been haphazardly placed in the man cave. I can't stand going in there. First mice and then a family of chipmunks have moved into the structure. There is also a hole in the floor that needs to be repaired. It's dirty, cramped, smelly, and unorganized.

Likewise, there is a host of interesting art including sculptures, paintings, and found object art that hang haphazardly on the walls. A small deer skull, minus an antler, peers down suspiciously as you enter. Rusty fishhooks that will never see the ocean decorate the worn rafters. Lining the walls and resting in orange Home Depot buckets are identical tools that will never be used. Why do we have so many of one item? Because you never know when you are going to need five pitchforks or seven rusty shovels!

Undecipherable graffiti from the former homeowner is painted on the plywood walls and a moldy dartboard hangs by the entrance reminding all who enter of their glory days.

Fecal matter from frequent visitors –mice, chipmunks, opossums, squirrels, and other rodents - can often be found on the counter tops of his workspace. I hold the spoon at a distance and grimace when asked to get a dab of peanut butter for the mousetraps.

I'd like to knock the entire shed down and build him something nicer. "You might have more room if you organize the space better," I offered.

"Stay out of my shed. I know where everything is."

"Every time I come in here I trip over the compressor...the snow blower is taking up so much space I can't get to my bike..."

"Then you shouldn't be in here," he cautioned as he glared at me suspiciously.

"What do you want? Why are you in here anyway?"

I don't recall what I wanted. "Fuh-ged-da-boud-it. I corralled the dogs. "Come on guys, we're leaving. I don't want them to get hurt in this mess. We can't afford another trip to the vet."

The next morning, my girlfriend comes into my office and I inquired how she felt about man caves.

Taking no time, she answered quickly, "I'm going to build a life-size shed in the back yard for him. Do you want to know what he did this weekend? He got mad because I was putting the liquid soap his mother gave us in the new soap dispenser!"

I stopped typing at my computer and looked up. I scratched my head and gestured with my palms, "So what, I don't see the problem."

"He had a melt down because he wanted some stupid generic brand that claims to have added moisturizer in it! It's going to be a large dog house with a cot!"

"At least you have a basement," I added. "In our house there is no basement, extra rooms, no place to go unless it's outside on the deck or to the shed!"

My girlfriend continued, "We spent all this money over the weekend on things for the kitchen and bathroom since the remodel is almost complete, and he has the nerve to start a war over soap! I threw his pillow down the stairs and told him to sleep on the couch! If he ever gets that shed, he's getting a bed in it."

I resumed typing. "Humph! You should have told him he's not a fucking bachelor anymore!"

I thought about the size of my husband's shed. "You know in my husband's shed there is a small loft. I could put an air mattress up there for him. The only problem is that the mice will chew holes in it like they did to the outdoor chair cushions!"

The problem with the conversation was that she was serious and I was not. I believe men should have a space for themselves, shed, basement, man cave; whatever you want to call it. But they need to be sleeping with their wives at night. Despite your issues and arguments, it's never going to work if you don't learn to work things out.

When you live in a small house, you need to learn to do a lot of compromising. It's best to start with the bedroom closet. My husband has one quarter of this real estate and I have the rest. We designed the closest around our clothing. He has a few ties, dress shirts, and pants. I have dresses, skirts, pants, long and short sleeve blouses, shirts, hats, dress jackets, suits, scarfs, pocketbooks, and shoes! It all fits nicely. He argued he didn't have any space.

"Space for what? You don't have any clothes. You wear a uniform to work! All the rest of your stuff is in the armoire."

"Of which you have the two bottom drawers," he laughed.

"You're right. They contain my winter sweaters. When you start wearing suits, ties, or sweaters to work, then we'll re-design the closet." It's a very practical and realistic design. Eventually, he conceded. We compromised!

I found ways to gain more closet space when we remodeled the bathroom. In order to get a bigger bathroom, I sacrificed closet space in the bedroom. My husband was upset when he saw the finished product. "The closet is too small. I can't fit any of my stuff in there."

Eyebrows raised I looked at him incredulously and continued the *same* conversation we had about his clothing. "You don't wear suits anymore. All your clothing fits in your armoire. Unless you are going to start carrying pocket books, wearing scarfs, dress shoes, and long dresses, you don't need to put anything in this closet except the space that is allotted to you for shoes, dress pants, and shirts!"

If my husband wore suits and ties and had an extensive wardrobe, we would have designed it differently.

The hall closet is packed with recreation items, coats and jackets for all seasons. The dining room closet is for dishes and the closet in the office is for office stuff.

"The dogs have more damn space than me," remarks my husband.

"You have your shed outside. They have a few pallets around the house," I laughed jokingly.

One of the most challenging events that happened during our marriage was the summer when my husband was laid off from his job and he decided to try his hand at interior decorating.

In addition to looking for jobs, I left him a list of things to do since he was now home all day. He was always good about emptying out the clean dishes from the dishwasher but not good at putting them away; most of the time he would stack pots, pans, and all the Tupperware on the counters. Now, because he was home, he began putting everything away.

When I arrived home and started cooking, it felt as if I never left work. We had this receptionist who was always misfiling files and paper work. We were always looking for something; therefore, it took longer to complete work. This was the way I felt in my own kitchen. The Tupperware was mixed with the pots, the plastic colander was with the pans, and cooking and bakeware were mixed wherever there was a spot!

Then he started moving the dog pallets. I'd come home and move them back. The dog's toys were relocated to the other room. "The dogs can't play with them in here. What's wrong with you?" I'd ask as I returned the basket to its original location.

I had enough when he started with the knick-knacks in the living room and then my stuff in the bathroom.

"If you move one more thing, I'm going into your shed and will start moving all your tools around! You're not a fucking bachelor anymore."

By 2016 the clutter in our house had spread. The closet was stuffed with clothing that needs to be given away. My artwork for my business was in every room.

"Why is that Christmas tree still in the kitchen? It's March, this is fuckin' ridiculous," he says.

"It belongs in the attic. It needs to be taken apart and brought to the attic. *We* haven't had time. Every weekend *we* have been busy." I put extra emphasis on the word *we*. "And I can't go up and down those pull-down attic steps with all this stuff!"

Piano music was in piles for an activity I was working on for work. Art books overflowed from the bookcases and the stuffed duck glared at me from the top of the shelf, wondering if he was going to ever return to the wall. He was removed to make room for *Chester*, the deer mount. Chester is a five-point buck, who, Bentley stares and growls at every night. I often remind my husband that Bentley, our lab, is a hunting dog and it's in his DNA to hunt. As I watch Bentley looking at the deer mount, I believe he is plotting to take Chester down. I am not sure how I would break the news to my husband if his beloved sculpture was attacked.

Years earlier I remember calling him at work one evening to tell him there was another incident in the house. I was referring to the deer tail, which was eaten by one of the dogs. Since then, all wildlife has been relocated to higher ground. But Chester, I believe, is in danger.

Back to the clutter. The hallway was packed with light fixtures for outdoor repair projects as well as stuff from his mother's house after she passed - silverware, and a tote of baseball cards. Her taxes, not a few statements but *every* tax statement she ever recorded sat in piles waiting to be shredded. Miscellaneous dishes were stacked in the dining room, while more figurines gathered dust in the attic. There was an area in the living room with the paperwork for his mother's estate – all of which I had been navigating. Organizing receipts, bank statements, paperwork for the attorney, and our taxes - the entire process had been daunting. In the midst of it all, my husband had the nerve to expresses his concern about the clutter. "Fuh-ged-da-boud-it. I want my hallway back, just throw it all out."

"It's from your mother's house. You said you wanted it," I replied, stunned by his admission.

"Throw it the fuck out!"

I offer dishes and figurines to someone at work and later call my husband to make sure he wants to part with it.

Now he wants to know if they are going to pay for it.

"Seriously?" I asked. "First you want to throw it out and now you want money for it. Put the tote in my truck tomorrow and I'll bring it to work. Or take it and scrap it."

"Do what you want. I'm tired of looking at it."

"No, it's your mother's. Either sell it, give it away, or scrap it," I snapped, angrily.

"Ok, just give it to them and throw out the tote of baseball cards."

His mom's old Singer sewing machine was in the back seat of the truck, along with the tote of silverware. Together they had been riding around Ocean County, their destination still undetermined.

The tote of baseball cards had a planned spot – the trash. I added to his misery by telling him a story about someone in the news who recently found a rookie baseball card in a book and it was worth a million dollars.

Suddenly, the attic was the new location for the tote of baseball cards because, according to my husband, they were going to be worth something someday. Ugh!

In our spare time we had looked at bigger homes, with more closets and rooms, but didn't want to do any more construction work.

I suggested moving out of state…but that would involve driving, directions, packing, and paying someone to cart all our stuff to the new location.

My husband suggested we throw everything out.

Talk of adding more rooms had been discussed and eventually happened, only causing more clutter, and more items relocated to the attic. Once central air conditioning was added, the attic somehow became smaller. Now our attic officially looks like my mothers, filled with stuff, which I vowed would never happen to me. If we don't deal with it soon we will be too old to climb up and down the pull down attic stairs.

I was hoping to win the lottery, so I could pay someone to move it all.

We respectfully remind one another that we are not bachelors or bachelorettes anymore and need to deal with the clutter in the attic.

CHAPTER 48

Trash Days

You would think a family of ten lives in our house with all the trash we constantly have. Most of the stuff comes from the yard or my husband. If it's not generated by the dogs, he is bringing something home.

Trash needs to be taken out on trash days, which is twice a week and *on* trash days only or the neighbors will complain and code enforcement will be called. The recycling is taken out on another day. "What the hell is so difficult about this?" I calmly asked my husband, who had once again forgotten to take the trash out.

"I forgot."

The week before he remembered, but it was a holiday. Instead of bringing it in, he left it out by the curb all week. The neighbor complained. The township called wanting to know if we needed a special pick-up, and if we didn't to make sure we follow the scheduled trash collection dates according to the zone we reside in.

My husband had a puzzled look on his face. "How do you even know what *fucking zone* we live in?"

I point to the wall. "It's printed in the fucking calendar. You know, the one hanging on the wall? The town sends us one every year. It's in color; you can't miss it."

"This is fucking ridiculous," he shouted as he grabbed the calendar.

"For your information we live in zone one for recycling, trash is on Monday and Thursdays because we live in the south half of the town, and leaf collection in split into three cycles!"

My husband stared at me with his mouth hanging open, clearly in shock. It's as if I just recited the entire NFL schedule for the season.

I gave him the "Alice Look" and continued. "This is not some rural town in Pennsylvania. There are rules." I begin spitting out more information as if I am presenting a doctoral dissertation, "You need to call for bulk pick up…the recycling center is open and takes the following items…some upgrades to your property require permits…when it snows you can't park on the street… there is a schedule for Christmas tree pickup…the trash pails can be no more than thirty-two gallons…you just can't do what you want or we will get a fine!"

My husband started flipping through the calendar. He was agitated, and I didn't even have to look at him to know why. Reading the calendar is like reading an instruction manual, which he refuses to do. Further, in my husband's world, the trash, recycling, and leaf collection schedules should all be on one page. He should not have to flip through the calendar to find them! I refuse to discuss the design of the calendar. It's pointless.

I started making a pot of coffee.

"YOU'RE NOT A FUCKING BACHELOR ANYMORE," I sighed as I placed a coffee cup in front of him.

301

CHAPTER 49

Maintenance and Acquisitions

Maintaining property requires one to do just that - maintain it!

He slams the calendar on the counter. "What the hell do we need this for?" The dogs enter the kitchen to investigate the noise. "It's a waste of paper. This is why our taxes are so damn high! Why the hell should *we* get fined for putting a trash can out on the wrong day? Do you see that guy across the street?" He pulls back the curtain of the kitchen window. "It's like a fuckin' junkyard on his property. Boats, campers, washers, dryers, cars...that stuffed hasn't moved in decades...the only water that boat see's is when it rains...and the town wants to fine *me*...that will be the day... I'm fucking calling code enforcement..."

When you and your loved one are looking to purchase a home, make sure you look at the number of trees on the property and what the adjoining neighbors have in their yards. Clearly something my husband and I missed.

It took twelve years before the town finally enforced the code and made the neighbor start getting rid of the junk on the property. While the bulk of it is gone, you can still see items in the back of the property – a washer & dryer and other junk. The boat that will never see water remains proudly resting on its trailer. We celebrated when the property was eventually sold, remaining junk removed, and a new home was constructed. A fence was installed.

Finally, no more junk to look at, but we do have other problems – leaves.

"Can you clean that pile of leaves and the dog poop in the yard today? It's a mess out back. We had a mild winter and those leaves are going to attract fleas and ticks. The last thing we need is the dogs to get attacked. We can't afford another trip to the vet," I remind my husband.

Leaves are a big issue for us. When we bought the house we somehow neglected to notice *all* the trees that were not only on our property but in our neighbor's yards too. I'll never forget the looks on our faces when we pulled in the driveway and jumped out of the moving truck into a mess of leaves. There were leaves everywhere. Instead of snow, it was leaves! My husband and I looked at one another and said at the same time, "Where the fuck did all this come from?"

Why didn't we see all the trees when we looked at the house? Because we were too busy making sure the property had a *fence* for the dogs!

There is one huge maple tree in the front yard and multiple pine trees surround us, so we are always cleaning the gutters and raking the lawn. It's a mess because we don't have a big enough ladder therefore we are always stretching the hose and splashing water on one another. It also takes us longer because we don't have the right equipment.

"Get the step ladder…move the hose over here…now bring it over here…you have to give it more water pressure…what about the side of the house…bring the ladder back over here…and what about the front…you got the crap all over the fucking furniture… now I have to clean it…"

Unfortunately for my husband my father also had a gutter-cleaning business that my brothers and I helped with. I *know* about the importance of cleaning gutters, I *know* all the problems that can arise from gutter cleaning neglect and I *know* how to clean gutters.

One day at work my boss stops me in the parking lot and wants to know why the gutters on the buildings are not cleaned yet?

I could tell him how the maintenance guy is working on it by taking a ladder, climbing eight feet and throwing the debris from the gutters in a plastic bag, coming back down the ladder, only to move the ladder four feet and repeat the process. If this continues, it will take him the rest of the year to clean five, small, one-story buildings.

He is the vice-president and I know he has no time to listen to the reasons why it's not done or what the problems may be. He is a busy man and I totally understand. The work just needs to be completed. I am acutely aware of this and he is waiting for an answer. So, I simply offer to do it *myself.* His eyebrows narrow and he looks at me in disbelief as if there is *no way* I could possibly perform this task and why would I even *suggest* such a thing!

I am barely listening as he is discussing the importance of gutter cleaning – as if I didn't know…if he only knew my gutter cleaning education perhaps he'd reconsider… it would take me half a day to do the job…carrying the big aluminum ladder on my shoulders is not an issue… walking the roof doesn't concern me… thanks to my father I've been well trained and its imbedded in my DNA…instead he'll get the maintenance guy some help…and I should put this on a schedule…and that I've been with the company long enough to know better…

When I get back into the building my supervisor saw me outside and wanted to know what the vice-president wanted. I tell her and offer to clean the gutters. Now she has witnessed me carrying the big ladder around and knows my history and that I could do the job. "No," she snaps, firmly. "I don't want you getting hurt, then I will have nobody here to help me. Besides you don't like bees and they are all over the property. Call the exterminator again."

The only real problem I have cleaning gutters is the bees. I can't stand them. My husband forever laughs at my fear. In the spring the dialogue is the same and usually ends with me yelling, "Fuh-ged-da-boud-it! I'm not going over there with the ladder! Not with all those carpenter bees swarming around!"

When we are not cleaning gutters, we're raking leaves. And as with everything else there is a procedure.

"Why did you put all those bags by the curb? Leaf collection is not this week."

Bewildered is how I'll describe his facial expression.

Hand on my hip; I gave him the "Alice Look."

"Didn't you check the fucking calendar?" I laugh.

"Fuh-ged-da-boud-it. I'll just take them over to the recycling center myself," he grumbled.

"Make sure you dump the leaves in the area *designated* for leaves. They have cameras out and are taking pictures of the offenders.

I really can't complain about my husband when it comes to the yard. He works hard to keep it maintained. He made sure the lawn was cut and the grass was watered. Years later, we dug it all up and put stone down. Now he fights the weeds that pop up at varying intervals. We have lots of flowerbeds in the front and back, so he is always rotating and adding dirt.

The original fountain and pond he built was destroyed by Hurricane Sandy. He rebuilt it and made it bigger. Bigger means more maintenance. We spend summers weeding flowerbeds, digging up pond hoses, and patching leaks. He has plans to take the entire construction apart, stone by stone, and rebuild it *again*.

In the summer, we start planting the vegetable and flower garden on the other side of the house. It's a lot of work, but we like to be outside. It's our own little paradise.

There is something always going on outside in the yard to keep us entertained. The dogs are forever on red alert and like sentinels, always checking the perimeter of the property for intruders. A scuffle of some sort is imminent when there is a sighting of squirrels, cats, moles, or chipmunks.

For some odd reason, the dogs like tomatoes. Chasing them out of the tomato beds is a daily occurrence and always leads to some catastrophe – like plants getting knocked over, or my husband tripping in one of the multitude of holes they have dug throughout the yard.

Then there is the incessant barking between the fences with the neighborhoods dogs or other canines just passing by. Hurricane Sandy took out part of our fence and although we made repairs, a cat continues to sneak into the yard and has the nerve to wander on the deck, causing more scratching at the sliding glass doors, barking, and yelling from my husband who is allergic to cats!

Our dogs are also relentless gardeners. They regularly enjoy changing the landscape of the yard. They start first thing in the morning and their routine is the same: digging, rotating dirt, and fertilizing the plants and grass. By midnight there are holes that inevitably my husband will step in and trip or twist his ankle!

Many man hours have been spent taking care of our property and the last thing I want to do is mess it up. So what does my husband do? Like a hoarder, he starts collecting stuff. He considers himself a purveyor of fine merchandise – merchandise from the trash or things that his friends give to him.

Once again, the rewind button in my mind is activated and I'm transported back in time to the yard I grew up in. I see the spackle buckets, ladders, piles of wood, and shingles on the side of the garage. There was a section in the back of the yard behind the shed that was fenced off to hide the rest of the junk. I vowed that my yard would never contain so much clutter.

My declaration worked out for me like this: When I look at the side of our house, I think of the television show *Sanford and Son*. The side of the house is a mini-junkyard. My husband assures me these are things that can be used for projects.

Sanford and Son was a popular sitcom in 1972. Fred and his son Lamont owed a salvage yard. Lamont did the work, while Fred was always looking for ways to make a quick buck.

For example, there was the blue siding left over from a friend's house but unfortunately there was never enough to side our home. He eventually had to cut it all up for the trash men to take it. Next, are a variety of stone in different sizes awaiting the construction of some architectural miracle!

There are also three huge, plastic shells to create decorative ponds, a container of sand, bricks, 2x4s in a variety of lengths, automobile ramps, a giant ramp for the snow blower so it can be wheeled into the truck, scrap metal, pet taxis, the old sink from the bathroom, more spackle buckets, fence panels that are no longer useable because the squirrels ate the tips off, buckets of paint that need to be taken to recycling and other junk…

How did we accumulate all this stuff? I really don't know. It just happened.

I was looking at all the crap one afternoon and expressed my concerns to my husband. "What do we need it for? Can't you just get rid of it? What the hell do we need all these fuckin' spackle buckets for? The dogs are going to get hurt...can't you just throw everything out?"

His solution was to install a gate. This keeps them from using the side of the house as their restroom. He likes it so much that he added four more around the property - not only to keep the dogs from going on the side of the house, but behind and on the other side of the shed, near the fire pit, and in the garden.

My mother jokes about it and says the dogs live in a "gated community."

The stuff on the side of the house started to move the year my husband was laid off from work.

It was the beginning of the summer. I was sitting on my canopy-covered swing in the garden and was on the phone with my mother. "I can hardly hear you," she yelled. "What is all that noise?"

"He's building a bird house."

"What?" My mother asked.

"He's constructing it from all the scrap wood and stuff we have on the side of the house!"

By the end of the summer the birdhouse resembled a miniature log cabin. Only it was so heavy it took both of us to move it. The façade and fireplace were constructed of stone pebbles from my garden. For the birds to use it, it needed to be supported by at least three or four six-by-six posts in the ground.

Years later my prayers were finally answered. I came home to find him cleaning up the side of the house. It was a miracle. Once it was cleaned, he built storage bins for the logs and kindling for the wood burning stove. We spent the end of the summer and fall collecting wood. Hurricane Irene was kind enough to start us off. Like rats we scoured the county for wood. Every time there was a log on the side of the road we would stop and pick it up. Friends also helped us fill our woodpile for the winter. There was no longer room for anything else on the side of the house – or so I thought.

I arrived home from work and discovered more stuff in the driveway. I immediately called my husband at work. The "Alice Look" is transmitted through the phone as I spoke. "What the *hell* is that thing in the driveway? Where did you get it? What do we need it for?"

He found it in the dumpster at work; he was going to put it in the shed.

"Are you fucking kidding me?" I yelled into the phone. "Now you're dumpster diving? What the hell is wrong with you?" It looked like it was used to hold brochures of some sort. "What the fuck are you going to do with that?"

"I can use it to separate all the screws and nuts."

More obscenities and I hung up.

The rack was huge. It sat in the driveway for three weeks. I didn't need a measuring tape to tell that it was too big for the shed, which was already crowded with other stuff. I knew once he dragged it back there, he was going to drag it right back to the curb. But before it made it to the curb, it would make a pit stop to the side of the house. That was exactly what happened!

Weeks later, my mother was visiting, and we were getting ready to go shopping. She was patiently waiting for me in the truck. I saw my husband talking to the neighbor as I exited the house. I could tell by the illuminated look on his face he was making some kind of deal – just like *Fred Sanford*! And sure enough they were discussing the removal of the junk from the neighbor's property across the street!

"Where the hell does he think he is going to put that?" My mother asked, aghast.

"Probably on the side of the house," I calmly replied.

The neighbor across the street had a homemade log splitter. It'd been sitting in his yard for more than twenty years, exposed to all types of inclement weather. It needed a lot of work before it would be able to split a log. He wanted to give it to my husband.

"It could be an antique," my husband reminded me. My mother smirked, "Antique, are you kidding me?"

My husband ignored us. He had a plan for it. He and his friend were going to try to repair it – without having to spend any money. He told me not to worry.

"Where are you going to put it?" I ask.

"On the side of the house."

"You can't be serious," I scream. "That is not going to fit on the side of the house…it's huge…I won't be able to get the wheel barrel through when I have get wood…and there is all that other junk…are you crazy…it's becoming a junk yard again…what the hell is wrong with you…"

Monday morning while at work, I conveyed my annoyance to my girlfriend.

My other colleague laughed and said, "My husband is the same way. I told him don't even think about bringing more crap to the house. I said to him just the other day that if he brings something else home he would be sleeping in the yard."

She got infuriated just thinking about it and has enough stories to write her own novel. "There are things in our yard and shed that have not moved in years. My husband's contention is that he never knows when he will need to use one of the items. I had my son put this ugly table out for the bulk trash pick-up. I arrived home and discovered it back in the yard on the side of the shed!"

I couldn't stop laughing. I told her, "If I had the space, they could go into business together."

She continued, "Sometimes, anything he sees in the trash will be brought home. Then he has the nerve to complain about the clutter from his trash collection. I remind him it's his and he has to get rid of it!"

I feel better. Knowing I'm not suffering alone and there is somebody worse puts it all in perspective.

CHAPTER 50

Ancient Artifacts

Three weeks later – the giant brochure rack worked out so well that it is sitting on the curb with the trash. Apparently, it's too big for the man cave. In its place, is the homemade log splitter. It is five feet long and rests on a small trailer. Hoses of varying sizes and shapes arc into the air and connect to odd pieces of scrap metal. It reminds me of a homemade distillery. The trailer was never going to make it alongside the house. Everything that was currently on the side of the house now would have to be moved if he wanted to try to get it into the yard via the side of the house.

I don't have to measure anything because I can tell just by looking at its size that it will not fit along the side of the house! Why couldn't he see that? Why did he think it would make it?

The tires on the trailer are already flat, after having been pumped with air twice. Moving this will require the help of a friend, who is coming to assist on the weekend. The driveway smelled of some spray that supposedly would loosen the rust and grime.

My mother gives my husband the "Alice Look" and shouts, "Are you kidding me! What the hell is that?"

My husband attempted to explain his acquisition. Like an archeologist who has discovered some ancient lost artifact, he excitedly described in great detail how it operated and its function.

I kissed my husband told him I loved him and that we were going shopping as I direct my mother toward the truck before she has the chance to respond.

Sometimes it's just best not to say anything.

I show a picture of the acquisition to my friends at work.

"Why the hell did he take it? What does he need that for?" my girlfriend asked, shocked as she flips through the photos of the monstrosity. "Where does he think he is going to put it?" I looked up from my computer and calmly stated, "Along the side of the house."

My girlfriend laughed sarcastically, "Did you suddenly acquire an additional ten feet of space from your neighbor? You can't even fit a wheel barrel along that side," she said, her eyes wide with disbelief as she continued to stare at the photographs.

"I know," I said quietly, glad that there was another rational person that recognized this.

"What the hell is he going to do with it?" She asked, as she returned the photos to me.

"I don't know. Ask him, he's a man," I pointed to a male employee standing nearby.

"It's free, it's another toy, and something to tinker with," he replied easily, as he marveled with a childlike quality at my husband's new gadget.

A year later, it was still sitting in the driveway, covered with a blue tarp. There were more repairs needed than originally thought. It was going to cost money. We would not be using it to cut wood this year or the following year.

The defunct log splitter sat in the driveway for many years until I finally had enough. Two guys in a van were driving up and down the street and picking through trash. I told my husband to see if they wanted the log splitter.

His face dropped. It was as if I had committed a sin. I knew exactly what he was thinking and the look on his face said it all. It read, "What you want me to just give it away?"

I didn't give him a moment to debate. "I am sick of looking at it. You haven't touched it in years, and it's taking up room in the driveway. You have an electric log splitter, so we don't even need this thing. ...perhaps if we lived in the mountains and were chopping gigantic trees down...but no you are cutting logs to fit fuckin' sixteen inches of space in the wood burning stove...we don't need this. Stop those guys and see if they want it."

It took these two men, in their late sixties, the entire day to move this thing out of the driveway; my husband helped by constantly pumping the tires with air when they deflated. These guys hooked the ancient log splitter to their van and towed it to some unknown destination.

The departure of the log splitter only ignited the flame that burned deep within my husband for acquiring items to facilitate splitting logs the fastest way possible.

Over the years there would be a flurry of borrowing and repairing of chain saws. I was sent on missions to Home Depot to purchase chains, parts, and oil. The shed was always a mess and friends were always coming and going with machinery to help us cut wood.

One Sunday at church I prayed that I would win the lottery, so I could purchase my husband a new electric log splitter and chain saw. The Lord has a sense of humor and answered my prayers by sending me plastic; a new credit card, with a high interest rate, which enabled my husband to purchase a brand-new log splitter.

Finally armed with a new log splitter we were missing one thing – wood. Purchasing wood cost money, which at that time was a difficult expense. I prayed to God and asked him to provide wood. The following month God answered my prayers and sent Hurricane Irene. Wood was so plentiful we had enough to build an ark, like Noah.

Hurricane Irene helped us survive another cold winter. We didn't know where we were going to get the money to purchase firewood the following year. I told my husband to pray about it. Hurricane Sandy answered his prayers weeks later. The wood was plentiful. We filled our truck with pine trees that fell on our property and deposited them at the dump. While there, we took the maple and oak and other logs people were leaving at the site.

Once again we combed Ocean County for wood. Sandy was generous and my husband's obsessive-compulsive behavior took over as the race for acquiring wood began.

I will never understand why junk and other stuff could stay on the side of the house for weeks, months, or years and not bother my husband, but when it came to the firewood in the driveway, my husband turned into a maniac. He worked like a man possessed by demons, day and night, to get all the wood cut and stacked in neat piles along the side of the house.

"Don't you think we have enough?" I asked, as he turned off the chain saw late one evening.

His rationalized he had to have it cut and ready for the winter. It was cut and stacked and piled in his neat little bins separated by plywood; organized by size and thickness too.

Hands on my hips, I gave him the "Alice Look." I said, "It needs time to cure, and it's still wet." What he heard was, "We need more wood."

My girlfriend's husband stopped by one weekend to pick up some wood. My husband filled his truck with logs. She later told me what he did when he got home. "Would you believe he worked well past dark, until he cut every piece of that wood? He had stacked it in neat little piles. Like a man possessed, he wasn't going to be satisfied until every piece of wood was cut and neatly stacked!"

Was I surprised? Absolutely not! I was happy knowing that I wasn't the only one suffering from more obsessive-compulsive behavior.

I once again consulted God and I prayed I would win enough money to buy a new home and with a gas fireplace. We are getting too old to be collecting, moving, and chopping wood. I was getting tired of carrying logs in, out, and around the house. God has yet to answer this prayer.

I was in the kitchen and I heard the sliding door opening and closing. My husband was carrying in firewood to fill the hopper. Moments later I heard the shower running. I shook my head because I knew exactly what had happened and he was trying to hurry up and destroy the evidence before I found out.

Too late. I frowned and yelled, "Did you step in dog shit again? Can't you watch where you're going? I told you to clean it up, I hope you didn't bring it in the house, I just washed the floors, You're not a fucking bachelor anymore!"

He put his shoe back on, laughing as he ran back toward the sliding glass doors dodging the towel I threw across the room. "What the fuck do you want me to do? You know the outside water is turned off…its to cold to carry all this wood around the house. Now open the window and I'll hand the logs to you through the window."

My mouth hung open in disbelief.

My mother smirked at the insanity and continued reading her newspaper.

"Yeah, yeah...I know; I'm not a fucking bachelor anymore! Well, you're not fucking single anymore either. Just open the damn window and help me..."

CHAPTER 51

The Return of the Ladder

In February 2016, we sold my mother-in-law's house in Pennsylvania. My husband insisted we stop by the house to pick up a few items. Unfortunately, I already know what they are. His best friend meets us to remove a small refrigerator and then helped strap and secure a twenty-foot aluminum ladder to the truck; the ladder his mother forbade him to take years prior because she perhaps needed it to get on the roof.

I can't help but find some sort of weird inexplicable humor in it all as we drive down I-95, the ladder rattling noisily in the wind. I wonder, "Do we really need another ladder?" We already have an aluminum ladder and a six-foot stepladder, which allows us to get on our roof easily.

"You should pull over and make sure it's secured," I suggested to my husband. I know this by the sound it's making, that the ladder needed to the tightened. While he was checking the cinches, I wondered if people have as many stories as I do about ladders. I felt there is some relevance to my father, my husband, my mother, and his mother – all linked by some sort of bizarre, indescribable insanity.

I thought about how the aluminum ladders were stacked in my yard as a child, and my brothers and I and the neighborhood kids would climb up and jump off pretending we could fly. I thought about my fear of bumble bees which resulted from the bee that flew in my long hair from the lilac bushes by the fence as we climbed on the ladders to jump off in our attempts to fly. I can hear the rattling of the ladders, piled high on my father's truck as he pulled into the driveway every evening, as I wondered how much he had to drink. I thought about the ladder that flew off some truck down the parkway during rush hour, smashing into the front grill of my truck. I thought about my husband's eighty-year old mother yelling at us on that hot summer day to put the ladder back because she might need it to go on the roof.

The door slammed, my husband adjusted the radio, and we were on the road again. He laughed at my memories but didn't want to hear anymore ladder stories.

Like some sort of trophy, the ladder will reside next to the other aluminum ladder attached to the fence, hidden in the shadow of the trees on the side of the shed. It will get more use from the squirrels and chipmunks rather that its intended function. At its new home, it will suffer the consequences of exposure to existing in the salt air down at the Jersey Shore. Years later the ladder will be given away, but every time I look at the side of the shed, I can't help thinking about that ladder, forever evoking childhood memories.

CHAPTER 52

Acceptance and Change

It's Saturday.

I've just come back from the convenience store with two extra-large coffees in my hand. My husband finished the last of the coffee and neglected to tell me we were out. The container holding the pods for the Keurig was empty too.

Wawa now follows and tracks my every movement. A co-worker and I were getting coffee at the convenient Wawa and convinced me to sign up for the Rewards Program. My iPhone notifies me constantly when I will receive free coffee, discounted food, and other free items, all of which I am happy to take advantage of.

I eventually applied for the Wawa gas credit card, which promised us savings on gas when used. And when we are getting gas, one of us is always running in for, you guessed it, coffee.

It's not about the coffee, but rather the technology. I feel a sense of accomplishment that I have conquered this application and can successfully navigate through the iPhone with relative ease.

When I'm with my husband, he will naturally super-size his coffee and purchase other items. Like a pro athlete, I move quickly and easily around the Wawa coffee bar. I am surrounded by candy, cake, and beverages and get sucked into the vortex of end cap displays so strategically placed, as I must walk past them to get to the coffee. I could have bought a bag of M&M's or coffee cake at the grocery store for what I just paid, but I'm not going food shopping until Sunday and the money is on the app, in the iPhone; hence, the convenience of shopping in the convenience store is paying off.

I don't really believe all this, but it's the only way I could rationalize it.

I walk out to the shed and hand him the super-sized cup of coffee from Wawa.

I inform him the oil-light came on in the truck.

He gives me a kiss and thanks me for the coffee before telling me that he is busy cleaning the yard. He must get it ready for the winter. Again, obsessive-compulsive behavior is taken to another level. It's early fall, but it doesn't matter. There is stuff in the yard still to dispose of such as leaves, trash, broken fence sections, and other junk all in a heaping pile in the garden bed. He also has to make a trip to the recycling center. Plus, tomorrow is football Sunday, and everything must be finished by tomorrow.

He tells me to make an appointment and bring the truck to the tire place down the street and let them take care of the oil! He says he is going to let tire place change the brakes and oil changed on his car next week.

The Ford Taurus loves going to Mavis Tire, formerly STS Auto, which is conveniently located, up the street from our home. I don't like taking my truck there because it usually takes some sort of specialist to make the repair. After one hundred thousand miles, three lights came on, and the convenient auto store could not make the repair and suggested we go to the dealership. I looked it up in the manual. "It has to do with the four-wheel drive," I read to my husband. "Fuh-ged-da-boud-it. Take it to the dealership," he said easily.

My husband had accompanied me to the dealership the weekend prior. The dealership couldn't fix it until Monday because they were too busy. The cost was six hundred dollars just to replace some sensors. To my amazement, my husband remained calm and said to charge it on the credit card.

I was given a rental car, which I refused to drive. It was frightening going from siting up high in a truck to a low in a compact car. On the way home we stopped at the Ford dealership. The salesman told me the F-150 is too much truck for me. My husband was fuming. "She drives a truck now," he exclaimed, clearly annoyed at the entire haggling process. We vowed to spend the rest of the year visiting dealerships and test-driving vehicles.

While we are enjoying our coffee from Wawa, I ask him about the crack in the windshield, he says leave it. There is still time we can wait before the winter arrives. No sense dealing with it now. I agree.

My eyes do a quick scan of his area. There are tools and stuff all over his man-cave. It's a mess, and he has the nerve to complain about the house! We live in a palace compared to the disgusting crap that's piled in the pseudo man cave. I don't know what he is doing and don't care to ask. I retreat to the house in fear that I will get attacked by some rodent who will appear from the hole in the plywood floor. "This fuckin' hole has been here since we moved in! Don't you think you can do something about it," I calmly ask. He enters the shed, returns with a can of spray foam, and shoots it into the hole. He uses the entire can.

He looks up and smiles proudly, "Problem solved."

"Very funny," I laugh. "At least we don't have to make a trip to Home Depot."

I grab some birdseed, fill the feeders around the yard, and leave some on top of the aluminum ladders alongside the house.

The ladders have become a freeway for the squirrels, chipmunks, and birds, allowing them to navigate more quickly around the shed and trees. The squirrels know the dogs can't get through the gate and like to sit on the ladders and taunt them, while the dogs bark incessantly.

Back in the kitchen I stir the gravy cooking on the stove for dinner later on. Afterward, I open the refrigerator and search for the meatballs I asked him to make earlier. I stare in amazement at the perfectly round, tightly packed orbs of meat, which substanti-ate his obsessive-compulsive nature that has again risen to another level this morning.

The meatballs are large, like balls on a pool table. I have too much to do and decide not to re-do them. My grandmother is jumping out of her grave. I can hear her voice, telling me how they are too hard and will not cook properly. I smile and add them to the pot before heading to the living room.

I walk around the blue plastic laundry basket full of clean clothing that sits in the middle of the room. It's been there for at least two weeks. I grab my iPhone, snap a quick photo, and send it to my girlfriend with a text message, "It's still here!" I make a mental note to throw it out and purchase something else. If we are going to have a laundry basket in the living room it should at least match the furniture!

A glass and plate sit on the coffee table – evidence of another late-night living room picnic. The television is already on. It's been on since my husband got up this morning.

I carry my coffee, bowl of cereal, and Pop-Tarts to the worn couch and sit and watch some TV. I unconsciously reach deep between the cushions and retrieve the TV remote and change the channel to catch up on the latest news in the NFL. The dogs park themselves in the drop zone at my feet. I give them each a piece of my Pop-Tart.

I observe huge tumbleweeds of dog hair, slowly rolling across the floor, triggered by the breeze from the overhead ceiling fan. I ignore it but look over at the vacuum and shake my head as I notice another grocery bag full of dust hanging from the handle, evidence that my husband vacuumed sometime during the week. I make a mental note to take the bag to the trash. My husband is home all day and doesn't go to work until four – he can at least take the bag out to the trash instead of watching the TV. I think about cancelling the cable package for there is too much for him to watch. My best girlfriend had suggested I block the channels.

I sit on the couch and cut coupons for grocery shopping on Sunday. I stop to momentarily check to ensure the TV trays are clean for tomorrow's football game and add hot wings, Stromboli's, chips and dip to the shopping list. I am not cooking tomorrow. It's all frozen food and will be heated up.

I add coffee. I need coffee for the coffee pot in my office that the girls gave me for my birthday. After having a cup in the morning at home, I get to work and the girls make more. Sometimes they run to Wawa and bring back coffee. Nevertheless, there is always coffee and we drink it all day. When I come home I make more coffee.

My husband peeks through the screen, "Do we need to take the dog back to the vet today?"

"No, the appointment is next week," I answer without looking up.

"Ok, just checking on our precious babies."

The dog had to have his ass expressed again and it was infected. Four trips to the vet, antibiotics, urine, stool samples and another three hundred dollars; it never ends.

"Make sure you cut one of those coupons for the K-cups for the coffee pot. We can stop at Bed, Bath, and Beyond later if you want?"

I smile. "You're lucky to have me. The coupons are in the truck."

"Love you, babe. We'll stop after we ride bikes."

My mother calls to see how the dog is feeling.

"Much better. The anti-biotic is working."

We have a lot of errands to run and are planning to take a bike ride on the trail later this afternoon. I throw some laundry in the machine and notice some towels and a shirt are mixed in with the white clothing. I close the door instead of removing them.

In the kitchen I do some quick surface cleaning and then bring the dog's toys to the basket in the bedroom. The bed is unmade, the sheets and comforter are rumpled. The decorative pillows rest on top of the armoire. My mother would be appalled.

I enter the bathroom to gather the wet towels for washing and gasp as I look at the scene before me. I feel the blood rushing to my face as I continue to stare…

"What the *fuck* is wrong with him," I shout.

The dogs raise their heads but continue to lounge on their pallets. Instinctively they know they haven't done anything and are not in trouble. They would have been up and at attention if I had asked, "Did you do this?" I listen as I identify my husband's current location from the racket he is creating.

Like a tornado, I rush to the front of the house and dash out of the door. The storm door slams loudly against the frame as it's still in need of repair. My husband is cleaning the front gutters and leaves on the roof. His back is to me. I wave my arms to get his attention. Blower in hand he turns slowly and looks in my direction. He immediately starts laughing when he sees what I am holding in my hand.

Roll of toilet paper in one hand and attachment in the other I once again demonstrate the mechanics of how one attaches the toilet paper to the roller. At the same time, I am screaming, "You're not a *fucking* bachelor anymore!"

Hand gestures from the both of us slice through the air. He dismisses me with the wave of his hand and the revving of the leaf blower. He thinks he is some sort of God as attacks the massive pile of leaves with his machine and blows them off the roof into the neighbors and our front yard.

I return the hand gesture, and the door slams behind me as I retreat into the house.

"Fuh-ged-da-boud-it." The dogs are now at my feet wondering what daddy has done now. They follow me into the bathroom as I complain about the stupidity of men.

I smile wickedly and as I rummage through the cabinet. "Do you know what this is?"

They sniff at the item in my hand, angle their heads to one side, and give me the "we'd rather have a biscuit look."

I slap a brand-new roll of toilet paper onto the roller. I only bought it because I had a coupon.

"This is *one*-ply toilet paper. Look at it guys; it's so thin you can see right through it. Maybe this time your father will finally understand that he's not a *fucking bachelor* anymore!"

S. WHEELER.
WRAPPING OR TOILET PAPER ROLL.

No. 459,516.   Patented Sept. 15, 1891.

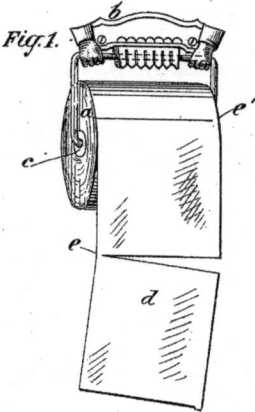

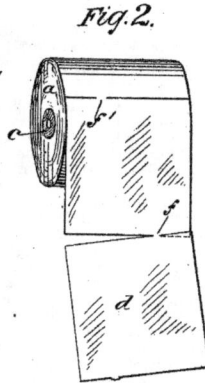

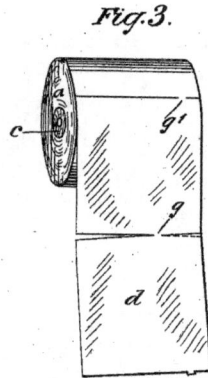

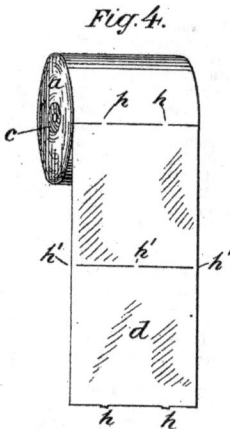

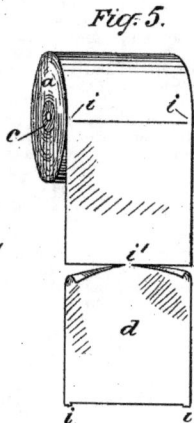

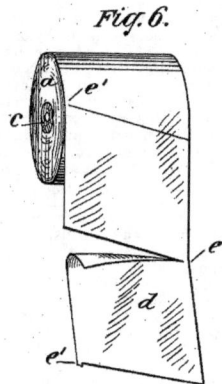

Fig.1.   *Fig.2.*   *Fig.3.*

Fig.4.   *Fig.5.*   *Fig.6.*

INVENTOR,

Seth Wheeler.

WITNESSES:

UNITED STATES PATENT OFFICE.

SETH WHEELER, OF ALBANY, NEW YORK.

WRAPPING OR TOILET PAPER ROLL.

SPECIFICATION forming part of Letters Patent No. 459,516, dated September 15, 1891.

Application filed June 10, 1891. Serial No. 395,758. (No model.)

To all whom it may concern:

Be it known that I, SETH WHEELER, of the city and county of Albany, and State of New York, have invented certain new and useful Improvements in Wrapping or Toilet Paper Rolls; and I do hereby declare that the following is a full, clear, and exact description thereof, reference being had to the accompanying drawings, forming a part of this specification.

My invention consists of a roll of paper for wrapping or toilet use so constructed that the points of attachment and severance between the sheets will be alternately out of parallel lines running through the whole body of the sheets, so that a pull upon the free end of the web will not be transmitted in a direct line through a series of sheets, but will be diverted by the spaces opposite the connecting points of the sheet pulled upon, thereby producing a transverse strain upon the next line of connecting points sufficient to break them.

In carrying out my invention the sheets of paper are only partially separated, having their points of attachment arranged in a novel manner, whereby each sheet will easily separate from the series as it is drawn from the roll, there being no litter occasioned, and any waste of paper is thereby prevented.

Since the advent of rolls of paper for the above-named uses many devices designed to prevent waste have been patented; but all effort in this direction has been apart from the roll of paper—namely, in the construction of holders for the rolls provided with means to prevent free unwinding of the roll and cause the sheets to separate singly at their connecting points. All these devices have been more or less complicated, liable to derangement, and expensive to both manufacturer and consumer, and consequently are little used now.

My improved roll may be used on the simplest holders.

Heretofore in the manufacture of rolls of paper the web of which is divided by lines of weakness into sheets it has been the practice to arrange the connecting points or bonds in parallel lines, or nearly so. Consequently, however slight the connection might be, it is evident, if the free end of the sheet be grasped at a point in line with the preceding connecting points, a long series of sheets may be drawn from the roll unless the free movement of the roll is prevented by friction or other means.

In the drawings, Figure 1 is a view of my improved roll suspended on the simplest form of fixture with a sheet of paper hanging therefrom, the points of attachment and severance being very near the margin of the sheets. Figs. 2 and 3 show my improved roll, the points of attachment and severance being nearer the line of center of the sheets than shown in Fig. 1. Figs. 4 and 5 are views of my improved roll, showing two points of attachment and severance which alternate with one point of attachment and severance in the same sheet. Fig. 6 is a view of my improved roll as applied to a different or oblique form of sheet.

a is my improved roll, being composed of a series of partially-connected sheets, and in Fig. 1 is applied to the simplest form of fixture.

b is the fixture, the arms of which pass through the core *c* of the roll.

d represents a sheet of paper ready to be detached from the roll.

In Fig. 1, *e* and *e'* represent the points of attachment and severance between two sheets and which alternate through the whole roll of sheets. By so arranging these points near the margin they may be of considerable width and still pull under slight strain. If the points of attachment and severance are arranged as at *f* and *f'* in Fig. 2, they should be narrower to avoid any probability of tearing into the body of the sheets when separating them. The points *e* and *e'*, Fig. 1, also *f* and *f'*, Fig. 2, are so arranged that one will be on one side and the other on the other side of the central longitudinal line of the roll. I prefer to so arrange the points of attachment and severance, although they may be arranged in many other different positions with respect to each other, as shown at *g* and *g'*, Fig. 3, where they are both on one side of the central longitudinal line of the roll, also as seen at *h h* and *h'*, Fig. 4, where it is shown that two points of attachment and severance may alternate with one, and it is clear that more than two points may be arranged so as to alternately sever without departing from the spirit of my invention. These points are partly on both sides and also upon the central longitudinal line of the roll.

In Fig. 5 the points of attachment and severance *i i* are shown on the margin of the sheets, where in Fig. 4 the points of attachment and severance *h h* are midway between the central longitudinal line of the roll and the margin of the sheet. Different forms of sheets may be wound in roll form, as shown in Fig. 6, having these alternating points of attachment and severance.

The principle of this invention, as shown applied in Figs. 1 and 5, is to so arrange the points of attachment and severance that those upon one edge of a sheet will be out of line with the points of severance uniting its opposite edge with the next sheet. By this method it will be seen that a pull upon the free end of the web will not be transmitted in a direct line through a series of sheets, but will be diverted by the spaces opposite the points of attachment and severance of the sheet pulled upon, producing a transverse strain upon the next line of connecting points sufficient to break them.

I claim—

1. A roll of paper for wrapping or toilet use so constructed that the points of attachment and severance between the sheets will be alternately out of parallel lines running through the whole body of the sheets, so that a pull upon the free end of the web will not be transmitted in a direct line through a series of sheets, but will be diverted by spaces opposite the connected points of the sheets, thereby producing a transverse strain upon the connected points sufficient to break them, substantially as described.

2. A roll of paper for wrapping or toilet use so constructed that the points of attachment and severance between the sheets will be alternately out of parallel lines running through the whole body of the sheets, such points of attachment and severance being upon both sides of the central longitudinal line of the web or series of sheets, so that a pull upon the free end of the web will not be transmitted in a direct line through a series of sheets, but will be diverted by the spaces opposite the connecting points of the sheet pulled upon, thereby producing a transverse strain upon the next line of connecting points sufficient to break them, substantially as described.

SETH WHEELER.

Witnesses:
  E. WHEELER,
  WM. A. WHEELER.

Endnotes

Ciao America, Beppe Severgnini c 1995 R.C.S. Libri & Grandi Opere S.p.A Milan. Broadway Books, a division of Random House, Inc. Broadway Books edition published in 2002.

Collectors and What They Collect, by Michele A. Fabiano, River-Views Magazine November-December 1997 Volume V Number VI c. Times Daily, Inc.

River Views is printed by Slaton Press in Moulton Alabama 205-974-4005.

About the Author

Michele A. Fabiano was born and raised in New Jersey. She earned a bachelor's degree in Art History from Rutgers University and master's degree in Art History from The City College of New York. She is the author of *The Agony Continues: Michelangelo's Search for Art in 20th Century NYC*.

Michele has taught art history courses at the City College of New York, The University of North Alabama, Brookdale Community College in Northern New Jersey, and Ocean County Community College in central New Jersey.

She has worked as a free-lance writer and photographer for Riverview's and Neighbor's Magazine. She also authored the college textbook, *From Cubs to Lions Your Guide to Success at the University of North Alabama*.

Michele resides in New Jersey with her husband Joe, and two dogs.

Author's Note

Dear Reader,

I hope you enjoyed reading *You're Not a Fucking Bachelor Anymore* as much as I enjoyed writing it. Please do me a favor and write a review on Amazon. The reviews are important, and your support is greatly appreciated.

Thank you,

Michele A. Fabiano

KCM Publishing
a division of KCM Digital Media, LLC

www.ingramcontent.com/pod-product-compliance
Lightning Source LLC
LaVergne TN
LVHW051223080426
835513LV00016B/1373